RECONCEPTUALIZING CHILDREN'S RIGHTS IN INTERNATIONAL DEVELOPMENT

Building on recent human rights scholarship, childhood studies and child rights programming, this conceptual framework on children's rights proposes three key notions: living rights, or the lived experiences in which rights take shape; social justice, or the shared normative beliefs that make rights appear legitimate for those who struggle to get them recognized; and translations, or the complex flux between different beliefs and perspectives on rights and their codification. By exploring the relationships between these three concepts, the realities and complexities of children's rights are highlighted. The framework is critical of approaches to children as passive targets of good intentions and aims to disclose how children craft their own conceptions and practices of rights. The contributions offer important insights into new ways of thinking and research within this emerging field.

KARL HANSON is Professor of Public Law at the Children's Rights Unit, University Institute Kurt Bösch (IUKB), Sion, Switzerland.

OLGA NIEUWENHUYS teaches International Development Studies at the Graduate School for the Social Sciences, University of Amsterdam, the Netherlands.

RECONCEPTUALIZING CHILDREN'S RIGHTS IN INTERNATIONAL DEVELOPMENT

Living Rights, Social Justice, Translations

Edited by

KARL HANSON

OLGA NIEUWENHUYS

CAMBRIDGE
UNIVERSITY PRESS

CAMBRIDGE UNIVERSITY PRESS
Cambridge, New York, Melbourne, Madrid, Cape Town,
Singapore, São Paulo, Delhi, Mexico City

Cambridge University Press
The Edinburgh Building, Cambridge CB2 8RU, UK

Published in the United States of America by Cambridge University Press, New York

www.cambridge.org
Information on this title: www.cambridge.org/9781107031517

First published 2013

A catalogue record for this publication is available from the British Library

Library of Congress Cataloguing in Publication Data
Reconceptualizing children's rights in international development : living rights,
social justice, translations / [edited by] Karl Hanson, Olga Nieuwenhuys.
p. cm.
Includes bibliographical references and index.
ISBN 978-1-107-03151-7 (hardback)
1. Children–Legal status, laws, etc. 2. Children's
rights. I. Hanson, Karl. II. Nieuwenhuys, Olga.
K639.R435 2012
323.3′52–dc23
2012019710

ISBN 978-1-107-03151-7 Hardback

CONTENTS

CONTRIBUTORS

TATEK ABEBE is Associate Professor at the Norwegian Centre for Child Research, Norwegian University of Sciences and Technology (NTNU) in Trondheim, Norway, where he teaches postgraduate courses in childhood studies and development studies. His research interests include children's rights and well-being, children's work, young people's livelihood pathways, child-focused research methodologies and how children in Africa are affected by and respond to processes of rapid socio-cultural and politico-economic transformation. He has contributed several chapters to books and, as a sole author or co-author, has published articles in various international journals.

SARADA BALAGOPALAN is a Fellow at the Centre for the Study of Developing Societies (CSDS), New Delhi, India. Her research interests include the politics of childhood, schooling and children's labour. She has published in the journals *Childhood, The Journal for the History of Childhood* and *Youth and Feminist Theory*. Her manuscript on marginalized childhoods in India and the politics of reform are due to be published in 2013.

EVA BREMS is Professor of Human Rights Law at the Human Rights Centre, Ghent University, Belgium. She studied law at the universities of Namur, Leuven and Harvard. Her research interests include many areas of domestic, comparative, European and international human rights law. Throughout her work there has been a recurring interest in issues relating to cultural and religious diversity and in the protection of the human rights of specific groups, such as women and children.

KRISTEN E. CHENEY is Senior Lecturer of Children and Youth Studies, International Institute of Social Studies in The Hague, the Netherlands. She is also co-convener and advisory board chair for the AAA Anthropology of Children and Childhood Interest Group.

Her research focuses on children's survival strategies amidst difficult circumstances in sub-Saharan Africa. She is author of *Pillars of the Nation: Child Citizens and Ugandan National Development* (2007) and is currently working on a manuscript based on her Fulbright-funded ethnographic research with orphans and vulnerable children (OVC). Her work takes an explicitly child-centred, rights-based approach to the hegemonic practices of government, development industry, and family, and their effects on children's choices.

COLETTE DAIUTE is Professor of Psychology and Head of the Ph.D. Program in Developmental Psychology at the Graduate Center, City University of New York. Before joining the Graduate Center faculty, she was a professor at Harvard University. She has published on foundational developmental theory relevant to children's rights, the politics of implementing children's rights, and issues of rights in armed conflicts. Recent related books include *Human Development and Political Violence* (Cambridge University Press, 2010), *International Perspectives on Youth Conflict and Development* (2006) and *Narrative Analysis* (2004). She was a featured speaker at the 2011 United Nations Psychology Day; she has lectured and convened research workshops internationally, including at Tata Institute of Social Sciences (India), Universidade Católica de Rio de Janiero (Brazil), University of Florence (Italy), University of Warwick (UK), University of Zagreb (Croatia), University of Belgrade (Serbia) and University of Manizales (Colombia).

YVAN DROZ is Senior Lecturer in Anthropology and Social Development at the Graduate Institute of International and Development Studies in Geneva, Switzerland. As a social anthropologist (Ph.D., University of Neuchâtel on Kikuyu Migrations in Kenya), he did extensive fieldwork in Africa, Latin America and Europe. From 2003 to 2007 he was Deputy Director and Head of the Research Department at the Graduate Institute of Development Studies, Geneva (now the Graduate Institute of International and Development Studies). He currently leads several teams of researchers on religious mobility in Kenya and Brazil, and on the transformations of family configurations and of images of masculinity and femininity in Switzerland. He also develops a comparative political anthropology of agriculture and of landscape in Switzerland, France and Quebec.

KARL HANSON is Professor in Public Law at the Children's Rights Unit, University Institute Kurt Bösch (IUKB) in Sion, Switzerland, where he teaches in the Master interdisciplinaire en droits de l'enfant (MIDE). He is also the Programme Director of the Master of Advanced Studies in Children's Rights (MCR) and a member of the Directive Committee of the European Network of Masters in Children's Rights. He obtained his doctorate in Law from Ghent University, Belgium, where he worked as Researcher at the Children's Rights Centre and as Senior Researcher at the Human Rights Centre. His publications and main research interests are in the emerging field of interdisciplinary children's rights studies and include international children's rights advocacy, child labour and working children, juvenile justice and the role of independent national children's rights institutions.

PATRICIA C. HENDERSON is a social anthropologist currently based at the Department of Sociology and Social Anthropology, Stellenbosch University, whose areas of specialization include medical anthropology and the study of children and youth in Africa. Phenomenology, theories of embodiment and performance contribute to her work in describing children's creative responses to the circumstances in which they find themselves. Her monograph, *AIDS, Intimacy and Care in Rural KwaZulu-Natal: A Kinship of Bones*, was published in 2011. The book charts the varied circumstances in which rural children orphaned by the AIDS epidemic live, helping to destabilize global stereotypes concerning 'AIDS orphans'. She is also part of a collaborative partnership between the United Kingdom, India, Brazil and South Africa seeking to theorize and critically examine the notion of children's participation.

MANFRED LIEBEL is Director of the Institute of International Studies in Childhood and Youth, International Academy (INA) and of the European Master in Childhood Studies and Children's Rights, Free University, both in Berlin, Germany. He is coordinator of the European Network of Masters in Children's Rights (ENMCR) and a member of the National Coalition for the Implementation of the Convention on the Rights of the Child in Germany. He also acts as a consultant of the Latin American Movement of Working Children and Adolescents (MOLACNATs). His research interests include children's rights and citizenship theory and practice, children's work, social movements and peer cultures of children and youth. He has published, edited and co-edited numerous books on childhood and children's rights including *Children's Rights from Below: Cross-Cultural Perspectives* (2012); *A Will of Their Own: Cross Cultural Perspectives on Working Children* (2004) and *Working to be Someone: Child Focused Research and Practice with Working Children* (2007).

PHILLIP MIZEN is Director of the Centre for Comparative Labour Studies, Department of Sociology, University of Warwick, UK, where he teaches sociology. His research interests are the sociology of youth and child labour. A major element of his work in this area has been an interest in how young people have been forced to bear a disproportionate burden of the costs of state restructuring as the Keynesian welfare state was repudiated through the rise of monetarism and, more recently, 'new Labour's' Third Way. These themes are elaborated in his books *Young People, Training and the State* (1995) and *The Changing State of Youth* (2005) and a number of related themes in a series of journal articles and book chapters. His interest in child labour has been pursued through a research project exploring the working lives of children in England and Wales, just before the turn of the twenty-first century. This project provided the basis for *Hidden Hands* (P. Mizen *et al.* (eds.) 2001). More recently he has been working with Dr Yaw Ofosu-Kusi to research the working lives of street children in Accra, Ghana.

OLGA NIEUWENHUYS teaches International Development Studies at the Graduate School for the Social Sciences and is affiliated to the Amsterdam Institute for Social Science Research both at the University of Amsterdam, the Netherlands. She is also editor of the journal *Childhood: A Journal for Global Child Research.* She studied sociology and social anthropology in Paris and Amsterdam and did most of her fieldwork in Kerala (India). She is the author of *Children's Lifeworlds: Gender and Labour in the Developing World* (1994) and has contributed widely to journals and book volumes. Her current research interests include the geo-politics of children's rights and postcolonial perspectives on childhood in the global South.

YAW OFOSU-KUSI holds a PhD in Applied Social Studies from the University of Warwick, UK. He currently teaches Economics and Social Studies at the University of Education, Winneba, Ghana where he is also the Director of International Relations. Since 2003, he has been researching into 'street life as labour' and has published book chapters and journal articles in that respect. In 2011 he directed the Child and Youth Studies Institute of the Council for the Development of Social Science Research in Africa (CODESRIA), Dakar, Senegal and has just completed the editing of a book on the year's theme, 'Children's agency and development in African societies'. He is currently working with Dr Phillip Mizen on street children in the informal sector in Accra, Ghana.

TOM O'NEILL is Associate Professor at the Department of Child and Youth Studies at Brock University, St Catharines, Ontario, Canada. He is a cultural anthropologist who has conducted extensive fieldwork in Nepal since 1993. His research in the Tibeto-Nepalese carpet industry dealt with petty-capitalism, 'bonded' child labour and youth who worked as carpet weavers. He has also investigated transnational labour migration, and the effects of Nepal's Maoist insurgency on its children and youth. His most recent research has been on second-generation Tamil–Canadian youth and transnational political identity. He is a co-editor, along with Dawn Zinga, of *Children's Rights: Multidisciplinary Approaches to Participation and Protection* (2008).

NEIL STAMMERS is Honorary Research Fellow in Politics at the University of Sussex, UK and is affiliated there to the Justice and Violence Research Centre. Recent publications include *Human Rights and Social Movements* (2009) and *Global Activism, Global Media,* (co-editor 2005). He has also published a range of journal articles and book chapters. His research interests include power, social movements, human rights and globalization. These are tied together by his exploration of the possibilities for positive transformative change. He is now working further on what he calls 'the paradox of institutionalization'.

ARNE VANDAELE obtained his Ph.D. in Law at the University of Leuven, Belgium, in 2003 on International Labour Rights and the Social Clause, and has published in various legal journals on human rights law, constitutional law and administrative law. He has worked at the University of Leuven as Senior Researcher for interdisciplinary research projects on children's rights and human rights. He is currently working as a lawyer at the Brussels Bar specializing in administrative and constitutional law.

ACKNOWLEDGEMENTS

During the several years in which we have been working on this volume we have had the chance to meet and talk to many people, whose encouragements and insights have contributed to its quality and consistency. We thank Pamela Reynolds and Neil Stammers for their warm support and involvement as keynote speakers in the research seminar in Sion, Switzerland where we presented an initial version of the theoretical framework of this book. The intensive and open discussions during this seminar with participants, paper contributors and chapter authors helped immensely to enrich our ideas and the material collected in this volume. We also express our gratitude to the administrative staff at the University Institute Kurt Bösch, in particular Sylvie Dubuis and Sarah Bruchez, as well as to Kalen Iwamoto, research master student at the University of Amsterdam, for their excellent administrative and logistic support, which enabled us to make the seminar an inspiring and pleasant event.

After the seminar, the chapter authors contributed a great deal by being not only critical but also bearing with us as the project advanced. Their readiness to revise their contribution several times to get the core notions that we propose here into sharper focus has helped to turn the volume into a truly collective endeavour.

We would like to give credit to our colleagues Frédéric Darbellay and Michele Poretti with whom we have collaborated intensively in an interdisciplinary research project funded by the Swiss National Science Foundation (Project no. CR11/1_127311), which has explored further the living rights, social justice and translations themes in the field of international children's rights advocacy. Their intellectual engagement with the interdisciplinary approach to children's rights studies, and our many discussions during formal and informal gatherings, has contributed significantly to developing the theoretical questions addressed in this book. The input by members of the research project's interdisciplinary steering group, Colette Daiute, Yvan Droz, Neil Stammers and Daniel Stoecklin, has been extremely valuable in helping to clarify our position.

Among the students at the Graduate School for Social Science Research, University of Amsterdam, who felt inspired by the ideas in this book and applied them in their fieldwork research on children's living rights, we would like to thank Joey Boink, Edward van Dalen, Maartje Gardeniers, Marianna Närhi, Chanida Pakdeebanchasak, Allison Ozero, Stefano Pezzoli, Lorenza Righetti, Joyce O. Robert-Orhue, Elseline Verkerk and Jessica van Wijk for the stimulating and frank exchange of ideas. We are also thankful for the constructive comments on earlier drafts of the manuscript by the anonymous reviewers. They have helped us bring our argument into focus and position it more firmly in the contemporary literature on human rights and on international development. The editorial assistance from Finola O'Sullivan and her colleagues at Cambridge University Press have equally been a great support.

We are also grateful for the financial support for organizing the research seminar on the themes developed in this book that we received from the Swiss National Science Foundation (Grant no. 10CO11–124243) and from the research group Governance and Inclusive Development, Department of Human Geography, Planning and International Development Studies of the University of Amsterdam.

Among family and friends who have supported us during the years while we were working on this book, Olga would like to thank particularly Karl's wife Hélène for her warm reception during her several stays in Geneva, her son Emile for an expert listening ear and for suggesting the cover image and her sister Martha for her gracious permission to use the image of her painting *Le petit cirque*. Finally, Karl wishes to thank his wife Hélène and his children Juline and Artus for their affectionate support and enduring understanding.

Introduction

1

Living rights, social justice, translations

KARL HANSON AND OLGA NIEUWENHUYS

Where do children's rights come from? Since the adoption of the UN Convention on the Rights of the Child (CRC) in 1989 the recognition that children are holders of rights, not only in the wealthier part of the world but perhaps especially in the least developed areas, has been gaining coinage among both practitioners and academics. This recognition has often been based on the implicit assumption that children's rights are the product of the lengthy process of legal negotiations that took place at the UN in Geneva during the decade preceding the ratification of the CRC by all but two (the USA and Somalia) countries in the world. This assumption has generally led to scholarship and policy-making being mainly concerned with issues of implementation. In this book we want to propose another approach. We emphasize that law always represents an unstable translation of ideas of right and wrong that exist in the real world and are based on lived experiences. From this it follows that children's rights are not merely the product of deliberations that are fixed in international legislation but that many of their underlying ideas already exist before they are translated into legal principles. Children, their parents and their communities continue to craft these conceptions of rights as they actively engage with the issues that confront them in the contexts in which they live and in which they establish the conditions for developing common grounds for action.

This introductory chapter proposes the outline for a theoretical framework that captures the complexities of children's rights as an open-ended endeavour that is responsive to the world that the young construct as part of their everyday life. It is built around three key concepts that we see as interrelated and impacting upon each other: living rights, social justice and translations. Most of our case-study material comes from the developing world, because, as we explain below, it is there that the contrast between legal principles and daily practice makes it dramatically clear that an alternative conceptualization of children's rights, that goes beyond issues of implementation, is necessary. Below we firstly explain how we arrived at our approach and then move on to a detailed discussion of its three buttressing notions: firstly *living rights*, secondly *social justice* and finally *translations*.

From one to many centres

If there is one city geographically associated with the CRC then it is Geneva, where the Convention was drafted between 1979 and 1989 and where, since 1992, the Committee on the Rights of the Child that monitors states' compliance with its provisions holds its three annual sessions. An important number of UN specialized agencies, intergovernmental and non-governmental organizations such as UNICEF, the International Labour Organization (ILO), the World Health Organization (WHO), the International Committee for the Red Cross and Save the Children have their headquarters or maintain offices a few kilometres from where the CRC is monitored. It was while walking through the parks located within this neighbourhood that we first asked the question 'where do children's rights come from?' Did children's rights really come into being in the gatherings of children's agencies in Geneva to irradiate as a *deus ex machina* throughout the world, in particular the developing world? We concluded that children's rights have not one but multiple geographical centres. Even if they are undeniably codified in international and national legal documents and further specified in international jurisprudence and development programmes, they were already alive in the minds and lived realities of children throughout the globe before that. Children do not simply discover their rights after exposure to metropolitan rights discourses, but become aware of their rights as they struggle with their families and communities to give meaning to their daily existence. This perspective on children's rights differs from the position of natural law scholars about the inherent character of human rights and comes close to what Dembour (2010) coins as the protest school of thought in human rights. Children engage with, interpret and give meaning to their rights; it is from this bottom-up perspective that their rights can be seen as 'living'. Thinking of them as living rights questions dominant views on the relation between the centre and the periphery of children's rights, and challenges the relevance of the centre–periphery binary itself.

Our Socratic walk in the geographical centre of official children's rights in Geneva led us to discuss the dimensions of the relation between global and local understandings of children's rights. We were particularly interested in theorizing the findings of a growing body of scholarship on how children's rights are put into practice from such diverse disciplines as sociology, anthropology, developmental psychology, international development studies and human rights studies. Facile, scandalous and extreme representations of the child in developing countries unduly cast the issue of children's rights in static binaries that almost force both scholars and the public at large into what has evolved as 'correct political thinking'. We wanted to offer an approach that would lend support to researchers attempting to escape from this type of thinking. Being critical of the ways children's rights are interpreted did not, in our eyes, result in a denial of the importance of rights to enhance children's lives and expand their agency. As we hope to demonstrate in this volume, rather to the contrary.

Finding inspiration in feminist theory, particularly its claim that women can produce knowledge on their own terms (Sunder, 2007), we thought that an interdisciplinary approach would help open spaces for children's production of knowledge about their rights. An interdisciplinary approach that takes complexity, circularity and interrelations into account offers a promising path to negotiate both the top-down 'paternalistic' implementation and the bottom-up 'empowering' uses of children's rights and to overcome sterile 'us vs. them' binaries so present in theorizations over power.

A few months before our promenade in Geneva, we had published with Pamela Reynolds a special issue of the journal *Childhood* titled 'Refractions of children's rights in development practice'. Taking an anthropological approach that focused on the lives of vulnerable children in a variety of contexts across the globe, we were concerned with the complex ways in which rights-based policies mesh with the practice of development and in the process become entangled, weld together or clash with children's ideas of right and wrong. We saw some danger in 'our use of rights to abstract and universalize at the expense of efforts to imagine the stake we have in mutual comprehensibility and to be responsive to other forms of life, especially those under construction by the young' (Reynolds *et al.*, 2006: 300–1). We suggested that an anthropological perspective could help demonstrate that children are not passive recipients of ideas that come 'from above' and that, if children's rights are to be entrenched, children should be party to the shaping and implementation of these rights. We now felt that the time was ripe for a more interdisciplinary approach and planned a workshop in Sion (Switzerland) where we invited a number of researchers coming from a range of disciplinary backgrounds, including socio-legal studies, communication sciences, human geography, social anthropology, sociology, developmental psychology and political science to write an original contribution on the theme of children's living rights. The discussions during the workshop provided us with further ideas for the theoretical framework developed in this chapter. We subsequently engaged carefully with and commented upon the various contributions, out of which twelve papers were finally selected to be included in the present volume.

As already indicated, the contributions all make reference to the three interrelated key concepts, living rights, social justice and translations, which also serve to organize the different parts of the book. In this theoretical introduction, we further develop the three concepts and indicate how the individual chapters contribute to conceptualize children's rights in developing societies. Starting from the lived experiences in which rights take shape raises the issue of how they become entrenched. We propose the notion of social justice to capture the broader shared normative beliefs that make rights appear legitimate and beyond question for those who struggle to get them recognized. These struggles result in what we call translations to designate the complex fluxes between different beliefs and perspectives on rights, their codification and the unstable interpretations given to these codified forms. Whilst the three proposed concepts each have some explanatory power, it is our contention that it is in their interrelatedness that we can start to grasp the complexities of how rights take shape in children's lived realities and daily struggles.

Living rights

The concept of living rights highlights that children (amongst other people), while making use of notions of rights, shape what these rights are – and become – in the social world. The concept challenges the idea that children's rights are exclusively those defined by international institutions or states. Offering the opportunities for empirical investigation of how co-existing, non-hierarchical forms of children's rights influence a given social arena, the notion creates a critical distance facilitating study and evaluation (see Tamanaha, 2000).

Children's notions of rights vary from seemingly inoffensive pleas, as when children demand the right to playgrounds, safe streets or a healthy environment, to more contentious claims that question hegemonic interpretations of what children are entitled to. When asked about their rights, children of Johannesburg, for instance, talk about the right to safely cross roads and to neighbourhoods that are free from crime (Swart-Kruger and Chawla, 2002). In India they demand play spaces in crowded slum areas (Driskell *et al.*, 2001). In Ethiopia girls take a critical stance against NGOs that interpret their rights in terms of autonomy and the pursuit of individual interests, arguing that they have duties as well and that they do not want to be obliged to earn their lives begging on the streets (Nieuwenhuys, 2001). In India, West Africa and many Latin American countries, the right to work and to be respected as workers has come forward as an important issue that children want to see addressed (Liebel, 2003 and Chapter 11 of this volume). The right to beg (Abebe, 2008; Invernizzi, 2003; Swanson, 2007), the right to take up arms (Denov, 2010; Peters and Richards, 1998; Rosen, 2005; Trawick, 2007), the right to work safely on the streets (Hecht, 1998 ; Kilbride *et al.*, 2000; Kovats-Bernat, 2006; and see Balagopalan in Chapter 7 of this volume), to an education that is respectful of communal political traditions and priorities (Baronnet, 2008), to protected marriage and motherhood (Bunting, 2005; Melchiorre, 2009; Merry, 2009; and see Henderson in Chapter 2 of this volume), and to be a family head (Evans, 2002; Kesby *et al.*, 2006; and see Cheney in Chapter 8 of this volume) are all rights that problematize top-down translations of children's rights.

The expression of rights often includes explicit demands addressed to local authorities and both national governments and international development agencies. Children may for example demand that NGOs address police violence on the streets, maltreatment, rape and murder while in custody, not hesitating to bear witness against the police at their own peril and risk. Their criticisms may often be shrewdly levelled against the interpretation of their rights – the right to survive figuring prominently and often being mentioned as overriding the rights of the urban middle classes to an environment free of beggars and street sellers (see for example: Berman, 2000; Droz, 2006; Godoy, 1999; Khair, 2001). Kovats-Bernat cites a former street child, now a staff member of the NGO Lafanmiselavi in Haiti's capital city of Port-au-Prince, expressing ideas about children's rights in these political terms:

> I remember when I was living on the streets. My heart would break when I saw other children going to school and participating in activities myself and other children living on the streets could never do. It's humiliating, because people who see you on the street treat you like an animal, and you can do nothing to defend yourself. Instead you feel very sad, and the sadness never leaves you … We need laws to force the government to take care of these children. They have a right to live like children who have parents.
>
> (Kovats-Bernat, 2006: 131).

The critique of market-led globalization is reiterated time and again, sometimes plainly voiced but more often craftily practised in subtle reverse manipulations of powerful global discourses. Child soldiers in Liberia and Sierra Leone manipulate NGO representations of victimhood to gain access to education or other resources (Hoffman, 2003; Shepler, 2005; Utas, 2005); HIV-orphans in South Africa overturn the very discourse of orphanhood by claiming that the whole of society has been orphaned by a government that has abdicated its duty to protect the vulnerable in times of crisis (Meintjes and Giese, 2006). The very way NGOs interpret children's rights may also be reinscribed in terms that subvert entirely their meaning, as when street children in Guatemala say: 'Our right is the right to be killed' (Godoy, 1999).

We look at children's rights as a 'living practice' shaped by children's everyday concerns. The question of how to understand the other's perspective when the other is a child is addressed in many contributions in this volume. Patti Henderson's ethnographic description of 'informal marriage' among rural 'AIDS-orphans' in KwaZulu-Natal, South Africa (Chapter 2) draws attention to the ambiguities with which girls especially have to deal in real-life situations. While the right to education and the absence of bodily violence may be formally championed as the hallmarks of girls' emancipation, limited real-life options for securing livelihoods entice girls to revive ancient practices of informal marriage that obstruct this very same emancipation. Courting repertoires and their outcomes are sufficiently embedded within local worlds to draw young girls towards what for them is an 'obvious' solution to waning family ties. Entering informal marriage therefore makes strategic sense for teenage girls in a context of unfolding HIV/AIDS-related deaths within their family and unemployment amongst their older siblings.

Phillip Mizen and Yaw Ofosu-Kusi in Chapter 3 make a case for using photographs of their living environment taken by street children to get a sense of their perspectives on their everyday lifeworld. The authors argue 'in defence of' the use of photography in social science research, in particular as a means of seeing and knowing the lives of street children. Photographs have the capacity to reveal the intimacy of children's everyday lives, to which aspects of their lives other research techniques such as observations, interviews or group discussions do not give access. Having the children picture and thus comment on their lives in the streets, on road junctions, waste grounds and derelict buildings in and around Ghana's capital city of Accra, teases out elaborate patterns of sharing and mutual help that makes their lives both bearable and meaningful.

Acknowledging the difference between 'reality' and the representation of that reality in photographs, the authors adopt what they call a critical realist stance in their use of photography to understand the lives of street children. This stance helps them uncover such important issues as personal hygiene, the sharing of food and the maintenance of moral standards of behaviour revealing the children's ingenuity and creativity. The photographs are not 'images of the pathological, the isolated, sick or diseased', but picture 'children doing what children often do; joking, playing and having fun, sharing friendships and creating relationships, doing nothing, passing time'.

Two contributions engage with working children's living rights. In his chapter on children's role in collective livelihood strategies in rural Ethiopia, Tatek Abebe proposes the notion of 'interdependent agency' as an alternative to all too individualistic interpretations of children's rights (Chapter 4). Claiming that in many parts of the world children are regarded as interdependent beings, he teases out how their daily livelihoods are entwined with the family collective and wider social structures. Focusing on the interrelatedness of rights, duties and obligations, Abebe unearths the multilayered nature of children's agency and the social, personal and spatial context in which it unfolds. Children's agency becomes real in the ways their work is entwined in wider networks of long-term support and in the collaboration between extended family networks (the family collective). Underlying the argument is an effort to link interdependent agency with living rights and to demonstrate that for Gedeo these rights are embedded in the family collective. There is a critical distancing from global top-down policies to grant children abstract rights in order to confer them agency, as this would not only ignore what they already have but also represent a form of denial of their way of life.

Tom O'Neill explores how young carpet weavers (both boys and girls) learn to negotiate their livelihoods and demonstrate a capacity for practical self-determination that enable them, against all odds, to shape their own lives (Chapter 5). The chapter reflects on the authors' fieldwork experience in Nepal by comparing the situation in three different factories and remarking on how children form a footloose labour force that moves in and out of the factories according to the available work and opportunities they may find further afield. Claiming that child protection efforts may often restrict working children's construction of their own futures, the paper takes issue against applying strict age limits in child labour legislation. The young weavers' experiences at work only imperfectly teach them the necessary skills to act in their own interests on a day-to-day basis, and what they would need most is support in buttressing their emergent ability to navigate the world of work.

These contributions underscore that children's rights cannot be limited to codifications in international or state law, nor to interpretations produced by development agencies. They must include the ways in which children practice their rights. Or to quote Tamanaha's conventionalist way of identifying law emptied of any essentialist feature: 'Law is whatever people identify and treat through their social practices as "law" (or *recht*, or *droit* and so on)' (2000: 313). Children's rights, in other words, are 'all of the many ways in which social actors across the range talk about, advocate for, criticize, study, legally enact, vernacularize, and so on, the idea of human rights in its different forms' (Goodale and Merry, 2007: 24). The approach implies that the *social practice* of the actors involved at both the local (e.g. children, their families, guardians or representatives; social movements) and the global level (e.g. institutions involved in law codification and agencies intervening on that basis on children's behalf) is what makes children's rights real.

From this perspective, children's rights cease to be a metaphysical abstraction of moral norms or the embodiment of universal natural rights. They are an imperfect compromise negotiated at a certain moment in time and in specific contexts by individuals representing different local and organizational interests and possessing different kinds of knowledge, skills and power. An illustration of this are human rights norms pertaining to children in the context of armed conflict that ban the use of child soldiers by prescribing age limitations for recruitment and participation in hostilities. This international legislative framework has been shaped as the outcome of successful humanitarian advocacy efforts and is largely informed by a 'protectionist' approach to children's experiences of armed conflict that leave aside more 'emancipatory' concerns (Hanson, 2011). International law in the context of armed conflict is but one of the many possible understandings of the rights of the child along with more marginalized or local conceptions, such as those embodied in the social practices of young people that express different forms of agency during armed conflict. We do not, however, suggest that social practice should override international norms. The point we want to make is that there exists a huge distance between the imagined child in the normative framework and the social practices of children, and that children's rights can therefore be made to carry many, even contradictory, meanings (see also Reynolds *et al.*, 2006).

In sum, all social practices that are conventionally identified as rights may be understood as 'living rights'. They are alive through active and creative interpretations, association and framing of what constitutes in a given context a child's right in people's hearts and minds. In this sense, children's and communities' understanding of rights are equally 'living' as the interpretations of experts and agencies acting on children's behalf. But even if we claim that children's rights are rights under construction and that their interpretation is a multifaceted and at times even contentious exercise, can we still unravel a broader, common concern for social justice in the ways they become entrenched?

Merry *et al.*'s study on how social movements in New York City mobilized human rights to deal with systematic race and gender discrimination may hold a beginning of an answer. The authors claim that the value side of human rights expressing broader social justice ideas had a particularly strong appeal in drawing people together and inspiring a sustained effort to support the movement (Merry *et al.*, 2010: 106–9). It is to the normative arena, which drives people to work for children's rights and in which children's rights get entrenched, that we therefore now turn.

Social justice

The term social justice encompasses three interlocking conceptual areas: the moral economy, where the ethos of reciprocity and inter-generational exchange informs how local communities and families in the developing world meet the challenges of organizing their daily life; the state as the primary guarantor of access to crucial resources (land, water, employment) and services (health, education and food); and social movements, the 'collective challenges [to elites, authorities, other groups or cultural codes] by people with common purposes and solidarity in sustained interactions with elites, opponents and authorities' (Tarrow, 1994; see also Stammers, 2009). While the justification for these collective challenges lies in the moral economy, the state figures as the main institution to which social movements can petition to forward claims and redress grievances. As we shall see, the rolling back of the state and the measures taken to reform the economy of developing countries under structural adjustment programmes during the 1980s and 1990s have made petitions to states increasingly futile and have opened a space of indeterminacy that induces social movements and more specifically NGOs to cast their claims and grievances in a human rights idiom.

In this section we make two points: first of all that the anthropological reading of children's narratives of their rights unveils the strength of social relations based on solidarity, defence of collective interests and a sense of communal harmony – in other words, as Stammers reminds us, the stuff which has historically provided the building blocks for the expression of collective rights (Stammers, 2009: 83). These social relations play a fundamental role in informing children's perceptions of social justice and the extent to which their individual interests are embedded into those of the collective. Secondly, that the post-cold war codification of international children's rights offered opportunities to social movements to gain leverage against states that failed people's sense of social justice towards the young and to appeal for support to the global community. We contend that this support is crucial in making children's rights alive today.

To begin with our first point, the living rights approach discussed above makes it possible to unveil a deep-seated, recurrent theme that articulates the ancient language of reciprocity in all human rights thinking. This language refers to what anthropologists have termed the moral economy (see Thompson, 1991 [1963]; Scott, 1976; Edelman, 2008). This economy is most manifest in the world of work, as in the absence of a welfare state the family collective, to use Abebe's term (Chapter 4), is the sole source of support and long-term security. It is to make their contribution to this collective that many poor children start working from an early age. Most of this work is by the side of parents, few children in the developing world entering in direct competition with adult workers. Particularly in the rural countryside families work together, the children generally performing subsidiary tasks, such as fishing, catching birds, collecting fallen fruits and fuelwood and so on to supplement the diet and earn a few coins (Nieuwenhuys, 1994). Children's work is often indistinguishable from the host of domestic chores necessary to make ends meet with the meagre proceeds of labour. In urban areas this work is often more visible, particularly when undertaken outside the child's home in limelight zones of the urban economy (Abebe, 2008; Hecht, 1998; Invernizzi, 2003; Kenny, 1999; Kovats-Bernat, 2006). Activities such as begging, porterage, retrieving useful materials from dumps, recycling and entertaining tourists have not only been labelled 'worst forms of child labour' by the ILO but are also the target of numerous NGO interventions all over the developing world. These interventions have to come to terms with the problem that, even if undesirable, much of this work is vital in enabling children to maintain their social worlds. Writing on life in the *favelas* of Recife (Brazil), Hecht uncovers how the ideal of children as nurturers of the family informs young boys' feelings of injustice and their resentment against society when they find themselves unable to live up to that ideal (Hecht, 1998).

Feelings of injustice are today typically voiced through social movements promoting ideas of solidarity, dignity and social justice. This has not always been the case. With decolonization following the Second World War, states in developing countries had embarked upon bold development programmes in which improving the fate of the young occupied a prominent place. As young people below the age of 18 formed the majority of the population, this was hardly surprising. But the role of the state in these newly independent nations changed as the cold war drew to an end in the 1980s.

The new world order that followed put developing states under heavy pressure to restyle their economies and societies according to the rationale of free-market economics propounded by the USA. This was to be the goal of the Structural Adjustment Programmes (SAPs) that were carried out under supervision of the IMF and World Bank in virtually all developing countries. As amply documented, the high proportion of children in many of these countries (between 50% to 70% of the population) simply meant that cuts in government spending deeply undermined whatever child and youth welfare services had been put in place in previous decades. Governments stopped feeding programmes, closed clinics, introduced school fees and threw hundreds of millions of parents of young children out of work (Bradshaw, 1993; Cornia *et al.*, 1987). The remaining funds were reserved to extreme cases that were identified as 'targets' of minimal interventions geared towards encouraging the beneficiaries to become self-sufficient as quickly as possible. The cuts provided a fertile ground for the emergence of social movements and non-governmental organizations specializing in fund-raising for child welfare. A vast array of organizations ranging from philanthropic societies and foundations, missionary churches, professional associations, political parties and trade unions to neighbourhood self-help groups and other social movements – their common trait being in fact only that they were 'non-governmental' – became involved in addressing children's welfare issues. These NGOs claimed to be more transparent, efficient, accountable and reliable than government bureaucracies and to be able to provide better support to targeted children at lower costs, not in the least because they could rely on alternate sources of income from their 'targets' such as voluntary labour as well as donations of both money and goods from both local and global civil society. The number of NGOs for children has since been growing both locally and internationally at an exponential rate, submerging not only public child welfare services but even state-led development programmes (Bornstein, 2005).

In their search for social justice, NGOs and the social movements they aim to support seek in international human rights instruments to translate the moral notions in which their beneficiaries' sense of social justice is embedded and adopt a supra-local idiom that is gaining coinage in global civil society. This is also the case with the now increasingly popular child rights' approach. The approach represents a translation of (parts of) the CRC and appeals to national and international civil society to bring justice to the young. As with other post-cold war human rights, the child rights' approach tells the young that even if their 'developing' states have failed them, they are not left behind, as these rights make the sovereignty of the erstwhile post-colonial nations 'contingent upon compliance with a minimum of human rights principles towards its residents' (Merry, 2006: 101).

NGOs have justified their roles as agencies occupying a strategic intermediary position between the most forgotten and downtrodden in society and their neglectful and inept governments. Their transnational support networks enable them to criticize and act without fear in exposing situations of children's rights violations and this is crucial for their very existence (Manzo, 2008). As we shall see in the next section, NGOs also find themselves in a position of advantage to act as translators of children's living rights. By their very nature, they need to find support among their beneficiaries, informing a process of constant negotiation with children and their communities over the normative framework that should guide translation, or, in other words, over how social justice for children is to be understood and realized.

As the contributions in this volume illuminate, both children and adults adhere to strong ethical norms that are sources of tensions and negotiations in their dealings with NGOs. Underlying these, as Yvan Droz argues in Chapter 6, may be a deeply held belief that the language of children's rights as busied by foreign NGOs or even the country's government could well undermine vital notions of social justice. In his contribution Droz confronts the Kikuyu people of Kenya's childhood *ethos* (a pervasive and implicit system of values) with the explicit politico-philosophical *ethics* that undergirds the readings of the CRC that have gained currency in the country. In the Kikuyu *ethos* the child represents the vital link between generations, social status as an 'accomplished person' critically depending on one's ability to successfully bear and raise children and grandchildren. In contrast, the *ethics* that finds its inspiration in the CRC views children as individuals endowed with inalienable rights that bear no relation to their social roles. Within this *ethics* parents' duties towards their children are geared towards enabling them to become free and autonomous individuals. For the Kikuyu, so runs Droz's argument, this *ethics* is merely a rationalised conception of a specific (Western) *ethos* presented in a way that makes it incompatible with their own. Only when the components of local *ethos* are highlighted and acknowledged can a fruitful conversation develop between the proponents of a universal *ethics* and local children and parents. This conversation could help prevent possible misunderstandings that arise when readings of children's rights that are grounded in pretensions of universality are imposed from above to the neglect if not denial of the existence of contending *ethos*.

Also Sarada Balagopalan draws from narratives about street children in Kolkota (Calcutta), India, to tease out 'metaphors of dissonance' that challenge readings of children's rights that all children possess rights-bearing subjectivities (Chapter 7). The author contends that rather than reading international treaties such as the CRC textually, more can be gained from trying to capture the ways in which the universal gets read within local webs of signification. Balagopalan's discussion of the idea of universal rights suggests ways of thinking (such as 'friction' and 'cultural translation') that may help enrich our understanding of how children's rights get entrenched in local notions of social justice and continually engage with the universal. Grounding their ideas of rights in notions of community and belonging, the particular historical context of street children in Calcutta make them ambivalent towards local NGOs' readings of their rights. While on the one hand they see in the NGOs allies who support them in their work on the streets and therefore defend what they feel is their right, they are also diffident, so she argues, against victimhood and individualism that may transpire in their policies.

That this diffidence can also entice children into attempting to manipulate and subvert what NGOs make of their rights in order to secure resources is the subject of Kristen Cheney's contribution in Chapter 8. Much of transnational children's rights activism, she observes, emphasizes a protectionist approach over an empowering one. The problem of implementation of the CRC hence does not lie, she feels, in children's lack of morality and agency, but in how adults abuse their power to ignore issues of social justice and use children's rights for their own self-interest. This drives children as those living in the context of AIDS in Uganda to adopt an identity of victim as a method to secure what they need. Orphans use similar tactics to those employed by former child soldiers, describing themselves as victims, which seems to be the only vocabulary that literally pays. The actions taken to secure rights, Cheney comments, thus paradoxically reinforce the denial of children's empowerment in favour of a protectionist reading of children's rights. But children capitalizing more on the figure of the 'vulnerable child' than on the active citizen claiming his or her rights also reveal their ability to strategically manipulate powerful social categories to procure resources. So while the codification of orphans' identities recreates children as sites for both local and global humanitarian intervention, children learn how to work the victimhood discourse and, by the same token, how to appropriate it.

Marginalized urban teenagers tend to get a disproportionate amount of interest from NGOs and to garner sympathy, support and funds. What their issues have in common is the potential threat they represent unless at least a semblance of action is undertaken. Armed teenagers in guerrilla armies; footloose young labourers who destabilize the international division of labour; street children in drug trafficking and robbery; girls upsetting the tourism industry and offering sexual services as a means to challenge their subordinate position in society; young children harassing the public to get alms or sell overpriced goods: these are highly political issues that threaten the governance of the global order and interventions in their favour may therefore count on support of international civil society. No child-related issue is politically innocent and we should remain aware that even if an unequal global order gives some agencies and governments an inordinate power to define, specify and prioritize children's rights, this does not necessarily imply a lack of resistance or struggle over which notions of social justice should prevail and how they should be translated into law. This brings us to our third concept.

Translations

The concept of translations is about what happens with rights in the encounter of children's and other actors' perspectives, movements for social justice and the elites, authorities and opponents. As claims and grievances get translated into law a process of implementation is set in motion. In General Comment No. 5 (2003) concerning general measures of implementation of the CRC, the Committee on the Rights of the Child defined implementation as 'the process whereby States parties take action to ensure the realization of all rights in the Convention for all children in their jurisdiction' (Committee on the Rights of the Child, 2003). The ultimate aim of human rights implementation is for international norms to have an impact on the ground in children's real lives. As argued in the previous section, the question of how to bridge the gap between the text of international legislation developed and interpreted in Geneva and the conceptions and practice of rights of real-life children in their localities in the developing world has taken centre stage.

When NGOs with politically sensitive agendas around such issues as child labour, child refugees, child prostitution and child soldiers began seeking the limelight, the stage was set for sparking intense debate among policy-makers and practitioners about the ability of children to really have a voice and the veracity of their narratives. This was most apparent during the meetings leading up to the adoption of ILO Convention No. 182 on the Worst Forms of Child Labour in 1999. While the NGO caucus organized a global march of working children converging on Geneva in support of the elimination of the worst forms of child labour as advocated by the new Convention, dissident NGO representatives of the international movement of working children assembled in the remote town of Kundapur in South India to make a case for protecting their right to work in dignity (see Liebel in Chapter 11 of this volume). While the former questioned the ability of exploited children – whom they likened to 'slaves' – to have any genuine opinions about their work unless they were first liberated from their exploiters and sent to school, the latter claimed that the CRC granted them the right to have a voice in matters that affected them. For both parties, the justification for involving children was that they faithfully translated the principles of the CRC into practice. But they clearly had divergent views as to how this was to be done.

NGO interventions and accompanying policy-oriented interpretations of rights find a resonance among children that, while being supportive, is also critical, transgressive and subversive. NGOs depend for their legitimacy, as already said, increasingly on children expressing their problems in a language of rights. Some authors have noted the perverse instrumentalization and manipulation that 'rights-talk' may engender (White and Choudhury, 2007). While we believe that 'facipulation' should not be discounted, we do think that, as women's and children's rights movements' recent attention to 'child marriage' or 'early marriage' exemplify, children under 18 are too easily assumed to be unable to exercise agency. As Bunting observes, maintaining minimum age as an inflexible legal standard may in fact exacerbate the underlying socio-economic problems informing girls' and adolescents' decisions in developing countries (2005: 18).

Several contributions in this book address the complexities of the translation process of children's rights, in particular localized development practices. Children's creativity and ingenuity in the invention of social practices is at the core of Colette Daiute's notion of 'living history' (Chapter 9). The author contends that children and youths growing up in the aftermath of war not only suffer from human and environmental destruction wrought by the previous generation but also from a range of symbolic consequences that limit their rights to shape society in response to their lived experiences. Inadequate assumptions about the nature and development of childhood that represent children and youth during and after war as damaged and helpless exclude them from activities requiring critical thinking. Turning history into an instrument of oppression, these representations ignore that those who grow up during and after war may have a very different approach to the past. To illustrate her point Daiute draws from a study with 12- to 27-year-olds who grew up in three countries (Bosnia, Croatia and Serbia) that were part of the former Yugoslavia as well as refugees living in the USA. Ideas of violence prevention, she argues, implicitly (and incompletely) draw on child development theories that emphasize biological maturation or socialization to cultural ways of knowing. Drawing from Vygotsky, she proposes an alternative approach that embeds child development in the daily interactions between children and society. It is in these interactions that children develop capacities, like language and thought, to make sense of the threats and opportunities they meet while growing up. These capacities make them critical of oppressive readings of the past and enable them to identify problems and solutions in the light of the situation in which they find themselves, in other words to engage in the creation of living history (see also Habashi, 2008).

How such a conversation could be grounded in legal practice is the subject of Eva Brems' contribution, in which she discusses contending interpretations of children's cultural and religious rights (Chapter 10). Discussing the general principles of the CRC (non-discrimination; best interests of the child; right to life and development; right to be heard), Brems situates her theory of inclusive universality within the current literature on universality/cultural diversity of international human rights. Writing from a legal perspective, Brems argues that the international legal human rights framework provides space to accommodate a variety of different readings of children's rights claims. The author elaborates a three-step model which, when parents and children have conflicting views about children's rights in the field of cultural and religious practices, can guide the (inherently normative) job of judges and lawyers in prioritizing particular human rights over others.

The two subsequent contributions deal with working children's rights, which were also addressed in previous chapters (Chapters 4 and 5), and analyse how the international movement of working children has travelled between local and global understandings of the rights of children at work. After reminding us of the three cities where the world meetings of working children have taken place (Kundapur, 1998; Berlin, 2004 and Sienna, 2006), Manfred Liebel positions working children's struggle for the translation of their right to work in dignity in international law within a wider social justice framework (Chapter 11). Opposition to anti-child labour legislation and campaigning, including the threat of trade sanctions, translates children's critique of how powerful economic interests drive market-led reforms that harm children (Liebel, 2003; Nieuwenhuys, 2005). Adopting the language of organized labour and substituting the rights-bearing subjects 'working children' for the objectifying term 'child labour' used by the ILO, the movement deeply unsettles the ILO's official claim of being the international labour organization. Its unquestioned endorsement of the binary adult vs. child labour reveals not only the perverse effects of this thinking but more deeply conceals the ILO's failure to support precisely those it says it wants to protect from exploitation.

Elaborating the issue further, Karl Hanson and Arne Vandaele (Chapter 12) argue that working children's claim to have their right to work in dignity recognized can inspire the rethinking of how international labour law addresses child labour and working children's rights. The *difference dilemma*, which addresses issues of equality and difference between adults and children, in particular between adult labourers and child labourers, helps them explore alternative ways of looking at existing international labour law. Their position on similarities and differences between working children and working adults forms the basis for reconceptualizing working children's participation rights and their right to work in dignity within international labour law. From their analysis of regulations regarding age limitations, rights in work and instrumental work-related rights, Hanson and Vandaele argue that such a translation is not, a priori, impossible.

The translation of children's rights into practice is never solely either a top-down or a bottom-up activity, as many contributions in this volume show, but a circular process whereby source and target languages constantly engage with one another giving rise to unforeseen complexities that produce a state of constant indeterminacy. Frustrating as this may appear to practitioners, translation must acknowledge difference and lend some recognition to children's representations of their lives and situation. This provides children with room to negotiate meanings and influence practitioners' interpretation of their rights that find their way, ultimately, into some kind of acknowledgement in the circles of legal experts. Sally Engel Merry (2006: 211) points at the double movement involved in translation, whereby international human rights are not only translated 'down' into local systems, but local stories are also translated 'up' into a common human rights idiom. Mark Goodale and Sally Engel Merry (2007) suggest that focusing on a third space, the 'betweenness' in which the dialogue between individual and groups on values and norms takes place, may help bypass the binary of the global and the local. It is in this in-between space, where the exchange of equally legitimate sets of values and norms takes place, that new social practices emerge.

Koen De Feyter stresses the need for human rights to be situation-specific, or *localized*, which implies that they have to take into account the human rights needs as formulated by local people; if global human rights are to be relevant to all, they need 'an infusion from below' (2007: 68). De Feyter proposes a bottom-up networking approach to human rights, which includes grass-roots organizations, local human rights movements, international human rights NGOs and governmental and intergovernmental institutions. This model requires that the human rights experiences of local communities set the agenda for the entire network (De Feyter 2007: 83), which is unlikely to happen. For Clifford Bob (2009) gatekeepers such as Amnesty International and Human Rights Watch wield decisive influence on which issues get onto the international human rights agenda and are more likely than local populations to inaugurate claims. Rather than the victims of human rights violations looking for gatekeepers to transmit their claim to the international bodies, gatekeepers would formulate claims in line with the organization's mission and with an eye on donor preferences (or the reverse) and then look for local 'victims' who fit the predefined violations. As Cheney (Chapter 8) illuminates, Bob's view may, however, underplay the astuteness of the 'victims' in navigating the landscape of children's rights violations.

We should be particularly wary of how transnational human rights networks active in the field of children's rights address the 'problematic of representational power' (Baxi, 2002), especially given the leading role of adults in activism around children's rights (see Stammers in Chapter 13 of this volume). Whose interpretations, and whose priorities of children's rights, are being defended? How do children's living rights coalesce with top-down international child rights implementation strategies? What are the trajectories of both approaches to children's rights? Where and how do bottom-up and top-down interpretations meet, if they meet, and what are the consequences of such an encounter? The 'translations' concept seeks to capture the tensions at work between global and local formulations of children's rights (see Wilson, 1997: 23) when actors taking part in the exercise of power, be they individuals, agencies or institutions, interact with one another (Gallagher, 2008: 402–3). Hence translation is, in our view, a multiple-way process that transforms the power relations of all actors involved. Robert J. C. Young terms such a dynamic view of translation as *Carribbean creolization*, which 'comes close to a foundational idea of postcolonialism: that the one-way process by which translation is customarily conceived can be rethought in terms of cultural interaction and as a space of re-empowerment' (2003: 142).

Interrelations and flux

Looking back at fifty years of legal anthropology, Sally Falk Moore discusses how the attribution of agency to the anthropological subject and the importance attached to action and choice have become the central concern of cultural and legal analysis. Small-scale fieldwork is being used to comment on large-scale issues, whereby the two levels are harnessed to ask 'whether the field work data show that there are major obstacles that stand in the way of realizing the freedoms and accountabilities that are part of the ideal of a liberal democracy' (2005: 361). Commenting on three books published at the end of the 1990s that she uses to illustrate her point, Moore writes:

> They [the authors] are moved to question the damaging effects of many laws and legal institutions. But they are also mindful that in some countries and in some international institutions, law is being used for reconstructive purposes. It can make social disasters, but in some situations it can help to prevent and repair them.
>
> When anthropologists are moved to ask under which conditions legal institutions can contribute to democratic practice, they are inadvertently showing some small signs of optimism about the possibilities of intentional action. Such enquiries demonstrate that even a habitually sceptical profession can acknowledge that perhaps things could be better. At the very least, situations could be better understood.
>
> (Moore, 2005: 361)

We believe that the concepts living rights, social justice and translations may help us to understand the complex ways in which children's rights come into play in today's developing societies, that they hold a capacity for theorizing that goes beyond the children's rights field and that they are also relevant for making sense of emerging patterns in human rights studies more generally. In his concluding chapter (Chapter 13), Neil Stammers reflects on the issues raised in the volume and positions the analytical themes 'living rights', 'translations' and 'social justice' within the broader framework of his research on human rights and social movements. He argues that starting from a triadic conceptualization of actors, agency and structure may offer a more fruitful way forward for grasping the complexities of the social world than the more usual binary agency vs. structure. For the author the three notions have a wider applicability than the field of children's rights alone and may contribute to minimize or mitigate the worst problems of what he describes as the paradox of institutionalization and the problem of representational power.

References

Abebe T (2008) Earning a living on the margins: begging, street work and the socio-spatial experiences of children in Addis Ababa. *Geografiska Annaler: Series B, Human Geography* 90: 271–84.

Baronnet B (2008) Rebel youth and Zapatista autonomous education. *Latin American Perspectives* 35(4): 112–24.

Baxi U (2002) *The Future of Human Rights*. Oxford University Press.

Berman L (2000) Surviving on the streets of Java: homeless children's narratives of violence. *Discourse and Society* 11(2): 149–74.

Bob C (2009) Introduction: Fighting for new rights. In: Bob C (ed.) *The International Struggle for New Human Rights*. Philadelphia: University of Pennsylvania Press, pp. 1–13.

Bornstein E (2005) *The Spirit of Development: Protestant NGOs, Morality, and Economics in Zimbabwe*. Stanford University Press.

Bradshaw Y W (1993) New directions in international development: a focus on children. *Childhood* 1(3): 134–42.

Bunting A (2005) Stages of development: marriage of girls and teens as an international human rights issue. *Social and Legal Studies* 14(2): 17–38.

Cornia G A, Jolly R and Stewart F (eds.) (1987) *Adjustment with a Human Face: Protecting the Vulnerable and Promoting Growth*. Oxford: Clarendon.

Committee on the Rights of the Child (2003) *General Comment No. 5. General Measures of Implementation of the Convention on the Rights of the Child (Arts. 4, 42 and 44, para. 6)*. 27 November 2003 (CRC/GC/2003/5).

De Feyter K (2007) Localising human rights. In: Benedek W, De Feyter K and Marella F (eds.) *Economic Globalisation and Human Rights*. Cambridge University Press, pp. 67–92.

Dembour M-B (2010) What are human rights? Four schools of thought. *Human Rights Quarterly* 32(1): 1–20.

Denov M (2010) *Child Soldiers: Sierra Leone's Revolutionary United Front.* Cambridge University Press.

Driskell D, Kanchan B and Chawla L (2001) Rhetoric, reality and resilience: Overcoming obstacles to young people's participation in development. *Environment and Urbanization* 13(1): 77–89.

Droz Y (2006) Street children and the ethic of work. New policy for an old morale, Nairobi (Kenya). *Childhood* 13(3): 349–63.

Edelman M (2008) Bringing the moral economy back in … to the study of 21st-century transnational peasant movements. *American Anthropologist* 107(3): 331–45.

Evans R (2002) Poverty, HIV, and barriers to education: street children's experiences in Tanzania. *Gender and Development* 10(3): 51–62.

Gallagher M (2008) Foucault, power and participation. *The International Journal of Children's Rights* 16(3): 395–406.

Godoy A S (1999) 'Our right is the right to be killed': making rights real on the streets of Guatemala City. *Childhood* 6(4): 423–42.

Goodale M and Merry S E (eds.) (2007) *The Practice of Human Rights: Tracking Law Between the Global and the Local.* Cambridge University Press.

Habashi J (2008) Palestinian children crafting national identity. *Childhood* 15(1): 12–29.

Hanson K (2011) International children's rights and armed conflict. *Human Rights and International Legal Discourse* 5(1): 40–62.

Hecht T (1998) *At Home in the Street.* Cambridge University Press.

Hoffman D (2003) Like beasts in the bush: synonyms of childhood and youth in Sierra Leone. *Postcolonial Studies* 6(3): 295–308.

Invernizzi A (2003) Street-working children and adolescents in Lima: work as an agent of socialization. *Childhood* 10(3): 319–41.

Kenny M L (1999) No visible means of support: child labor in urban northeast Brazil. *Human Organization* 58(4): 375–86.

Kesby M, Gwanzura-Ottemoller F and Chizororo M (2006) Theorizing *other*, 'other childhoods': issues emerging from work on HIV in urban and rural Zimbabwe. *Children's Geographies* 4(2): 185–202.

Khair S (2001) Street children in conflict with the law: the Bangladesh experience. *Asia-Pacific Journal on Human Rights and the Law* 2(1): 55–76.

Kilbride P, Suda C and Njeru E (2000) *Street Children in Kenya: Voices of Children in Search of a Childhood.* Westport, CT: Bergin & Garvey.

Kovats-Bernat J C (2006) *Sleeping Rough in Port-au-Prince.* Gainesville: University of Florida Press.

Liebel M (2003) Working children as social subjects: the contribution of working children's organisations to social transformations. *Childhood* 10(3): 265–85.

Manzo K (2008) Imaging humanitarianism: NGO identity and the iconography of childhood. *Antipode* 40(4): 632–57.

Meintjes H and Giese S (2006) Spinning the epidemic: the making of mythologies of orphanhood in the context of AIDS. *Childhood* 13(3): 407–30.

Melchiorre A (2009) Marrying protection and autonomy. *CRIN Review* 23: 28–9.

Merry S E (2006) *Human Rights and Gender Violence: Translating International Law into Local Justice*. University of Chicago Press.

(2009) Relating to the subjects of human rights: the culture of agency in human rights discourse. In: Freeman M and Napier D (eds.) *Law and Anthropology. Current Legal Issues*. Oxford University Press, pp. 385–407.

Merry S E, Levitt P, Rosen M Ş and Yoon D H (2010) Law from below: women's human rights and social movements in New York City. *Law and Society Review* 44(1): 101–28.

Moore S F (2005) Certainties undone: fifty turbulent years of legal anthropology, 1949–1999. In: Moore S F (ed.). *Law and Anthropology. A Reader*. Malden: Blackwell Publishing, pp. 346–67.

Nieuwenhuys O (1994) *Children's Lifeworlds, Gender, Welfare and Labour in the Developing World*. New York/London: Routledge.

(2001) By the sweat of their brow? Street children, NGOs and children's rights in Addis Ababa. *Africa* 71(4): 539–57.

(2005) Child labour. In: Sherrod L R, Flanagan C and Kassimir R (eds.) *Youth Activism: An International Encyclopedia*. Westport, CT: Greenwood Publishing, pp.113–21.

Peters K and Richards P (1998) Why we fight: voices of youth combatants in Sierra Leone. *Africa* 68(2): 183–209.

Reynolds P, Nieuwenhuys O and Hanson K (2006). Refractions of children's rights in development practice: a view from anthropology. *Childhood* 13(3): 291–303.

Rosen D M (2005) *Armies of the Young: Child Soldiers in War and Terrorism*. Piscataway, NJ: Rutgers University Press.

Scott J C (1976) *The Moral Economy of the Peasant: Rebellion and Subsistence in Southeast Asia*. New Haven, CT: Yale University Press.

Shepler S (2005) The rites of the child: global discourses of youth and reintegrating child soldiers in Sierra Leone. *Journal of Human Rights* 4(2): 197–211.

Stammers N (2009) *Human Rights and Social Movements*. London: Pluto Press.

Sunder M (2007) Introduction: Feminism in the power/knowledge age. In: Sunder M (ed.) *Gender and Feminist Theory in Law and Society*. Burlington: Ashgate, pp. xi–xxiii.

Swanson K (2007) 'Bad mothers' and 'delinquent children': unravelling anti-begging rhetoric in the Ecuadorian Andes. *Gender, Place & Culture* 14(6): 703–20.

Swart-Kruger J and Chawla L (2002) 'We know something someone doesn't know': children speak out on local conditions in Johannesburg. *Environment & Urbanization* 14(2): 85–96.

Tamanaha B Z (2000) A non-essentialist version of legal pluralism. *Journal of Law and Society* 27(2): 296–321.

Tarrow S (1994). *Power in Movement: Collective Action, Social Movements and Politics.* Cambridge University Press.

Thompson E P (1991 [1963]) *The Making of the English Working Class.* London: Penguin.

Trawick M (2007) *Enemy Lines. Warfare, Childhood, and Play in Batticaloa.* Berkeley and Los Angeles: University of California Press.

Utas M (2005) Victimcy, girlfriending, soldiering: tactic agency in a young woman's social navigation of the Liberian war zone. *Anthropology Quarterly* 78(2): 403–30.

White S and Choudhury S (2007) The politics of child participation in international development: the dilemma of agency. *European Journal of Development Research* 19(4): 529–50.

Wilson R A (1997) Rights, culture and context: An introduction. In: Wilson R A (ed.) *Human Rights, Culture and Context: Anthropological Perspectives.* London: Pluto Press, pp. 1–27.

Young R (2003) *Postcolonialism. A Very Short Introduction.* Oxford University Press.

PART I

Living rights

2

Ukugana: 'Informal marriage' and children's rights discourse among rural 'AIDS-orphans' in KwaZulu-Natal, South Africa

PATRICIA C. HENDERSON

The chapter examines permutations of gendered identities in relation to the discourse of young persons' rights. Drawing on a research period from March 2003 to December 2005, it documents girls' strategies for survival in Emfuleni, a settlement in some of the high mountain reaches of Okhahlamba, a sub-district within the province of KwaZulu-Natal, South Africa.[1] In a context of HIV/AIDS and multiple deaths accompanied by diminishing kinship networks, five out of a group of twenty-one girls, ranging in age between 14 and 20, sought what I have termed 'informal marriages' with young men. Each of the girls had lost one or both parents to the disease. Such relationships are more broadly taken up throughout the region by young people who are not as overtly affected by the presence of HIV/AIDS, but who cannot afford the high cost of a fully achieved marriage. These relationships are publicly sanctioned through ritual, the participation of younger people in celebrations around a couple's agreement and the exchange of gifts between their families – exchanges that mirror those involved in the formation of a completed marriage in which substantial bridewealth is given to a girl's family.

Despite marked gendered differentiation, in terms of the emerging subjectivities of boys and girls, and a hierarchical gendered social organisation that increasingly constrains the comportment and expressive

[1] Emfuleni is a pseudonym, as are the names of young people to whom I refer in the text. Data for the chapter were gathered during a five-year research project (March 2003–March 2008) into the experience of people living with and alongside HIV/AIDS in Okhahlamba, a sub-district in KwaZulu-Natal, South Africa. The following organizations sponsored the research: The Centre for HIV/AIDS Networking (HIVAN), the Rockefeller Brothers' Fund, Atlantic Philanthropies, the Carnegie Corporation and the National Institutes of Health (NIH). Extracts of interviews that appear in the chapter were recorded in isi-Zulu and translated into English. I would like to thank Pamela Reynolds and Shirley Pendlebury for discussions in relation to the chapter.

possibilities for girls in the process of becoming 'young brides', courting repertoires and their outcomes create threads of meaningful sociality. In relation to girls who have lost parents to the AIDS epidemic, and who have few other relatives on whom to rely, contracting an 'informal marriage' becomes one possible response to the shrinkage of family ties. Given the low standard of education in the region, a history of little education for girls and the increasing difficulty of finding employment in the wider society, the insistence on the girls' right to education on the part of local non-governmental organisation (NGO) personnel seems of less importance to some young women than increasing the set of people whom they legitimately call upon as relatives.

Courting styles, as described in the chapter, are considered alongside notions of children's rights, as promulgated in the Convention of the Rights of the Child (CRC) that have entered the community through NGO activities. For example, at a one-week workshop, children's rights, as listed in the Convention, were discussed with only three out of a group of thirty-four with whom I worked. Presenters and local facilitators spoke of rights in a manner that assumed their immediate cogency and transparency, and that extricated young people from their complex ties and responsibilities with and in relation to adults. Embedded forms of interaction and social life that might have had a bearing on local interpretations of rights were omitted from discussions. The facilitators did not consider that they might have importance in relation to a cultural translation of rights. NGOs in the region generally approached local communities with a degree of naivety, as if they were predominantly characterised by overarching forms of lack, and as if in their own practice NGOs were purveyors of neutral forms of knowledge. Social repertoires that NGOs thought of as being 'traditional' were dismissed as having no relevance to contemporary worlds and to efforts in forging a democratic state. Rights were couched in a way that assumed their unproblematic universality, and that were upheld in relation to a particular construction of personhood. This was a form of personhood that insisted on the discrete individual as being the quintessential rights-bearing subject.

What I will explore in the chapter has resonance with the ideas of another contributor to the volume, Sarada Balagopalan, who, drawing on Judith Butler (Zižek *et al.*, 2011), unsettles the notion of the universal by suggesting that it bears the trace of the very particular that it seeks to negate, and that what is promulgated as universal is in fact a parochial idea of dominant, hegemonic power that cannot be separated from histories of colonialism and imperialism. If the universal is imagined as aspirational rather than rigid law to be imposed, it becomes important to document how global notions of universality engage with the local in forms of unusual friction (Tsing, 2005). Returning to the CRC, in relation to courting repertoires in Okhahlamba, notions of universality will therefore be considered alongside already established practices in which young people find pleasure and social status, and in which they form collective spheres of independence and recognition. These are repertories embedded in social life in which pleasing aesthetics contribute to their longevity, and are nevertheless conjoined with differential forms of power.

Therefore, whilst acknowledging the pleasing aspects of courtship and the importance of local forms of relationship, the chapter traces nodes of ambivalence in courting repertoires, and in particular the blurring of distinctions between metaphors of violence and its actuality, as a process of aestheticisation. Despite the above paradox, *ukugana* (informal marriage), as it is practised, retains contingent qualities where a girl can negotiate a choice of lover and sometimes the conditions under which she enters such a relationship.

Although not everyone practises courting rituals as I will describe them, they cannot be dismissed as 'archaic residues' of a distant past, but have contemporary salience, and are reclaimed and reinvigorated within the region and beyond.[2] In relation to constructions of tradition within contemporary settings, Deborah Battaglia argues that nostalgia is powerfully deployed within post-colonial situations in marking peoples' 'attachment of appropriate feelings toward their own histories, products and capabilities [and] their detachment from – and active resistance to – disempowering conditions of post-colonial life' (1995: 77). Similarly, Elizabeth Povinelli (2006) explores differing forms of sociality and their ideological scaffolding in the form of discourses within neo-liberal post colonies: one based on what she terms 'stranger sociality' and the paramount importance of individual quests for freedom, where freedom emerges from the severing of prolonged bonds with others; and the other, embedded in the metaphoric deployment of the notion of genealogy, where differing freedoms are generated from ties that bind, and the practice of sustaining lines of generosity with others. The question then emerges, do local constructions of personhood in Okhahlamba in some instances dislodge the notion of rights from their usual location, in relation to the discrete

[2] The most extended contemporary investigation of young girls' group involvement in rituals of affinity, or rituals around courtship and marriage may be found in Fiona Scorgie's (2003) work. See also Eileen Krige (1968).

individual as a set of entitlements to a place where broad, intermingled ties, where socially recognised roles may be drawn upon, or emulated in attempts to provide forms of protection, for example?

Geographies

Okhahlamba occupies a position of marginality in relation to the economic centres of South Africa. It is made up of the trust-lands of the amaNgwane, the amaZizi, African freehold settlements, white-owned commercial farms and tourist resorts. Most African people who regard Okhahlamba as their home seek employment for parts of their lives outside the region in major cities. A few are employed within the local tourist industry, or work intermittently on white-owned farms as labourers.

Emfuleni and its surrounds are cattle country. Most cattle herds are small with many households having lost their herds altogether due to encroaching impoverishment and stock theft. Maize is grown on spread-out valley floors. Dispersed homesteads are scattered over foothills and along some higher mountain reaches.

The surrounding natural environment beyond their homesteads into which young people venture constitutes a valued, independent space, where their activities, although threaded through with responsibilities in relation to the running of their homesteads, provide opportunities for courtship. The contemporary formation of groups of boys and girls around courtship and rituals of affinity more broadly come to mirror in certain respects the age-set social organisation of the past (see Scorgie, 2003: 113; Krige, 1950 [1936]: 81). Strong bonds of friendship therefore develop between young people, and have the effect of cementing a notion of home and place, in spite of the peripatetic lives they may later lead through forms of migration.

Terminology

In isiZulu, *ukugana* may be translated as 'to marry' (Doke *et al.*, 2006: 230). The term is, however, used across a range of relationships in Okhahlamba, indicating the intention to marry, or to choose a husband on the part of a girl (Scorgie, 2003), but not necessarily the achievement of full marriage marked by the passage of bridewealth from a man's family to that of his bride. *Ukugana* is sometimes translated as to be 'engaged', or as 'elopement' (Scorgie, 2003). Women in the region who declare they are 'really' married, use the phrase, *Ngi shadile* ('I am married'), meaning that full bridewealth has been paid. Many women involved in lasting relationships, where full bridewealth has *not* been given, refer to their status, using the word *ganile*. There are often protracted and incomplete preparations for and exchanges within marriage, suggesting ways in which de facto relationships are open to interpretation and to change.

Pathways to 'informal marriage'

In Okhahlamba, the journey of *ukugana* or 'informal marriage' is accomplished in three ways: through a girl, once having chosen a lover (*uqomile*, see below), 'disappearing' and staying overnight at her boyfriend's homestead; through forced abduction (*ukuthwala*) of a girl by a group of boys on behalf of a particular boy against her will, and through 'staged' abduction, where a boy and girl have come to an agreement that they want their family to recognise their relationship, but do not have sufficient means for bridewealth payments. After a girl has stayed overnight at a boy's homestead through one of the above ways, a negotiator (*umkhongi*) is usually sent to the girl's home the following day. Unless a girl escapes from an unwanted *ukuthwala* situation, or after a member of her own family has questioned her as to whether she accepts the relationship, and she has refused it, a fine is paid to the girl's family for precipitating an elopement, culpability for which is always regarded as the boy's. Thereafter a series of exchanges, visits and dance parties take place between the two families in which the relationship is accepted.

Gender, power and relationship

Ukugana ('informal marriage') constitutes a publicly negotiated relationship between a boy and a girl, where a girl comes to live in a boy's homestead, taking on many of the attributes and responsibilities of a *makoti* (young bride). In Okhahlamba, gendered power relations often seem starkly skewed as they unfold with the progression of courtship, and as a girl moves from her family home to that of her lover. The forceful and at times violent nature of the courting practices of boys and young men contrast with the increasingly 'muted' behaviour of girls as courtship proceeds – a 'muteness' that boys interpret in the initial stages of courtship as indicating that their words have 'struck home' and are having the desired effect on the girls they court. Once having moved to her boyfriend's homestead, a girl is expected to perform a series of verbal and physical acts of avoidance, connoting respect (*inhlonipho*) in relation to her lover's father and the older men and boys within the homestead, as well as towards her 'mother-in-law'. It is therefore unsurprising that boys actively propose love (*ukushela*) to woo girls, whereas it is regarded as shameful for girls to do likewise.

Boys pride themselves on their verbal dexterity, on the 'verbal traps' they set for girls. A girl, together with her peers, confront the 'verbal assaults' of boys with *izifenqo*, a form of witty repartee that overtly dismisses the boy (see, for example, Vilakazi, 1962: 48). *Izifenqo* constitutes a verbal art that upholds the ways in which girls are expected to defend their virginity and its aestheticisation, the high value of their potential fertility and the ideal of its actualisation in a legitimated agreement between families, despite the social and economic realities that often thwart or truncate such ideals.[3] Boys suggest, as intimated above, that their words are taking effect on a girl when she begins to fall silent, when she casts her gaze downwards and becomes shy. Boys' words are said to 'hit' a girl until they take effect. To speak privately of love to a girl is to 'bite her ear' (*ukuloma indlebe yakhe*). Boys try to make dramatic, sudden appearances in confronting girls they wish to court so that, to borrow Vilakazi's (1962: 48) phrase, girls are 'hit by apprehension' (*ishaywa uvalo*). Yet despite the ways in which girls are called upon to overtly ignore the approaches of boys, after she has received several proposals, a girl actively chooses a lover (*ukuqoma*) by informing an older girl, a leader (*iqhikiza*) in her vicinity, that she accepts a certain boy. Thereafter the leader, together with the girl's age-mates, inform the boy that he has been accepted by her. The girl marks her preference through the leader acting as emissary on her behalf, by giving the boy a beaded necklace (*iqabane*).

A collective description of *ukuqoma* (a girl choosing a lover) follows. It was composed in writing by six girls between 14 and 18 years old at a workshop I conducted with twenty-four young people from Emfuleni in July 2005. It reiterates the public and enjoyable aspects of courtship.

> [The girl] will want the *iqhikiza* [girls' leader] to make an *iqabane* [beaded necklace]. When the leader has agreed, you disappear at night from your home. You sleep at her home. The leader will go and look for girls. She will return with the girls to make the necklace and a white flag. The girls go together to fetch a long stick from the forest. They attach and sew a white cloth to the stick. The leader washes the necklace to cleanse it. Before

[3] Suzanne Leclerc-Madlala (1999, 2001) and Fiona Scorgie (2003: 110–11) show the irony of girls being held morally accountable for maintaining sexual purity in a context where they were often pressured into sexual relations and where they occupied the least powerful position in a gendered hierarchy of social relationships.

> dawn, they all go to collect water and to bathe themselves. The y take the necklace and the cloth. The leader carries the cloth and stick, and they sing on the way until they reach the boy's home. They sing, and when they enter the yard, they dance there. The women ululate. The girls go and stand in the middle of the yard singing and dancing. They stand for a long time in the yard. Then the boy will become the lover of the girl.
>
> Once he sees the girls in the yard he comes out and pretends to run away. The boy's family take the girl inside, and she will be asked, 'Who are you? Who is it that you have come to *qoma* [choose as a lover]?' The girls will reply that the girl has come to be a certain boy's lover. The family will ask, 'What is the name of your father?' Then they will cook food. When the girls have finished the food, the boy's family will ask, 'How much money do you want?' They will then give money to the leader.[4]
>
> The leader places the necklace on the young *umkhwenyana* ['son-in-law']. She will start hitting him on different parts of his body with the necklace. Then the young man will hit the leader with it. The leader then tears it away from him and places it on the young man. The leader says, 'Nonhleke [the name of the girl] said we should bring back those feet, your feet. You walked until your *takkies* [trainers] were worn out [in walking to court her]. She has said that you should not write her [name] on your left hand [the left-hand side of the body being the less valued side]. You must write her name on your right hand, because if you write her of the left hand she will grab hold of you for two weeks and then leave you.' The *iqhikiza* takes the money and we split it and go home.
>
> (Zinhle, Pretty, Ntombifuthi, Grace, Zolile,
> Gertrude: focus group 21 July 2005)

The example of the witty 'verbal assault' directed towards the chosen boy by the *iqhikiza* (girls' leader) in this hypothetical case challenges him to value the girl and not treat her badly.

Despite the ways in which girls 'speak' through their choice of a lover and through the words of the leader, metaphors of beating and combat are threaded through courtship, where on a general level force and forcefulness point to the distinct and rivalrous posturing of the two families that are slowly approaching one another to form a relationship through two of their children. In relation to sexual partnership, on a more personal level, force and forcefulness are aligned with boys' expected behaviour, whereas gradual acquiescence is aligned with what is expected of girls.

The most extreme form of courtship in Okhahlamba is the literally violent abduction of a girl against her wishes (*ukuthwala*) by a young man

[4] In a situation where a girl indicates her choice of lover, money is given to the *iqhikiza* to thank her and her companions for bringing a girl who has chosen their son into a relationship with his family.

and his friends who try to force her into sexual relations with the boy in his homestead by keeping her there overnight and making her ingest and inhale various medicines that are said to induce love.[5] Young couples, however, sometimes decide to elope, enacting abduction so that the girl saves face by appearing to have been taken to her lover's homestead against her will. A distinction may therefore be made between *forced abduction* and *staged abduction* (my emphasis), where negotiations quickly ensue with the girl's family to formalise the relationship with the boy.

Phumzile, a 17-year-old girl from Emfuleni, who lived with her maternal grandmother, expresses her fear of abduction by a stranger. After gathering wood one day she saw a man carrying a stick hiding in the bush, and when he tried to accost her she grew afraid and refused to speak to him, running all the way home to her grandmother's homestead. Of this experience she wrote:

> Let it be said that one day I went to gather wood to make fire. There was not even one stick left to beat a dog [*Kwakungekho ngisho nelokushaya inja ukhuni lolu*]. I woke up in the morning and washed my face. I took an *inkatha* [circle of cloth] and an axe and rope to tie the bundle. When I arrived in the forest, I put down my rope, the one used for tying bundles of wood, and my axe. I went to gather wood. When I had finished, I tied the sticks together. I took my *inkatha* and put it on top of my head, and then lifted the bundle of wood onto it. I then left. While I was still on my way I became aware that I was tired. I took down the bundle of wood and rested, thinking about the hill I would have to climb. And *hhe*! I did not ask from the sun [*Angibuzanga elangeni*, meaning something happened that she did not expect]! On the side of a small hill, someone was hidden. I continued on my journey. When I passed that place, there was a man. He said he wanted to ask a question. I said, 'From whom?' He said I should stop so that he could ask properly. I said, 'I do not want to stop. I am going home now.' He wanted to scare me with the stick he was carrying. I was afraid that he would try to carry me off [*Ukuthwala* literally means, to carry someone off]. Then I said to myself, 'Broken arm' [*Ngalo yephuka*] [meaning it was time to run and leave everything]! I ran until I reached home. I arrived and threw my bundle down. I rested in the shadow of the sun [shade] at home. It is nice to be here [in English]. It is nice to be here [in isiZulu].
>
> (Phumzile Makhanya, July 2005)

[5] *Ukuthwala* is found within other Nguni groups, for example within communities who speak isiXhosa. See Henderson (1999: 128); Ross (2008) (personal communication with regard to research in Worcester). Gcina Mhlope gives a moving description of the extreme violence and violation involved in unwanted forms of *ukuthwala* in her story, 'Nokulunga's Wedding' (2009: 203–12).

Returning to the theme of violence threaded through courting repertoires, another way that boys are said to take vengeance on girls who reject them as lovers is through the activation of sometimes particularly aggressive forms of love medicine. The girl, crying in an unbounded way (*umhayiso*), is compelled to run to the boy's home through the force that such medicines are said to exert. Here she is subjected to the ingestion of further medicines that work by converting rejection and hatred into love and acquiescence.[6] Seven girls, ranging from 14 to 18, described to me the effects of medicine on a girl once she had been abducted by a group of boys into a particular boy's homestead and into his private quarters against her wishes:

> They place *umuthi wothando* [love medicine] into the food that they give her. There are boys who carry *sjamboks*. They stand next to the [boy and the girl] saying that the boy should begin playing [having sex]. The boys will repeat themselves again and again, saying the boy and girl must sleep together. The girl will start by refusing. They will repeat themselves saying, 'Girl, have you or have you not heard?' The girl will hide near the door keeping quiet and holding onto the door. She will not respond. The boys will repeat themselves again, being very angry now. They will say, 'You have to do one of these things, either eat this food or go to sleep [with the boy]. What have you chosen?' She will then move closer to the food pretending that she wants the food. But no! She does not want it. The boys will then ask whether she is stubborn. They will say, 'Don't you see that you are not in your own home?' While they tell her that they play with their *sjamboks*. The girl ends up eating the food into which medicine has been placed ... The boy knows that she is beginning to agree [*igcizelela*] because of the medicine she has already eaten in the food. After she has inhaled [medicine burning on a pot shard] she will go straight to the bed to sleep. The boy then asks her what has brought her there and she will respond with a smooth voice, saying, 'It is your love'. That is love medicine for a girl. It is medicine that forces a girl to love.
>
> (Xoli, Phumzile, Bongi, Jabu, Busangani, Thandi, Sindiswa: focus group 21 July 2005)

The notion that girls may be 'forced to love' points to two nodes of ambivalence within the textures of gendered relations in Okhahlamba: one, where girls choose a lover and yet must suppress any overt expression of desire, and the other, where metaphors of violence may blur into acts of violence within sexual relations. The consequences of the above forms of ambivalence are the suppression of the possibility of articulation

[6] See Julie Parle and Fiona Scorgie (2004) for the most extensive contemporary account of *umhayiso*.

and hence the overt emergence of injury and distress girls and women may experience.[7] Such ambivalence raises issues in relation to the constitution of selves and subjectivities for girls. It is a widely accepted idea that, for a girl, travelling to live in a boyfriend's or husband's homestead is not easy; that it involves a transformation of self through which she accommodates herself to the demands of the household into which she has moved. She loses close proximity to her own family and becomes a stranger within the home of her lover, where for many years she may be regarded with suspicion, as a person through whom malevolence may be introduced to her boyfriend's or husband's family. It is therefore within the violence of culture that structures of gendered hierarchy are forged. For all the above shortcomings, a young bride is nevertheless regarded with respect, as someone who through potentially giving birth to children will contribute inestimably to her partner's family and lineage. She is also regarded as one who has left behind the playfulness associated with childhood and who bravely confronts the burdens of adult life.

In concluding the first section of the chapter, the discourse of love is therefore one in which force and decisiveness are linked to boys' desire and where female desire is increasingly constrained with the conversion of a girl from a lover to a young bride where the development of love on the part of girls may blur into capitulation, acclimatisation and accommodation.

Despite the aestheticisation of violence in courtship, not all boys in Emfuleni condone *ukuthwala* ('abduction') in its most extreme form. The boys also experience insecurities and anxieties in relation to love. Six boys from Emfuleni, in discussing what it was to propose love to a girl (*ukushela*), outlined the valued goal and importance of building a home, of publicly acknowledged courtship in which everyone knows whom a girl has chosen as her lover, and their personal anxieties in pursuing girls where girls take their time in deciding whether a boy is serious about them or not. Of the dangers associated with *ukuthwala* ('forced abduction'), they wrote:

> But it happens that a person will abduct you without loving you at all. That means that in the end it causes danger between the girl and the boy. You might find that the girl has a boyfriend whom she loves. The girl will then tell the boy to come and kill the one who has abducted her, or she might put poison in his food with medicine [*umdlise*] so that he dies. Because

[7] See Christina Toren (1994: 20–1) for an example of similar forms of silencing amongst girls within Fijian courtship practices.

> it is seen that there is danger, the boy should rather speak with the girl, and if she does not agree, he should move on because abduction is *abuse* [English word used]. It is not allowed. You may end up being jailed.
>
> (Nathi, Bongo, Sithembiso, Mzwakhe, Mthoko, Ayanda: focus group 21 July 2005)

Of particular interest within the above account is the way in which notions concerning bewitchment arise in tandem with reference to 'abuse' and consequently to children's rights within the boys' text. Their juxtaposition bears out the multiplicious nature of local worlds, the coexistence of aspects of social life that intertwine in surprising ways. Of interest also is that the boys are predominantly concerned with the ways in which girls may harm them in overt and covert ways when forced into a relationship, rather than with any injury a girl may suffer on her own account.

Pathways of children's rights discourse

My introduction to the young people of Emfuleni was through an NGO that defined the group as 'orphans', a name they dismissed (Henderson, 2006, 2011). The NGO involved the children in an agricultural project, teaching them organisational skills and planning. They were committed to building neighbourhood 'Children's Rights Committees' composed of groups of adults, mainly women, who monitored the living circumstances of 'orphans' and who directed them to the project. The Children's Rights Committee within Emfuleni brought to the project facilitator's attention specific problems the youth encountered, for example, difficulties in paying school fees and the consequent refusal of the headmaster to release their examination results. They visited the headmaster, pleading for the right of children to attend school and asking him to waive their fees, or at least to countenance a delay in their payment.

As mentioned above, three of the young people were sent on a week-long child's rights course through the local NGO convened by an organisation from the coastal city of Durban. The one 'right' that children and young people considered to be consistently flouted in their home areas was the right not to be physically abused, or not to be beaten. Many expressed sadness at being beaten by their parents, guardians or schoolteachers. In their view, to be beaten was not to be treated well, or as expressed in isiZulu, 'not to be carried well'.

In our interaction with the young people, the NGO facilitator and I made sure that children, regardless of age or gender, were able to 'speak out', to report and record problems within their project and to receive special attention through regular home visits in which we also sought to record their histories.

The five girls who eloped with their boyfriends did so before they had reached Grade 12, the last year of secondary schooling. Ntombikhayise was in Grade 10, Cebsile in Grade 11, and Bongi, Nonhlanhla and Tozi in Grade 9. All the girls, with the exception of Ntombikhayise, accepted that, as 'young brides' in their boyfriends' homesteads, they would have to give up going to school. Ntombikhayise expressed the wish that she would like to complete her schooling, but that this would only be possible if her in-laws allowed her to do so. As the burden of work within households fell specifically to young brides, and as the family with whom she had formed a relationship was particularly conservative, this did not seem a likely outcome. Despite the fact that the girls' right to education was truncated in *ukugana* relationships, they nevertheless entered them with a degree of pride and with excitement, due to widespread approval of such relationships and the pleasurable celebrations and aesthetic values associated with them.

Girls in *ukugana* relationships

I now briefly outline the living circumstances of the five girls who entered *ukugana* relationships and who consequently left schooling. Ntombikhayise began the process of *ukugana* in 2004, when she was 20 years old. She had completed Grade 10, with two years of high school still outstanding. As a child she had lived with her mother's mother, her mother – who while still at school had given birth to her – and her mother's brother. After her mother formally married when Ntombikhayise was 6 years old, she remained with her maternal grandmother while her mother moved to her new husband's home. Her father ceased to play a significant role in her life as she grew older. Her mother died in 1999 from *lesisifo* (this illness, as HIV/AIDS is commonly referred to in Okhahlamba). She retained a strong bond with her mother's mother and with her brother. Of the precise way in which she entered a *gana* relationship, Ntombikhayise said:

> [My boyfriend] pretended as if I was just visiting him. He then kept me there [by force] although I did not want to, but now I enjoy it. Then people went to report what had happened at home and they negotiated.

What Ntombikhayise implies is that her boyfriend precipitated an *ukugana* relationship with her before she felt ready to live within his homestead. However, once having settled, she enjoyed her status as a young bride. Ntombikhayise knew of six other girls from her neighbourhood who entered into similar *gana* relationships. She and the other girls were particularly praised in their decision to form such relationships because none of them had been pregnant at the time. She invited me also to some of the exciting dance parties that were held around the formation of the relationship. Ntombikhayise was proud that she had formed a relationship with a big family whom she described as *amaqaba* (usually used in a disparaging way to mean 'uneducated', but in this case meaning a 'traditional' family) and on whose behalf she had to work hard. Referring to the manner in which she worked in her boyfriend's homestead, she said:

> This side there is no time to play, unlike those girls who have 'married' at Zwelitsha, where there are a lot of little Christians (*amakholwanyana*).
>
> (Interview: 21 May 2004)

Her grandmother viewed the relationship with some flexibility and thought that in time the boyfriend's family might allow her to return to school.

Nonhlanhla was 17 when she eloped. When she was 10 years old her mother left her with her father before contracting a formal marriage. In the intervening years she had lived with her father, who did not provide adequately for her. When he was paid for casual work as a cattle herder, he often refused to share money with her and she was consequently often hungry. Both her mother and the woman whom her mother's husband subsequently married, died of HIV/AIDS, so she had no one to whom she could appeal for support. Jabu, one of Nonhlanhla's friends, said that she had entered an *ukugana* relationship primarily because of pressing circumstances. It was not clear to her whether Nonhlanhla would improve her situation greatly in going to live with her boyfriend, as his family were poor also.

Cebsile was 18 and Bongi, her younger sister, 17, when they became engaged and went to live with their boyfriends. Their story in particular brings out how entering informal marriages with their lovers made strategic sense in the context of unfolding deaths within their family and given difficulties in finding employment on the part of their older brothers and sisters (see Henderson, 2006: 313–16). They nursed both parents before they died of HIV/AIDS. Their older and younger brother departed for Cape Town to find work. One sister, who was later struck dead by lightning, married locally and the other also left for Cape Town to live with a boyfriend, although she herself was unemployed. Cebsile and Bongi were forced to live with neighbours and to offer their services to families whom they described as having humanity (*ubuntu*). On one of his visits home, their elder brother formed a *gana* relationship with a young local woman, resuscitating the homestead by coming to live in it. Cebsile and Bongi returned to their parents' former homestead to live with the new young bride and shortly thereafter formed similar *gana* relationships with their boyfriends.

Tozi became pregnant at 17. Her father died of HIV/AIDS when she was 14, and her mother just after the birth of Tozi's child. She then precipitated a *gana* relationship with her boyfriend by going to sit outside his family home. Her father's brother negotiated with the family on her behalf. Once the boyfriend's father had confirmed that his son, who worked in a mine in Johannesburg, was prepared to accept her as a young bride, Tozi came to live with her boyfriend's family.

Weighing up education and relationship

In the eyes of children's activists in the region, young girls who enter *ukugana* relationships are foreclosing their 'futures' in forfeiting their education. Yet the education people receive at the secondary school most of them attended is of a particularly low standard. In December 2005, four of the five young people who had reached their last year of secondary school failed their exams.

Although educational approaches have changed at a national level due to shifts in government policy, this does not translate into quality education for young people. Teachers are unskilled in the teaching methods that new integrated curricula require. Most lessons involve teachers copying sections of textbooks onto a blackboard and getting the children to read and repeat what is written there. A shortage of textbooks in the school reinforces the above method of instruction. Most lessons are written in English, a language that many of the young people speak hardly at all. Even young people in the last year of their secondary schooling cannot hold a prolonged conversation in English. Concepts described in often difficult English on the board are not explained to pupils. The political culture of the school emphasises deference towards teachers and unquestioning obedience, creating an atmosphere that discourages questions from young people, even when they do not understand what has been written on the board. Although corporal punishment is outlawed by the state, some teachers carry sticks with them to class, suggesting they may at times flout the law.

Teachers themselves are demoralised, something that seemed to be symbolised in a burnt-out classroom that remained neglected with its melted and contorted metal desk-legs on a blackened floor and collapsed roof for over nine months.

As many families in the region produce sufficient grain to feed themselves for seven months of the year, and as cattle are highly valued, boys and girls are sometimes called out of school to assist in harvesting maize, or in the case of boys to try to recoup cattle that have gone astray or are stolen.

That young brides no longer attend school is something that boys' families insist upon. From the perspective of the young women concerned, given the rapidly eroding family structures from which they come, such 'marriages' have the advantage of expanding the number of people upon whom they can immediately and legitimately call for assistance. Women in the region have historically had very little education and this fact perhaps influences girls' willingness to forfeit it in difficult circumstances.[8] The girls also know that the families into which they move, and with whom they have formed a publicly acknowledged relationship, will welcome any children born of their relationship with their young man.

Girls who continue with their schooling, and who often later travel to major cities in search of work or further training, are not necessarily better off. Within the cities, employment, even for people who have completed matriculation, is still hard to come by, and there is little public acknowledgement of the relationships young women form with boys or men, and therefore little social protection in the event of difficulties.[9]

[8] None of the mothers of the group of thirty-four young people had education beyond a primary school level. Some said that they had only sufficient education to write their own names.

[9] A growing literature now exists outlining the necessity of multiple sexual partners for both young women and men given a national unemployment rate of over 40 per cent and a decrease in jobs for men who find it increasingly difficult to provide the financial means for full marriage. For changing forms of masculinity and the economy of multiple partnerships see, for example, Kelly and Ntlabati (2002) and Hunter (2002, 2005, 2007).

Conclusion: *ukugana* and living rights

The chapter has explored how gendered hierarchies in Okhahlamba are threaded through social life in ways that are at once pleasing and traduced with power. I have therefore pointed to the aestheticisation of forms of violence in which metaphor and actuality begin to blur, and raise questions around the notion of choice and freedoms arising within the constraints of particular historical, economic and social horizons. Although such relations prescribe the parameters in which subjectivities emerge, the young girls whose *ukugana* relationships I have described drew on local repertoires of creating socially recognised bonds of affinity that are nevertheless threaded through with gendered distinctions. Given the above complexities, how do abstract rights – for example, the right to education, gender equality and protection – assume cogency within a context of marked gender differentiation, limited educational and employment possibilities, and where the state and its constitution, in which basic rights are enshrined, are experienced as remote?

In relation to the theme of the book – living rights – does *ukugana* leave room for the deployment of personal trajectories – or is it an end point that merely ensures survival? As we have seen in a brief accounting of the five instances of *ukugana* explored in the chapter, Ntomikhayise was in a much stronger position than the other girls in that although her *ukugana* relationship had been precipitated by her boyfriend, insisting that she remained in his homestead, her grandmother and the family with which she was forming a new relationship had sufficient means to exchange gifts and to host the dance parties attached to the formation of such a relationship in a way that was deeply satisfying to her. She received praise from her peers and the adults in the vicinity of her home for the way in which she had accomplished her relationship. Despite the volume of hard work she subsequently undertook in her new homestead, she took particular pride in it and perceived it as demonstrating her new social status. In contrast, Nonhlanhla's relationship grew out of the particularly dire circumstances in which she found herself living with her father and in this case, together with Cebsile and Bongi, formed *ukugana* relations to ensure her survival in the immediate future. It must be noted, however, that even in Cebsile's and Bongi's case, where both parents had died of HIV/AIDS and where they had sought support from willing neighbours, the resurrection of their father's homestead was of deep spiritual importance to them and to their brothers. Their older brother, contracting a similar relationship with a young local woman, ensured that the homestead could be reconstituted. Their own relationships confirmed the possibility of future exchanges between their brother, as head of their own family, and the families with which they now lived. In relation to Tozi, who was already pregnant when she initiated a process in which she hoped her boyfriend's family would recognise her as a potential young bride, she was successful. Embedded within courting practices in Okhahlamba, therefore, are ways in which girls can make their desires known, even if indirectly. They choose their lovers through *ukuqoma* where others represent them. They are also able in some instances to refuse relationships emerging out of what I have described as forced abduction.

As I have suggested at the beginning of the chapter, NGOs are largely ignorant of or do not consciously think of the ways in which local practices can resonate with certain children's rights. Although the NGO working predominantly with the children tried to suggest how important education was for the girls concerned, they did not provide them with the means of continuing their education. Given the erosion of social ties on which they could rely, girls entering *ukugana* relationships were finding for themselves local forms of social protection and new sets of relatives from whom they could ask for assistance. NGOs did not therefore try to negotiate or translate children's views of their right to protection, particularly in view of the poor quality of education and largely bleak prospects for educated youths. Careful consideration of the ways in which the details of everyday life may make visible means of protection and validation – although in a particular gendered form – are therefore ignored. The result is a shallow engagement with young people in relation to rights as promulgated in the CRC and a complete avoidance of the way in which local forms of sociality may begin to fulfil some of the aspirational demands contained in the document. In some respects this renders NGOs 'blind' to lessons they could learn through paying attention to the local.

Perhaps *ukugana* is not the most ideal future that a girl may wish for herself if she had real choices, but on the other hand, it is inappropriate to assume that it does not constitute a choice at all. The reference to Battaglia's (1995) ideas concerning nostalgia suggests that there are positive dimensions to the recuperation of what people claim as 'traditional' practices within the context of a post-colonial state.

References

Battaglia D (ed.) (1995) On practical nostalgia: Self-prospecting among urban Trobrianders. In: *The Rhetorics of Self-Making*. Berkeley: University of California Press, pp. 77–96.

Doke C M *et al.* (2006) *English Zulu Dictionary*. Johannesburg: Witwatersrand University Press.

Henderson P C (1999) *Living with Fragility: Children in New Crossroads*. Ph.D. Thesis, University of Cape Town, South Africa.

(2006) South African AIDS orphans: examining assumptions around vulnerability from the perspective of rural children and youth. *Childhood* 13(3): 303–28.

(2011) *AIDS, Intimacy and Care in Rural KwaZulu-Natal: A Kinship of Bones*. Amsterdam University Press.

Hunter M (2002) The materiality of everyday sex: Thinking beyond 'prostitution'. *African Studies* 61(1): 99–120.

(2005) Cultural politics and masculinities: Multiple-partners in historical perspective in KwaZulu-Natal. *Culture, Health & Sexuality* 7(3): 209–23.

(2007) The changing political economy of sex in South Africa: The significance of unemployment and inequalities to the scale of the AIDS pandemic. *Social Science Medicine* 64(3): 689–700.

Kelly K and Ntlabati P (2002) Early adolescent sex in South Africa: HIV/AIDS intervention challenges. *Social Dynamics* 28(1): 42–63.

Krige E (1950 [1936]) *The Social System of the Zulus*. Pietermaritzburg: Shuter and Shooter.

(1968) Girls' puberty songs and their relation to fertility, health, morality and religion among the Zulu. *Africa* 38(2): 173–98.

Leclerc-Madlala S (1999) *Demonizing Women in the Era of AIDS: An Analysis of the Gendered Construction of HIV/AIDS in KwaZulu-Natal*. Ph.D. Thesis, University of Natal, South Africa.

(2001) Virginity testing: Managing sexuality in a maturing HIV/AIDS epidemic. *Medical Anthropology Quarterly* 15(4): 533–52.

Mhlope G (2009) Nokulunga's wedding. In: Balseiro I and Hecht T (eds.) *South Africa: A Traveler's Literary Companion*. Berkeley: Whereabouts Press, pp. 203–12.

Parle J and Scorgie F (2004) *Bewitching Zulu Women: Umhayiso, Gender and Witchcraft in Natal*. Unpublished paper.

Povinelli E (2006) *The Empire of Love: Towards a Theory of Intimacy, Genealogy and Carnality*. Durham and London: Duke University Press.

Scorgie F (2003) *Mobilising 'Tradition' in the Post-Apartheid Era: Amasiko, AIDS and Cultural Rights in KwaZulu Natal, South Africa*. Ph.D. Thesis, Cambridge University.

Tsing A L (2005) *Frictions: An Ethnography of Global Connection.* Princeton University Press.

Toren C (1994) Transforming love: representing Fijian hierarchy. In: Penelope H and Peter G (eds.) *Sex and Violence: Issues in Representation and Experience.* London: Routledge, pp. 18–39.

Vilakazi A (1962). *Zulu Transformations: A Study of the Dynamics of Social Change.* Pietermaritzburg: University of Natal Press.

Zižek S, Butler J and Laclau E (2011) *Contingency, Hegemony, Universality.* London and New York: Verso Press.

3

Seeing and knowing? Street children's lifeworlds through the camera's lens

PHILLIP MIZEN AND YAW OFOSU-KUSI

This chapter considers photography as a means of seeing and knowing the lives of street children. Following what Ennew and Swart-Kruger (2003) note to be a 'paradigm shift' in thinking about the growing numbers of children who take to the streets of the cities of the developing world, in our research we have aspired to the production of collaborative and complementary research practices through the forging of research relationships with the children who we encounter that give meaning to their agency and purpose. In the course of this we have wanted to take seriously what we believe to be the fortitude and creativity of children surviving under terrible conditions by bringing to the fore their everyday experiences and lifeworlds, so that we may understand better the knowledge and meanings that they possess and how they can act upon these understandings in purposeful and sometimes decisive ways. Put in the terms of this book's purpose, we have looked to take seriously street children's capacity to make and remake their social lives, viewed the children as participants engaged with us in a process of mutual understanding and followed this commitment through by encouraging the children with and for whom we research to produce photographic accounts of their time spent living and working on the street.

We have done so because any understanding of children as the possessors of living rights, and the attendant forms of knowledge that flow from this, underscores the need for deftness and innovation in method. If we are to know better the worlds that children live in and through, and so avoid relying on what global orthodoxy says or assumes to be the case, then we must find more appropriate means for so doing. Among researchers of street and working children there have been some significant moves towards 'listening' to what they say (inter alia Katz, 2004; Liebel, 2004; Woodhead, 1999; Nieuwenhuys, 1994; Reynolds, 1991; see also James, 2007), understood as taking seriously their testimonials, seeking out their opinions and finding new and innovative ways for children to give voice to their knowledge and understandings. In our study we have sought to extend this emphasis on sympathetic methodology and research cooperation by complementing the need to listen more carefully to the 'voices' of children with a parallel interest in 'seeing' more clearly their social world, in the belief that by seeing we can more fully aid the processes of knowing and understanding. By using photography to encourage the children with whom we work to become agents of their own inquiry, we seek to utilize the magnitude and direction possessed by photographic images to create lines of communication between lives otherwise separated by time and space (Salgado, 2000). In allowing us to connect with the lives of the children, see what officially is often deemed not to exist and document what ordinarily goes unrecorded, the 'invaluable, if imperfect truth' (Tremain, 2000: 3) of a photograph, we believe, permits a significant means of knowing better the worlds that children create and inhabit.

This is the condition of how and why the images we work with come into existence. In utilizing photography in our research we extend and consolidate a collaborative venture between ourselves and the children we work with that is motivated by a mutual desire to create a source of unofficial truth and everyday insight, and to reconnect the children's photographs with the social and political context within which they are produced. We have written about the methodology adopted to this end elsewhere, so it is not our intention to repeat here the procedures and principles that we have adopted in the course of our research and the practical, technical and ethical difficulties that we have encountered (Mizen, 2005; Mizen and Ofosu-Kusi, 2006). In the present contribution we want to begin to reflect upon method and to clarify our mode of explanation and understanding that any consideration of method must require. By method we understand guidance and the ways we work in considering the world in order for us to understand it better. Method is the medium of research practice but it also necessarily involves questioning its outcomes. The outcome in this case is a distinctive collection of photographs produced by children living and working on the streets of Accra, a large and growing sub-Saharan African city. By drawing upon these photographs we want to consider their value as a means to bear witness to the everyday reality of street children's lives and, in the process, how they may assist in advancing our understanding of the emergence of new urban childhoods.

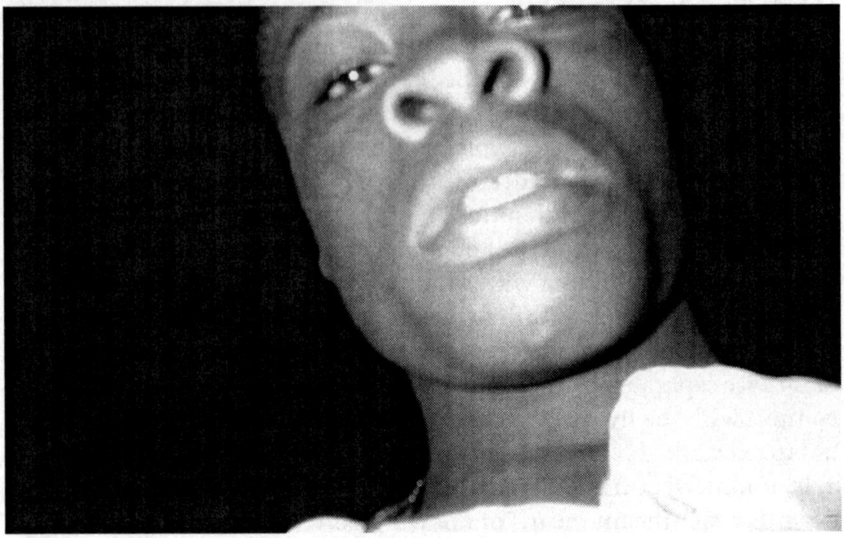

Image 1 Mustapha, male, 15 years old

Seeing and knowing

We begin with an image of Mustapha, a self-portrait by a 15-year-old boy who, according to the NGO Catholic Action for Street Children (2008), is one of more than 15,000 children under the age of 18 who live and work on the streets of Accra, Ghana's capital city. As one of the *Kubolo*,[1] that most pejorative of terms used to denigrate this steadily growing section of the urban poor, Mustapha is one of over seventy street children with whom we have worked with over almost four years of continuous fieldwork.[2] Our concern has been with 'street life as labour' and with how children like Mustapha who live and work on Accra's street set about (re)making lives under conditions not of their choosing. Rarely asked

[1] The general meaning of *Kubolo* is someone who sleeps outside their home, but it is specifically applied to children. Its etymology can be traced to the Ga language, where the action word is *kubo* (i.e. to be wayward, stay away from home, stay on the street) and the person engaging in the action is *lo*. Thus, *Kubolo* is a wayward child, or street child, although it can also be used to refer to a truant – someone who refuses to go to school or attends school infrequently.

[2] We would like to express our thanks to the Research Development Fund at the University of Warwick, Catholic Action for Street Children and the many street children who supported this research.

about their worlds (see Kovats-Bernat, 2006), our intention has been to undertake research *with* and *for* these children by giving testament to their experiences and by taking seriously their testimonials, views and opinions (Mizen and Ofosu-Kusi, 2006). Played out in terms that can be described as a 'dialogue with a purpose' (Burgess, 1988), we have pursued our research around a loosely structured series of exchanges conducted through face-to-face conversations, interviews, group discussions and observations. Carried out in the streets and road junctions in and around central Accra, its waste grounds and derelict buildings, and in some of the few places that offer the children some moments of respite, we have sought to provide opportunities for children to share with us what it means to live and work on the streets of Ghana's capital city.

Photographs, we believe, can extend our knowledge of the empirical, the domain of experience, what can be observed. Consequently, we have looked to develop our 'dialogue' by way of photography's powers of social exchange and its capacity to connect our sense of the everyday with the everyday experiences of children like Mustapha. By asking street children to participate in our research by making photographic accounts of a day in their lives and then to discuss these with us, (see Mizen and Ofosu-Kusi, 2010a), our aim has been to know better what it means to live and work on the street as a child and to explore a street child's life and labour in terms that allow for some element of self-definition. By giving some of the children relatively inexpensive, single-use cameras with a fixed focus lens, (fast) colour film and chargeable flash unit, we have encouraged them to use its twenty-seven frames to create photographic records, visual documents relating to significant or noteworthy aspects of their lives, putatively simple visual sources of knowledge and insight through which we can better come to know these children and the worlds they seek to make their own.

The meaning of photographs, the sociologist Howard Becker (1995) tells us, is almost all a matter of context. Placed within the context of our research, we hold the street children's photographs to possess evidential value, visual documents that are capable of bearing witness and testimony to the experience of a particular childhood that is rooted in a historical moment in which economic growth and rapid processes of urbanization have become decoupled from the supply of jobs and a living wage (Davis, 2006). Photographs like ours, we believe, serve as a means of disclosure that can communicate what is often beyond the capacity of language to convey, critical sources of knowing and understanding not easily reducible to linguistic description. These photographs tell vividly of the environs

Image 2 Stephen, male, 15 years old

and ecology of street life, its detail and design, fractures and strains, its palpable fragmentation. In the children's photographs we see glimpses of bustling marketplaces, busy thoroughfares and pavements, crowded transit stations and jammed-up road junctions where the children eke out their living. There are vistas of well-worn spaces and dilapidated buildings, concrete walkways, austere and uninviting stairwells and hard stone verandas, scruffy shop fronts and rickety market stalls, broken-down and battered vehicles, the bric-a-brac of pavement commerce. What we see in the children's photographs are discernible elements of a physical fabric and infrastructure under stress, and a burgeoning informal economy within which the children must work to survive. We also see a capacity to grasp something out of virtually nothing and to instinctively assert a right to space and time in a highly disorganized environment.

As a source of unofficial truth and everyday experience, this visual record of children's city life is given added force by the regularity with which its discrete elements are served up for our attention. Individually,

Image 3 Johnny, male, 14 years old

the photographs capture specific moments of the children's daily routines as they move, work, eat, play and sleep, but taken together they build a larger tableau of street living in which what is discovered in one child's photograph more often than not finds an echo and corroboration in an image produced by another. Patterns and themes emerge, as we are presented with photographs of children pushing barrow-loads of market produce, broad metal pans carefully balanced upon heads and weighed down with sachets of iced water, rigid plastic suitcases, large wooden boxes and tall wicker baskets heaved through hot streets and hectic markets. These are the intricate details of their survival, the goods they carry, sell and hawk. Elsewhere we are taken down the roads and pavements through which they wander into the markets, transit stations, lorry parks and road junctions where they seek out work, these habitual spaces crammed with items that are both identifiable and unknown, other workers in the informal economy against whom they compete and the faces of those they work for.

Image 4 Philomena, female, 14 years old

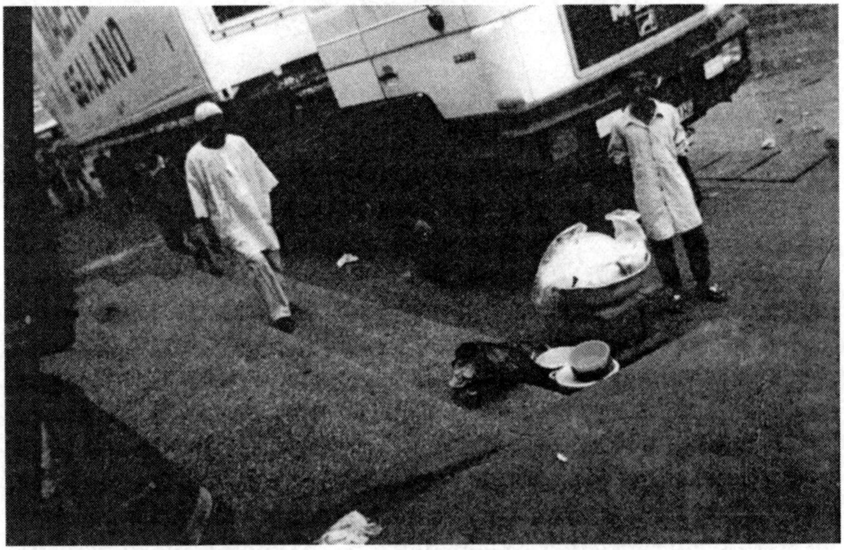

Image 5 Prince, male, 13 years old

The familiarity that the photographs bring to our knowledge of the children's daily lives finds a parallel in their value as confirmation. In what has elsewhere been likened to 'triangulation plus' (Bolton *et al.*, 2001: 515), the photographs not only allow us to corroborate what we have been told by children whose lives require artifice and ingenuity, but they also allow us to go beyond simple verification. To know from interview or discussion that a child works for a chop bar owner washing dishes or cleaning tables in return for money, food or a place to rest a while is, of course, to extend further our knowledge of the children's lives. But to see photographs of the roughly fashioned wooden benches, a charcoal brazier, aluminium cooking pots, a table densely stacked with instant coffee, sugar, bags of tea, several dozen eggs and numerous tins of condensed milk is also to simultaneously substantiate and add an otherwise unascertainable topographical dimension. It is, at once, to both confirm and valorize the children's accounts of how they live and what they must do to bring about their own survival in ways that go beyond repetition or restatement.

Some of this we have seen for ourselves as we have walked the same streets and marketplaces, sat at the same road junctions and meeting places, watching, observing and talking. Often, however, the children use their cameras to take us into places normally out of bounds, to the private and personal, to spaces and places that for us remain out of reach. In these photographs we find a connection between the children's lives and those of the wider urban poor as we see depicted the ramshackle buildings of the shanties and informal settlements through which they move and with whose inhabitants they live, work and are sometimes related; livestock and poultry crammed into dirty spaces between rickety huts and fences as rubbish burns in the background; densely packed spaces between shacks and alleyways almost too narrow for an adult to move through; playing football and having fun within the carcasses of Accra's many incomplete buildings.

More moving are those allusions to the private sorrows faced by some of Accra's poor contained within photographs that connect us with some of the major public issues of our time. In two images we view three smartly dressed men standing around a seated and equally well-dressed young woman, her head bowed down as she receives their dramatic prayer calling for her delivery from a life-threatening affliction. Elsewhere we are taken into the interior of a shack in an informal settlement, its inhabitants photographed sharing a meal from plastic containers spread across broken white and red plastic flooring, babies dressed in clean white lie on blankets and broken foam matting, the ruined white and red flooring,

Image 6 Steven, male, 15 years old

rough wooden walls and conspicuous absence of anything but the most basic necessities of life a powerful reminder of their grinding poverty.

The children's photographs also subvert the commonplace depiction that deprives them of child-like qualities or youthful spirit (Glauser, 1998). These are no ordinary children, at least when judged in terms of normative notions of childhood, but contained within these photographs is a powerful humanizing dimension. In their photographs they reveal themselves in ways suggesting humour, friendship, compassion and tenderness as, when faced with a camera, the children laugh, smile, point or strike a pose. In other images they dance and smile, raise their arms in celebration, look on one another whilst at play. Girls and boys dressed up to party, showing off recently acquired shoes, shirts and dresses or smoking a cigarette in quiet defiance. In other photographs we see them sharing food and drink with one another, playing games or staying close as they idle away empty time squatting in the shade, sitting with arms around one another's shoulders or caught in a moment of tender embrace. These are not images of the pathological, the isolated, sick or diseased, nor do they convey a sense of children of other worlds incapable of meaningful thought or action. These are children doing what children often do: joking, playing and having fun, sharing friendships and creating relationships, doing nothing, passing time.

Image 7 Pam, female, 14 years old

Representing visually children's living rights

We thus hold close photography as one means for children to better connect their lifeworlds with ours, to define and convey pictorially the detail of their existence and to take part more actively in the process of knowing and understanding by presenting us with visual information of the observable dimensions of their lived reality. These are terms we use advisedly since in our own disciplines, sociology and education, and in much of anthropology too, there has been a retreat from the idea that photography can play any part in establishing an intimacy with the everyday reality of existence – and in some instances from any connection between the real and photographic representation at all (see Pink, 2005). In talking of knowing something of the reality of children's lives and of what it means to know directly children's living rights, we thus refuse to enclose our commitment to realism within scare quotes since we are advocates of the existence of a childhood independent of our capacity to represent it, that what exists, the realm of objects, structures and powers, and of photograph's powers of critical disclosure.

To conflate reality with the empirical – with calls upon our experience of the world – is, as critical realists remind us, profoundly mistaken (Sayer, 2002). Much of what exists in the world lies beyond observation and thus beyond photography's immediate practical value. In our case, by viewing the photographs as either thin, cold, inert pieces of paper or as points of coloured light on a computer monitor, we grasp little of the children's human agency; tantalizingly few instances of the resourcefulness, intuition and creativity that lie behind the making of these lifeless photographic forms. And yet, at the same time, photography does connect us with these children's agency. It is in the act of making a photograph that the actuality of children's agency is clearly evident since, like all forms of knowledge, '[t]he photographic image does not belong to the natural world. It is a product of human labour' (Damisch, 2003: 88). By asking these children to observe their worlds and to communicate its empirical dimensions in photographic form is to necessarily invite them to draw upon their lived experience of that world and to engage in a more or less self-conscious process of practical activity in which they are required to isolate and select, discern and frame, 'point and shoot', as the flash unit is charged, the camera raised and the shutter button released.

By entertaining connections between a photograph and knowledge of the observable, we aim at going to the heart of the living rights concern with representational power. However, by arguing, as we do, that children's photography can better connect us to the actuality of their lifeworlds, we are exposed to encountering accusations of naïve objectivism. It risks a casual but misplaced identification of our work with those like Briski (2004), and her acclaimed photographic work with the children of sex workers in Kolkata, where the relationship between a child's photograph and what it means is held to be self-evident, one in which the making or viewing of their pictures requires little or no elaboration. Alternatively, by emphasizing that photographs presuppose acts of sensuous labour, we recall to mind that images like ours are made as well as taken. In asking the children to record the world in photographic form, we should therefore not confuse their photographs with the misplaced belief that what we have been doing is accumulating objective 'facts'; as if somehow by giving the children cameras we can establish a straightforward connection between ourselves and their social worlds, visions of absolute truth that disclaim mediation and intervention. To do so would be to participate in photography's 'ontological deception' (Damisch,

2003: 88) in which a child's photograph of an object is mistaken for that object itself. It would mean, in short, ignoring what the viewing of our first image of Mustapha must surely encourage us to do: to see him as fixed in a flat, two-dimensional, lifeless form, viewed from an awkward and unusual angle, the image of his face out of focus and marked by the traces of pitted negatives and the smears of chemical developer. To see him, that is, as a *picture*.

As something made, pictures are, of course, products of culture and convention. To accept that photographs are representations or constructions, however, does not necessarily lead us towards the view of those sceptics who assert that there is no direct or necessary relationship between the meaning of a photographic image and the object that is represented (Harper, 1998). In a critique of an earlier paper authored by one of us, for instance, our use of photography has been dismissed as little more than the actions of ventriloquists and voyeurs (Piper and Frankham, 2007). Instead of photography offering one distinctive way for us to know something of the detail of children's lives beyond that contained within official representations, our practice has been likened to a sociological conjuring trick where the meanings we have attached to the children's photographs have been dismissed as no more than expressions of our adult cultural power. In stumbling into the trap of holding photography as a means to know the lives of others, we are accused of being the perpetrators of a deceit in which our own imagination of what children's worlds might look like are projected onto a medium of communication that is incapable of establishing unambiguous or fixed meanings.

Conceding such arguments, however, would be to entertain a position as equally indefensible as that of the naïve realists with whom we are so casually associated. By reducing the meanings of children's photographs to what those like us wish to make of them would be to undertake a volte-face in which a photograph's representational force and function are disarticulated from the people, places and contexts of which it is both inscription and expression. Such an idealist position is neither logical nor desirable, since photography, unlike painting or drawing, is also 'a craft of given forms, rooted in a process of finding rather than making' (Edwards, 2006: 83–4). It may be mistaken to see in photography a direct line of vision to the nitty-gritty of children's 'other' worlds, but it does not follow from this that children's photographs do not possess value that includes their evidential worth.

How, then, can we make sense of the evidential value of the images we work with? How can we be sure that the meaning given to a child's photograph is not simply a reflection of our own ideology? To address these questions means going to the heart of the living rights project since we must clarify what we mean by *giving voice to children's voices* (James, 2007). For photography, it is sometimes said that 'seeing comes before words' (Berger, 1972: 7), that we learn to see before we can speak. For most people there is, of course, an undeniable truth to this statement but it also contains an important note of visual chauvinism since it is equally the case that for us to see, we must possess concepts or knowledge capable of allowing us to do so, where the very act of referring to something necessarily involves some idea of what is being referred to (Sayer, 1992). Observation, understood as calling upon our experience of sense-data of the world, is thus itself a mediated process of learning as we go about the manipulation of our world, categorizing and discriminating as we see and do, organizing our observations in particular ways as these observations, in turn, feed back into the determination of our understandings. Calls to the facts are thus never simply unambiguous observational statements or foundational claims, but rather statements about these observations. All observation is therefore knowledge-dependent and all seeing is concept-laden. To see we have to know, but in the process of seeing we are capable of altering our understandings.

It is important to recognize this because in so doing we can begin to appreciate that there is no contradiction between our belief in a childhood independent of our knowledge of it and our acceptance that this can only be known in theory-dependent ways (Sayer, 2002). To claim, as our critics do, that by invoking notions of the real in photography we are able to silence children so as to manipulate their photographs according to our own ideology, is to conflate the necessity of coming to the children's photographs in conceptually laden ways with conceptually determined forms of viewing. The former understands that we must make claims upon these photographs in order to understand them but that the concepts we draw upon to do so – for example street child, child labourer, informal economy, friendship, cooperation, living rights – retain their credibility only if they offer some element of correspondence or corroboration with what photography's indexical and iconic qualities hold out for us to see. Even if we do not fully understand the processes involved when we look upon a photograph, we know that the image is connected in some way to the thing it represents and that the arrangement of things, people and places depicted in a photograph presuppose their existence prior to the shutter button being depressed (Edwards, 2006). By insisting that we use photographs as a blank canvas for our own biases and theories, the sceptics confuse the process of construal and mediation necessarily involved in their observation with that of constitution and production. In doing so, they countenance the preposterous propositions that our concepts and understandings are neutral to a photograph's capacity to present us with visual information of that which the camera is placed in relation to, that our understandings can anticipate all empirical questions and, ultimately, that the children's photographs can be made to mean whatever we wish.

Lessons from the *Kubolo*

One of the clearest indications of how the children's photographs provide insight beyond those contained within our own discursive frameworks is not to be found so much in their role as affirmation, corroboration or embellishment, but in their capacity to surprise and question. If realism is no more than a rhetorical device through which we can impose our own stories upon an image and if the relationship between a photograph and the event it depicts is irrelevant or beside the point, then it becomes impossible to account for the surprises that the children's photographs invariably spring. It is here that our method comes closest to the theme of *living rights* because one of the most significant lessons from our work with the street children is how their photographs disclose the weaknesses and shortcomings of our comprehension of particular dimensions to their lives, new observations in photographic form that serve to question the status of our current knowledge and understanding.

Perhaps the only truth or certainty that we can take from our photographic work with the street children is the capacity of the children to use their photographs to surprise. To take one prominent example, in a series of three photographs we have been presented with images of street children engaged in acts of personal hygiene and cleanliness, what sociologists would describe as the 'body work' necessary if one is to maintain or improve appearance, health and hygiene (Schilling, 2003). In the first photograph we are shown four street boys in a narrow, dark space lit only by the feeble glow of artificial lighting. The boys are clearly in some sort of changing area indicated by a wall painting of a man's head undertaken in the Ghanaian vernacular, above which is written in capital letters the word 'male', and by three of the four boys clearly pictured in the process of changing their clothes. In the second and third images the boys are now shown stripped of most of their clothes, some of them are naked, standing in what appears to be a communal shower. In one of these images two of the boys are clearly laughing. There are no signs of the shower heads

Image 8 Prince, male, 15 years old

nor running water, but the roughly tiled walls and cracked, flaking blue paintwork above them, the light reflected from the water on the boys' bodies and the distinctive white soap foam is testament to the fact that these boys are showering.

In another example, two of the children have provided a series of personal, almost poignant, images of how they seek solace and protection by sleeping in makeshift tents. In each case the cameras belonged to girls, itself some indication of the peculiar vulnerability that girls feel when living and working on the street and the attempts they make to escape the dangers of rough sleeping. In one of the girl's images we see in profile two tents fabricated from rough sheeting fastened by strings to the closed metal doors of a shop front. In another image this tent is viewed from the front and standing before it we see two of its three occupants, a street girl and boy, in what may be some sort of embrace, and in a third image we are presented with a blurred close-up of the face of a sleeping occupant. In the second girl's photographs we are presented with a parallel series

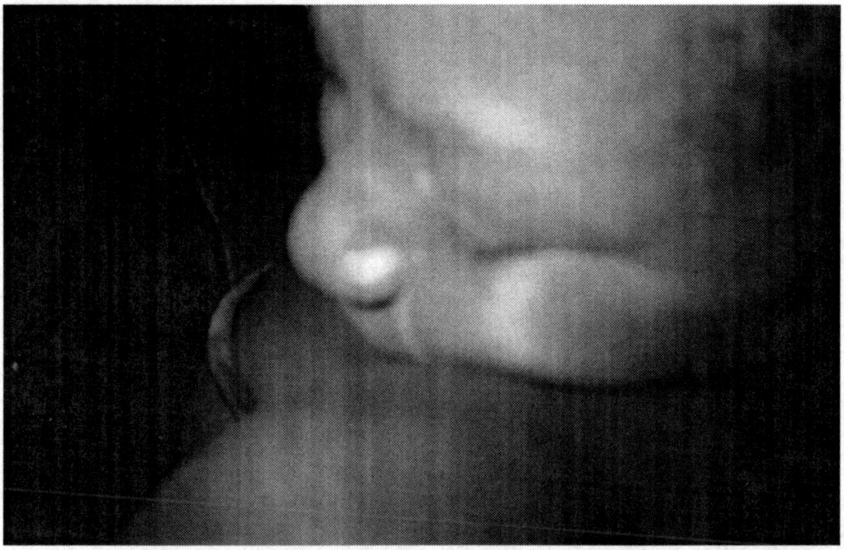

Image 9 Abena, female, 16 years old

of images. In one we observe in close-up the ripped and holed fabric of a tent, its bottom edges weighted down with rocks and stones, the small gash in its side a tiny window into its inner sanctuary. In a second image the inside of the tent is fully revealed as we encounter another child, her back (we know her gender from the photographer) turned towards us, as she lies fast asleep under the pitch of the tent. She seems fully clothed and a white sleeping cloth haphazardly covers most of her legs, while her head rests upon a grey pillow. The tent interior presents itself as a sparse affair with little else to observe other than the rough grass matting that covers the tent's floor and a dirty cushion and cover truncated by one edge of the photograph's frame.

In both cases we see these as keen instances of how the children's photographs reveal what is most likely beyond the capacity of researchers to observe directly, but they are also examples of how the images interrupt, shake and unsettle accepted understandings of street children's lives. Street children, it is commonly assumed, are neither interested in matters of personal hygiene nor does life on the street permit them the means to do so. Images like these thus surprise, they provide a startling riposte to both lazy conceptions of street children as feral, dirty and unkempt itinerants and those reports of nothing but street life's unending deprivations

Image 10 Abena, female, 16 years old

and hardships. So, too, with the images of tented sleeping and the unanticipated evidence they provide of the children's ingenuity and creativeness in separating themselves from the inhospitality of the street, if only by the thickness of a few millimetres provided by old fertilizer bags. Pictures of child tent dwellers in the heart of a city of some two million people point to the hardiness and remarkable ingenuity that children can bring to such austere contexts in ways that require the reappraisal of our understandings.

Our claims to realism also rest on how the photographs underscore the fallibility of our knowledge of the children's lives. Fallibility, 'the experience of getting things wrong, of having our expectations confounded, and of crashing into things' (Sayer, 2002: 2), provides justification for our belief in a world that exists beyond its representation, since if reality is simply a product of how we go about the business of representation and the knowledge that we claim as truth, then how could we ever be mistaken about the worlds that children inhabit?

Evidence for this comes from what are, for us, two especially significant photographs. In the first, four children, their ages difficult to tell, are laid out on matting spaced across a doorway. Beyond them it is possible that there lay other companions, but in the dimness of the

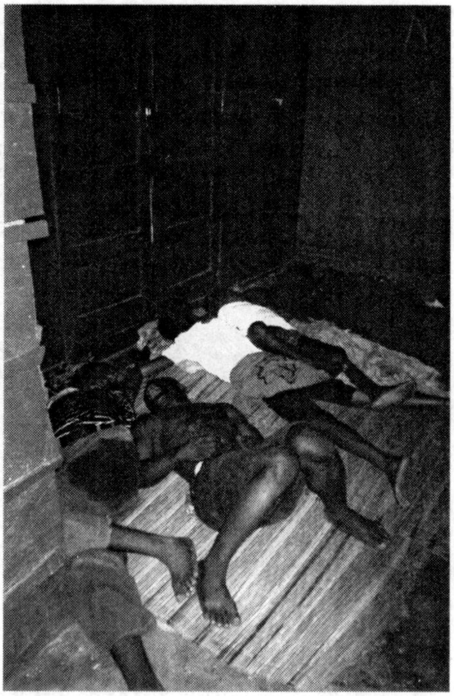

Image 11 Pam, female, 14 years old

photograph's periphery it is impossible to tell. The darkness circling these subjects nevertheless reinforces what is otherwise clearly evident: that this is an image of sleeping children. All are clothed to some degree but their stained garments, bare feet and lack of visible possessions allude to a sparse existence. An arrangement neither neat nor pleasant, it is one nonetheless which exudes design and purpose. The sleeping mat, a discarded sleeping cloth, makeshift pillow, a just-visible water sachet, the parallel sleeping positions, each of these provides a sign of clear intent. Less obvious but no less significant is a physical connectedness that binds these sleeping children together. The child closest to the photographer (a boy) lies with the sole of his left foot against the top of the foot of the second closest child (a boy), who in return rests his upper right arm against the first child's torso; the first and the third closest child (a girl) are united by touching elbows just above the head of the second child; the last visible child (a girl) embraces the back of the third child in the crook of her bent right leg, while her left leg bends

Image 12 Mustapha, male, 15 years old

backwards to also hold close her sleeping companion. This physical connection of children asleep in a doorway is an allusion to something of greater significance.

In the second example, three boys sit at a wooden table, a narrow, roughly fashioned affair, pitted and stained by frequent use. Arranged on the surface of the table lie a mug of pale plastic, an empty blue plastic bowl and partial glimpses of other now empty containers. The image suggests an intriguing equilibrium in that the right hand of each boy is poised over a large terracotta bowl, at the bottom of which lies a small pool of yellow, oily liquid that is most likely palm-nut soup. In the hands of two of the boys are chunks of *fufu* and another piece of the pale dough-like material lies at the bottom of the bowl. Held in the hand of the third boy is the head of a small fish, the whiteness of its protruding backbone providing almost cartoon-like proof of it having been picked completely clean of flesh. The bowl and its frugal contents utterly command the boys' attention. Communal eating, a meal enjoyed together; an instance of something shared.

Scenes reminiscent of these are evident throughout the children's photographs, the frequency with which both sleep and food feature itself an indication of their importance to the children's lives. Among the images of sleep we see photographs of children searching out and laying down the cardboard packing cases used as improvised mattresses, sleeping children stretched out across wooden or concrete benches on stone verandas and inside video shacks, groups of four or five laying on cardboard or foam, others huddled tightly together in doorways and in front of shops, and twos and threes fast asleep and almost entirely hidden by their sleeping covers. In another photograph the dangers of sleep are revealed, as two street children are pictured stooped over the sleeping bodies of three others rifling through their clothing. So, too, with the photographs of food. Here we are served up with images of street food vendors, charcoal grills, gleaming metal cooking pots and tables stacked with provisions, children being served by a roadside vendor, others gathered around as a woman pounds away with a large wooden staff preparing *fufu*. The occurrence of such images is more than matched by the regularity with which we see photographs of the children eating. Children are only very occasionally pictured eating alone; these photographs are much more likely to show groups of three or four children besides the photographer (and at times eight or nine) sitting or standing around together on pavements, verandas or walkways passing between them bowls of food or eating from the same receptacle.

It is the theme of sociality contained within these photographs that has forced us to reassess our knowledge of street life that allows for a much more important element of self-organization. Instead of the more usually invoked Hobbesian nightmare of childhoods overflowing with cruelty, resentment and rage, where '[i]n the street, boys tend to be highly individualistic' (Hecht, 1998: 45), fiercely competitive and violently opportunistic, the photographs have sensitized us to the existence of a much more open and cooperative culture among street children. For us, the children's photographs provide intimate visual evidence of a culture that is distinguished as much by friendship as it is by violence and competitiveness, as small groups of three, four or five children actively make and remake friendships in which considerations of reciprocity and mutual support are a significant feature, and where inclusiveness and cooperation are significant themes. It is the two photographs above that initiated our exploration of what we have elsewhere termed a 'sensibility of the reciprocal' among street children, evidenced by those small but selfless acts of support and solidarity so crucial to the children's survival (Mizen and Ofosu-Kusi, 2010b). Such acts may add an element of greater comfort to the otherwise harsh and threatening conditions in which children seek rest, or where the children's physical connections to another while sleeping constitute a source of emotional comfort and practical defence against the likelihood of molestation or harm. Gathering together for food also finds importance beyond the simple pleasures of ensuring company at meal times. To extend to a friend in need and without money the prospect of a meal today may produce a safeguard for tomorrow when that friend returns the favour.

Conclusion

We began this chapter by suggesting a role for photography as a means to connect our sense of the everyday with the everyday experiences and reality of others and, in doing so, building a better understanding of what may pass for children's living rights. Central to this has been our confrontation with the arguments of those who argue that in claiming a relationship between a photograph and the reality it depicts, we necessarily participate in the myth that a child's photograph is an objective truth, a direct and unmediated line between their understanding and experience of the world and ours. Believing that reality is hidden from us by the powerful and that photographs provide a means to communicate these hidden truths, we are blamed for promulgating the lie that photographs are true and for failing to acknowledge the constructedness of these accounts. Far from encouraging these children to 'speak' and to share with us those hidden aspects of their everyday lives, others see in our approach the silencing of these children's 'voices'.

Our response has been to resist what we see as a retreat from our engagement with the real world and of photography's role as critical disclosure by stressing a necessary relationship between a photograph and the event, place or person that it depicts. We do so because in stressing that images are constructed by the powerful as depictions of reality, including by us as researchers and adults, and as projections of cultural power, it seems to us that the necessary relationship between a photograph and its pre-photographic event has been lost; as if who holds the camera and what it is placed in relation to is irrelevant or beside the point. To construe what this relationship may involve and what a photograph may mean, as we must necessarily do in calling upon any form of sensuous experience, is not to be conflated with the constitution of their meaning. Our knowledge of the world, our conceptually dependent ways of seeing, are not neutral to the visual information that a photograph provides, nor can the understandings that we inevitably bring to photographs anticipate all questions that arise in the process of their viewing. The lessons from the *Kubolo* are clear in this respect. For, it is through the intimacy with the everyday lives of these children that these photographs have the capacity to both surprise and highlight the fallibility of our understandings.

References

Becker H (1995) Visual sociology, documentary photography and photojournalism: It's (almost) all a matter of context. *Visual Sociology* 10(1–2): 5–14.

Berger J (1972) *Ways of Seeing*. Harmondsworth: Penguin.

Bolton A, Pole C and Mizen P (2001) Picture this: Researching child workers. *Sociology* 35(2): 501–18.

Briski Z (2004) *Born into Brothels: Photographs by the Children of Calcutta*. New York: Umbrage Editions.

Burgess R G (1988) Conversations with a purpose: the ethnographic interview in educational research. In: Burgess R G (ed.) *Conducting Qualitative Research*. Greenwich: JAI Press, pp. 137–55.

Catholic Action for Street Children (2008) *Statistics*. Accra: Catholic Action for Street Children. Available at www.casghana.com/street_statistics.php (accessed 14 June 2012).

Damisch H (2003) Five notes for a phenomenology of the photographic image. In: Wells L (ed.) *The Photography Reader*. London: Routledge, pp. 87–9.

Davis M (2006) *Planet of Slums*. London: Verso Books.

Edwards S (2006) *Photography: A Very Short Introduction*. Oxford University Press.

Ennew J and Swart-Kruger J (2003) Introduction: Homes, places and spaces in the construction of street children and street youth. *Children, Youth and Environments* 13(1). Available at: www.colorado.edu/journals/cye/13_1/CYE_CurrentIssue_Articles.htm (accessed 14 June 2012).

Glauser B (1998) Street children: deconstructing a construct. In: James A and Prout A (eds.) *Constructing and Reconstructing Childhood: Contemporary Studies in the Sociology of Childhood*. London: Falmer Press, pp. 138–56.

Harper D (1998) An argument for visual sociology. In: Prosser J (ed.) *Image-Based Research: A Sourcebook for Qualitative Researchers*. London: Routledge Falmer, pp. 24–41.

Hecht T (1998) *At Home in the Street: Street Children of Northeast Brazil*. Cambridge University Press.

James A (2007) Giving voice to children's voices: practices and problems. *American Anthropologist* 109(2): 261–72.

Katz C (2004) *Growing up Global: Economic Restructuring and Children's Everyday Lives*. Minneapolis: University of Minnesota Press.

Kovats-Bernat J C (2006) *Sleeping Rough in Port-au-Prince: An Ethnography of Street Children and Violence in Haiti*. Gainesville: University of Florida Press.

Liebel M (2004) *A Will of Their Own: Cross-Cultural Perspectives on Working Children*. London: Zed Books.

Mizen P (2005) A little light work? Children's images of their labour. *Visual Studies* 20(2): 124–39.

Mizen P and Ofosu-Kusi Y (2006) Researching with, not on: using photography in researching street children in Accra, Ghana. In: Smith M (ed.) *Negotiating Boundaries and Borders: Qualitative Methodology and Development Research*. Oxford: Elsevier, pp. 57–82.

(2010a) Unofficial truth and everyday insight: 'voice' and visual research with Accra's poor children. *Visual Studies* 25(3): 255–67.

(2010b) Asking, giving, receiving: friendship as survival strategy among Accra's street children. *Childhood* 17(4): 441–55.

Nieuwenhuys O (1994) *Children's Lifeworlds: Gender, Welfare and Labour in the Developing World*. London: Routledge.

Pink S (2005) *Doing Visual Ethnography*. London: Sage.

Piper H and Frankham J (2007) Seeing voices and hearing pictures: image as discourse and the framing of image-based research. *Discourse: Studies in the Cultural Politics of Education* 28(3): 373–87.

Reynolds P (1991) *Dance Civet Cat: Child Labour in the Zambezi Valley*. London: Zed Books.

Salgado S (2000) Workers. In: Light K (ed.) *Witness in Our Time: Working Lives of Documentary Photographers*. Washington: Smithsonian Books.

Sayer A (1992) *Method in Social Science: A Realist Approach*. London: Routledge.

(2002) *Realism and Social Science*. London: Sage Publications.

Schilling C (2003) *The Body and Social Theory*. London: Sage. 2nd Edition.

Tremain K (2000) Seeing and believing. In: Light K (ed.) *Witness in Our Time: Working Lives of Documentary Photographers*. Washington: Smithsonian Books.

Woodhead M (1999) Combating child labour: listen to what children say. *Childhood* 6(1): 27–49.

4

Interdependent rights and agency: the role of children in collective livelihood strategies in rural Ethiopia

TATEK ABEBE

Every weekday, around noon, it is possible to see many pupils, both individually and in groups, going to Bora[1] (Gedeo district, southern Ethiopia) junior secondary school to take over the 'hot seat' from the morning-shift pupils. Messay, who is 15 years old and attends Grade 6, is one of them. Before she goes to school, she carries out most of the household chores and makes food for the family, comprising six of her siblings and their parents. Her father lives and works as a blacksmith elsewhere, while her mother earns money by chopping and processing *enset*, a root crop and a staple food source; this is her major source of income. Messay's elder sister is a primary school teacher in a peasant association,[2] not very far from Bora. If Messay performs well in school, she hopes to study medicine in the future, but given the poverty in her household, she also believes that instead she may have to retail commodities in the daily market or find a job in a relatively short time. Two of her eldest brothers work in the rural informal economic sector. One of them earns a little by selling fruits and *khat*,[3] a mild stimulant cash crop, and by working as a day labourer in the nearby town of Dilla (about 400 km south of Addis Ababa), while the other brother hires out and repairs bicycles. For this family, combining domestic work, education and participation in income-generating activities is evidently a vital livelihood strategy and one of the defining features of family life.

(Field note, April 2006)

[1] Pseudonyms have been used for individuals and schools to protect their anonymity.

[2] A peasant association is the lowest administrative unit in rural Ethiopian contexts, consisting of households and villages that are classed as grouped together according to their geographical proximity, and for administrative convenience, tax collection and service delivery.

[3] *Khat* is scientifically known as *Catha edulis*.

The above field note, prepared following an interview with Messay and accompanied by a visit to her household, suggests that for most children in rural Ethiopia working and contributing to family livelihood are important features of their lives. These children are valued for their socio-economic roles and grow up holding complex responsibilities and maintaining reciprocal relationships within the family. They are neither independent citizens nor autonomous individuals with separate rights but interdependent beings whose daily livelihoods are intricately entwined with and are inseparable from that of the family collective. In Ethiopia, as in many parts of the developing world, the desire to sustain family solidarity and interdependent lives often overshadows children's individual needs and interests. These children's lives represent the antithesis of the hegemonic model premised on the idea that children should have a safe and happy existence, and childhood is seen as a work-free and care-receiving phase of the life course. I argue that this is so not because of the inability of rural Ethiopians to acknowledge children's individuality but on account of an hegemonic model in which selected ideals from a once localised Western construction of childhood being exported to the rest of the world gains momentum (Kjørholt, 2004; Nieuwenhuys, 2001; Stephens, 1995: 8). Arguably, dominant interpretations of the United Nations Convention on the Rights of the Child (CRC) represent one such construct inscribed with 'premises that a child is a universal subject who should everywhere be enabled to be a free, autonomous, choosing and rational individual' (Wells, 2009: 166). By drawing attention to the individual rights of children, translations of the CRC into development policies and practices not only consolidate 'the superiority of the childhood model as it evolved in the West and the need to impose this model on a global scale' (Nieuwenhuys, 1998: 270), but also justify people's belief in the richer world that they have the 'right to reshape children in their own image and [remake] non-Western childhoods … in Western forms' (Matthews, 2003: 4).

Research *with* children and young people about their livelihoods in non-Western contexts is limited but growing. Such research includes studies that look at children's paid and unpaid work within the household, in agricultural activities, in marketplaces, and also within the wider rural and urban informal economic sectors (e.g. Bass, 2004; Bourdillon, 2001; Katz, 2004; Nieuwenhuys, 1994; Reynolds, 1991; Schildkrout, 2002). These studies have improved our understanding of the specific social, economic, political and cultural contexts in which work takes place. They have highlighted how work is a main signifier of children's lifeworlds, providing them with a sense of self-reliance, worth and self-respect because of their ability to help out and supplement the family income (Boyden and Levison, 2000; Kabeer *et al.*, 2003; Woodhead, 1998). Although survival, socialisation, participation, abuse and exploitation all mesh when children are at work, researchers have also underlined that children's ability to contribute to the family's livelihood is a source of empowerment (Aitken *et al.*, 2006; Ansell, 2005; Ennew *et al.*, 2005; Invernizzi, 2003; Robson, 2003). Many parents believe that hard work makes children more resilient as adults (Rwezaura, 1998 quoted in Ansell, 2005). As Punch (2002) argues, work also restores in young people culturally bounded notions of responsibility about the opportunities and constraints they face and enables them to make decisions about their work and future life chances.

This chapter draws inspiration from and aims to contribute knowledge to the small but growing body of literature that critically examines the value of the language of children's rights and the social significance of this language to working children (e.g. Burr, 2002; Reynolds *et al.*, 2006; Roche, 1999: 475; White, 2007). To develop my concept of interdependent agency and link it to rights, I particularly focus on how working children negotiate their rights interdependently with the wider social networks of the extended family system or, as I will call it from here on, the family collective.[4] Drawing on fieldwork on the role of children in household livelihood strategies in Gedeo, southern Ethiopia, I highlight how socio-economic contexts in which collective strategies are predominant shape or contextualise children's ability to contribute to daily and generational reproduction. This is so because the individual capacity and rights of children tie in with the familial, social and economic transformations in which their lives unfold. I argue that the human rights of children should be situated within the broader socio-cultural and politico-economic context of their livelihoods and that the focus of analysis should not be limited to the role of children within households and/or families but include the interrelatedness of rights, duties and obligations vis-à-vis the family collective.

[4] Family collectives incorporate kinship structures that are connected through livelihood circumstances and mediated by interpersonal relationships, social contracts (inter- and intra-generational) and expectations. Three interrelated dimensions of social support systems constitute family collectives in Ethiopia: (a) conventional families linked by kinship; (b) households in which different family members and fictive kin reside; and (c) expanding social networks of support – kith and kin – forged on the basis of friendship, religious affinity, livelihood systems, geographical proximity, ethnicity and social ties. Membership in the family collective endows one with particular rights, entitlements, activities and responsibilities.

I collected the empirical material for this argument during eight months of fieldwork spread over a period of three years using such techniques as life histories, focus group discussions, semi-structured interviews, observations, photo essays and story writing. Although most of the children I researched did not know their true chronological age, they knew their relative position vis-à-vis seniors and juniors in the family. The research explored, among other aspects, children's and their families' views on livelihoods, poverty, rights and social relationships. It examined the ways in which boys and girls go about their daily lives, with specific emphasis on their perspectives on what, how, where, why and with whom they work. I paid particular attention to how transformation in familial and communal livelihood strategies, noted in earlier research, have deeply altered the participation of children in diverse forms of paid and unpaid work (Abebe, 2007; Abebe and Kjørholt, 2009).

In the following sections I first briefly present recent theoretical debates regarding children's agency and social competence. Second, I situate Gedeo in a broader social and economic context and explore the ways in which, to maximise their potential for earning a living, children take part in various productive and reproductive work. Third, I focus on the intersection of children's agency and rights, arguing that children's rights being grounded in obligation towards family collectives are not necessarily in opposition to or clashing with those of adults. Finally, I will tease out the implications of the empirical material to reconceptualise children's rights as interdependence and suggest ways of contextualising their right to work within rapidly changing socio-cultural and politico-economic contexts.

Theoretical debates on children's agency

Although 'it is now possible to take it for granted that children are social actors' (Alanen, 1998: 29), there is still a 'ghettoisation' of children's agency that has not fully permeated into all social science disciplines (Holt and Holloway, 2006). There is also lack of consensus on the diverse ways in which agency is constituted in children's everyday lives. Existing literature often casts children and childhood in banal and oppositional terms, counterposing agency *against* dependency. Critiquing dominant perspectives within developmental psychology, scholars argue that children should not be viewed as passive, dependent and waiting-to-be-adults in need of protection but instead as people, that is, as active, competent social beings who can participate in matters affecting their lives (James *et al.*,

1998). I find viewing children as independent actors inherently problematic, however, because it implies that agency can best be exercised where individualism takes precedence over collective concerns (Abebe, 2008) and children are seen as right-claiming subjects (Kjørholt, 2004).

Robson *et al.* (2007: 135) define children's agency as the ability to 'navigate the contexts and positions of their life worlds, fulfilling many economic, social, and cultural expectations, while simultaneously charting individual and/or collective choice and possibilities for their daily and future lives'. This means agency neither suggests an innate capacity that is lost nor the rejection of the social structures that enable and constrain children's social actions (Holloway and Valentine, 2000). Although children have personal agency, which shapes their individual choices and desires, I contend that this depends largely on and is regulated by family contexts, livelihood opportunities/constraints and interpersonal relationships. Thus, children's agency should also not be confused either with 'autonomy' or with 'self-determinacy' or as the treatment of children on a par with adults (Kjørholt, 2004). Rather, it needs to be espoused in terms of power, that is, the power bestowed on children to participate, influence and control events in their daily lives, the lives of those around them and the societies in which they live (James and Prout, 1997: 8). That said, children's experiences of agency also depend on whom they are with, what they are doing and where they are (Robson *et al.*, 2007). They can be simultaneously dependent and independent with respect to different aspects of their social worlds including the ability to access land, work, schooling and shelter (in the short term), and to marry and establish a household of their own (in the long term). This means children's everyday lives move back and forth along a continuum of diverse experiences in relation to changing degrees of independence/dependence reflecting authority, rights, abilities, knowledge, responsibilities and so on (Punch, 2007).

Working children develop their capacities within the imperatives of culture, livelihoods, generation, gender and so on, only gradually. Their growing competencies – economic, cultural, and social – are not simply linked to chronological age but are born of social experiences and interactions, enhanced by exposure and practice. Children's agency at work is also enmeshed with adults' work particularly with that of women (Katz, 2004; Porter, 1996; Schildkrout, 2002). Although children in the Majority World tend to achieve relative independence earlier, family interdependence continues throughout the life course (Punch, 2002). As Punch (2007) argues, it is too simplistic to use the notion of dependency, whether of children on adults, or adults on children. Child–family relationships should be explained in terms of interdependencies, which are negotiated and renegotiated over time and space, and need to be understood in relation to the particular social and cultural context (Punch, 2007). I argue that the extent to which working children exercise agency depends on the interaction between personal agency and complex social, economic and political structures that shape livelihood opportunities and constraints. These structures constitute family contexts, institutions, traditions, rules and norms, as well as *interpersonal relationships* with other social actors in *material* contexts (see Bevan and Pankhurst, 2007). I will do so by contextualising the work of children belonging to subsistence agricultural communities experiencing rapid transitions in their livelihoods.

Gedeo children's social and material world

Gedeo District, located within the multi-ethnic Southern Regional State of Ethiopia, has a population of about one million, mostly farmers belonging to the Gedeo ethnic group. The Gedeo are largely patriarchal, and share relatively homogenous socio-cultural practices, religions and livelihoods (Tadesse, 2002). With a total area of 1330 km^2, Gedeo district has a population density of 618 people per km^2. The average rural household has 0.3 ha of land, compared to the national average of 1 ha of land and an average of 0.89 ha for the Southern Regional State, which makes it one of the regions with the most chronic land shortage in Ethiopia. As a result, about 38% of people are landless compared to the national average of 25% and a regional average of 30% (CSA, 2002). They mostly engage in non-farming-related jobs, including migrant labour.

The patrilocal family collective is structured by seniority, age and gender. A typical family structure comprises multiple wives who may reside in the same compound (Brogger, 1984), although this is more common among high status, wealthier families. To combine subsistence agriculture, cash crops and domestic tasks with raising children, co-wives work mostly together. Levirate marriage or widow inheritance, by which a man takes the wife of his deceased brother, is still widely practised and has three pivotal functions. First, it ensures the preservation of clan land from being inherited by members of other tribes, as inheritance rights follow the patrilineage, and girls are often married outside of their lineage. Second, the brother assumes the responsibility of taking care of the wife and children of his deceased brother as an 'heir' to his family (Bevan and Pankhurst, 1996; Brogger, 1984). Third, levirate marriage ensures that the reproductive power of the widow is 'not wasted', especially if the husband dies childless, children being both a family resource – as wealth in people – and a source of prestige and social status.

Fundamental to this structure is that Gedeo children's membership of the wider social system is not an automatic right. Children are 'born into families', and it is often the (male) member of the family who mediates a child's access to and full membership of the clan. The latter in turn bestows on the child his/her rights to physical, social and cultural resources (e.g. land, dowry, inheritance rights, social security etc.). In other words, Gedeo children are primarily members of complex family collectives to whom they owe duties and obligations for securing their rights, existence and well-being. In this web of relationships, children owe obedience and respect to the elders in whom is vested the power to exercise authority and control over minors.

Generational interdependence is a central organising principle of family life in rural Ethiopia. In her ethnographic account on children's life worlds, Poluha (2004) argues that social relationships are deeply rooted in caring and fulfilling mutual needs within and across generations:

> Life in Ethiopia ... is dependent on your neighbors and friends; you must live social life or *mahiberawi nuro* [literally meaning collective life] and do so through membership in various social associations. When you yourself or a member of your family becomes sick or dies your association will help you manage socially, financially and morally ... they are your social security.
>
> (Poluha, 2004: 55–9)

Livelihood strategies requiring cooperation and participation in various forms of associations (solidarity groups, redistributive groups, work groups, religious groups, funeral associations etc.), family and kinship relations shape Gedeo children's personal actions.

Gedeo people's livelihoods have for generations depended on growing *enset* in conjunction with cereals, coffee and a variety of fruits and vegetables, and dairy farming. Agricultural produce is destined to local and international markets and depends crucially on children's work. *Enset*, also known as the 'false banana', produces non-edible fruit, but the trunk and root are processed as food. It takes four to six years for the plant to build up a sufficient store of carbohydrates before it is suitable for use as food (Hamer and Hamer, 1994). Compared to other food crops, being drought-resistant and high-yielding, *enset* can support high population density (Tadesse, 2002). Believing that increasing national revenue is decisive for rapid economic development, the government has since the 1980s encouraged a shift from subsistence to cash-crop production. Small-scale farmers enthusiastically abandoned their diversified farming systems to grow coffee for the world market, thereby stimulating a set of changes in resource access and social relations that they did not anticipate. Because of an undue reliance on mono-cropping, Gedeo families' income became extremely vulnerable. There are three main reasons for this. First, there is the global restructuring of the coffee market following the collapse of the International Coffee Association (ICA) that formerly regulated supply and market prices. After the withdrawal of the USA – a major global actor in coffee trade – from the ICA in 1989, coffee roasting companies began to dictate the price and supply of coffee in the world market, making no distinction between high quality sun-dried organic beans produced by small-scale peasants as in Gedeo and cheap blends produced using chemical fertilisers and steam washing. Second, Structural Adjustment Programmes (SAP) increased land tax, withdrew subsidies and increased the cost of fertilisers, insecticides and pesticides, which had initially been subsidised in order to stimulate cash-crop production. Third, import tariffs on processed goods such as roasted coffee prevent producing countries in the South from exporting anything but the raw materials at very low prices. As a result, although the global coffee trade has a turnover of 14 billion dollars,[5] the income of small-scale producers has plummeted between 2000 and 2003, Ethiopia's coffee revenue dropping by almost 60 per cent (Oxfam, 2002). Considering that cash-crop cultivation has also affected income in kind, how do peasant families respond to such revenue drops? In the following section I begin with an answer as I explore children's involvement in diverse forms of household strategies and in the rural informal economic sector.

Rural poverty and children's views on work

Children in Gedeo are valued for their active contribution of labour to the household. Children are socialised early to help both men and women as they go about their various tasks:

> In childhood … girls learn to avoid laziness and to be helpful to all adults, but especially to assist their mothers in *enset* preparation and in caring for younger siblings … Boys by working with their fathers in [hoeing,

[5] *Black Gold* – a film on global coffee trade involving Ethiopia. Available at: www.blackgoldmovie.com (accessed 12 February 2008).

> planting, weeding and harvesting], gardening and pasturing animals, learn more community oriented values of wealth acquisition and its redistribution.
>
> (Hamer and Hamer, 1994: 94)

Boys and girls represent not only social security in old age but also perform different productive and reproductive activities as part of their daily responsibilities. In return, they may expect to be rewarded with praise, food, clothing, shelter, school materials and, when they come of age, inheritance rights including land. The child's ability to fulfil duties predates and is inseparable from his or her right to secure livelihood means from the wider family collective. Unlike most children in the Western world, Gedeo children *earn* their rights rather than being entitled to them because they are minors below 18 years of age.

Poverty is not only children's daily reality but also the main reason why they are put to work. Take the following case of a family composed of a widow, her four children and three grandchildren:

> All the household members reside in a small hut of approximately 20 m^2. The household is poor. Some of the children occasionally spend nights in their maternal uncle's household, which is also the main source of support, particularly during times of food shortage. Although their uncle works on the land of the children's parents under a sharecropping contract, the resource from it is not sufficient to cover daily means of subsistence. The family lives in extreme poverty: the children are barefooted, and sleep without blanket on a mattress made of dried grass. The day I visited the household, a torrential rain was pouring and water leaked through the thatched roof and running over the floor where the family slept. A cow – probably the household's only asset – shares the space with them. Abiti is a nine-year-old boy in the family and is in Grade 1 at school. However, unlike his friends, he does not have books or a pen to write with. He showed me his 10-page exercise book, which was already falling apart due to the sweat from his hands. Every page of the exercise book was filled with different subjects – science, maths and language, etc. Alaba, an elder brother to Abiti, is 13 years old although he looked underweight for his age. He dropped out of school because he felt that he could better spend his time looking after the cow together with other children in the neighborhood who do not attend school. The rest of the children combine work with schooling but said that most of the time they had to work to get food. The children work in other people's gardens as farmhands, and are remunerated in either cash or kind. They also work alongside their grandmother on their backyard plot of 0.65 hectare where they grow maize, sweet potato, *enset*, and coffee.
>
> (Field note, March 2005)

This is but one example of the many households whose poverty results in multiple forms of childhood deprivation making children's futures seem rather bleak. However, these children also demonstrated a considerable degree of *will agency*, that is, stamina and a strong desire to achieve viable livelihoods.

Deepening rural poverty, prompted by market-driven rural development, has impacted on the nature, type and intensity of work children perform. Shitaye (girl, 14 years old), currently living with her sister, says:

> I keep an eye on my sister's children, who are now three years and eight months old. My sister works for the coffee-processing firm, so when my grandmother is not around, I am in charge of them. I get them meals, wash their clothes, and bath them.

Shitaye's quote demonstrates that women's paid work increases the amount and quality of care available to children. This is because the domestic work normally done by women tends to be shared with children or is even completely transferred to them, adults keeping only a supervisory role (Jennings, 1997, cited in Boyden and Levison, 2000; Robson, 2003). Fikre wrote the following story about how she cared alone for her ailing grandfather:

> I had been helping my grandfather who was ailing for about two years before he died. I first told my father that he was ill, but he thought that it might be a simple cold. But as his cough got worse and worse, he became weaker. We went to the clinic, which referred him to the hospital where the doctor said that it was tuberculosis, and prescribed him medicine. We bought the medicines and got him home. I used to wash his clothes and take him to the clinic to get his regular injection. I got him his food and coffee, and I prepared his bed and helped him walk around. He was very weak, and I wanted to help him for as long as possible.
>
> (Fikre, girl, 15 years old)

Rural poverty has left many families with fewer resources to shoulder children's productive and reproductive burdens particularly when men are absent for work or have died. In the words of 13-year-old Kelemua whose father had died three years previously:

> We first went to live with our aunt, but since she was poor, I returned home with two of my brothers. Our mother remarried and kept two of the children, who assisted her with the farm work … but she then separated and we began to face problems … My father's relatives wanted to take us and the farm [according to the local tradition of widow inheritance]. But our eldest brother decided that we should remain here … He now works

> on the farm [and is the head of the family]. I do the housework and sell goods in the market.

The above quotes reveal that the activities and responsibilities of children are generally bound up with earning an income or production that has an important value to family collectives. They indicate that adult men and women benefit substantially from the labour – both paid and unpaid – of boys and girls. Despite various socio-economic constraints, children's access and contribution to the household-based resources of family collectives enhances their ability to obtain immediate and long-term means for their well-being. This means children's labour is pivotal to how they see and are seen by their families, shaping the nature of contributions they make. This is also evidenced in, as the above quotes demonstrate, the graduation of boys into men's work, while girls remain relegated to women's work including unpaid domestic work.

Migration is a way of escaping hardships in times of duress for many rural boys as it increases opportunities to earn better incomes than those obtaining in farming or trading in the home village (see Thorsen, 2006). Gedeo boys may also decide to migrate to learn new skills or be helped by wealthier family members living elsewhere (see Young and Ansell, 2003). Tigelu, who runs a small grocery shop in Gedeo with money earned in a town bordering Kenya, explains:

> There are a lot of opportunities there, because there is business. Jobs are better … I worked as a shop assistant in my uncle's store and with the money I earned, I opened this shop.
>
> (Tigelu, boy, 16 years old)

The ways in which domestic labour, farm work, trade and migration impact on young people's work highlight the growing importance of interdependent livelihood strategies. Tigelu's words highlight that children's lives, agency and capacities are an integral part of, and are shaped by, the web of social relations in which the household is enmeshed. The vulnerable nature of family livelihoods goes in tandem with children's capacity to adapt to adverse living conditions. Thus, children's role in collective livelihood strategies enhances their resilience in confronting their everyday lives.

Gender, birth order, family composition and social maturity influence the ways in which work is distributed within Gedeo households. They also shape children's opportunities and constraints in accessing resources such as schooling. Older children and physically stronger boys may be kept at home to help their parents with agricultural work, whereas weaker boys and/or academically bright children may be sent to school. Children's rights and duties are also shaped by gender. Even young boys may engage in selling farm produce and be in charge of managing household assets if the parents believe that they are 'wise'. Girls may be held responsible only for domestic chores and will have less invested in their education than boys. Patrilocality being the rule, they are considered as acquiring a 'new citizenship' after marriage and remain part of the family collective only until adolescence.

Agricultural entrepreneurship

Children acquire agricultural knowledge in conjunction with play, by observing and receiving instruction from adults and through trial and error. Parents encourage children from an early age to learn how to earn money and participate in cash-earning activities. As the cash economy is a pivotal source of family livelihoods, children grow up being socialised to become what has been termed 'agricultural entrepreneurs' (Hamer, 1987: 241), where they learn to tap resources from the physical environment and to sell commercial crops. Thereby children combine growing food crops (maize, *enset*, potato, root crops) and cash crops (coffee, *khat*, sugar cane, fruits), trading farm proceeds in marketplaces and working as farmhands or doing casual labour in nearby towns. 'Entrepreneur boys' are active in the daily and weekly markets of Gedeo. The important role boys play in the market begins with their work as *delala* or brokers, as 15-year-old Negara says:

> I help people who come from the towns to buy fruit in large quantities. I also work as *delala* [business boy] between the sellers and the buyers in settling the price of goods. [In doing so,] I make both parties happy and get a commission.

The brokerage service is not restricted to finding the right product and trading partners, but includes taking goods to the market, securing the means of transportation and delivering the products to the transport terminals. Negara adds:

> My friend has a rickshaw with which he transports items from the daily market to the roadside. He also takes to the market items which cars cannot deliver to the marketplace [due to accessibility problems]. So, whenever my customers demand a service like this, I recommend him to do it for them.

Negara was one of the many typical business boys in the daily market in Gedeo whose work revealed how children play a crucial role in the local economy and, in particular, in the various stages of commodity circulation. Buying and selling commodities on both a wholesale and retail basis is an important aspect of children's 'trading careers'. Says 12-year-old Digafe:

> I buy and sell seasonal fruits during different periods of the year. On a good day, I can make two to three birr [Ethiopian currency] in profit. I am now considering buying cane sugar from the lowland peasant associations and retailing it here. It is much more profitable than fruit [which also quickly becomes perishable, due to the hot and humid nature of the area] and is in high demand during the dry season.

Involvement in trade, then, enables young people to earn money while allowing them to acquire valuable skills, like making computations, dealing with customers, gaining experience-based and practice-based learning in the workplace as well as developing child–adult relationships.

Children's local work in trade cannot be detached from complex material realities, but needs to be situated in intersecting geographical scales and contexts (Aitken *et al.*, 2006) of the 'glocal space economy'. This is not only because the nature of their livelihoods is such that spatial mobility is very crucial but also because global capital is entrenched in their local livelihoods. Labour is intricately entwined with the seasonality of work and the intensive labour contribution children make during different agricultural work cycles, including land preparation, crop tending, harvesting, and marketing. During fieldwork, I observed that a substantial number of children picked coffee berries seasonally and worked for coffee-processing firms on a long-term basis. Peasant households collect coffee berries in two stages. In the first, deep-red berries are selectively picked, leaving behind the greenish ones to mature. After a month or so children and their families pool their labour to pick the remaining berries and carefully work on the coffee tree tops to ensure future productivity. Child labour in coffee production is particularly important because selectively picking only the mature coffee beans by hand is a tedious, labour-intensive job, which children are considered to be more adept at doing than adults.

As rural development failed young people, it not only created a spatial separation of economic production and social reproduction (Katz, 2004), but also accelerated the age- and gender-based divisions of labour. Such complex processes of social and economic change have altered children's living and working conditions in profound ways, and is discussed elsewhere (Abebe, 2007, 2008; Abebe and Kjørholt, 2009). Restructuring of the coffee market has led to, among other things, children being directly exposed to a deeply unequal and exploitative system of international trade. The migration of adult men and women to seek alternative livelihood strategies has transferred the burden of household reproduction onto children, particularly girls. On the other hand, with the prominence of commercial agriculture, more boys than girls become increasingly drawn into picking coffee beans, processing (washing, drying, sorting the damaged beans from the clean ones), carrying and trading them to the coffee cooperative shops, which, through niche markets, eventually export the products elsewhere. Further, the restructuring of the global coffee market has meant that international capital has become closely entwined with children's work and determines the value their work deserves locally. In this way, children's agency at work becomes embedded in 'glocal spaces' – situated in local contexts, but increasingly subordinated to the global capitalist system.

Although children are encouraged to trade independently and they begin managing small sums from an early age, relative freedom is achieved only gradually. As the main objective of their economic activities is family well-being, sharing resources is done in such a way that the child may keep only a part of the money he or she earns. In her study of Kano children in Nigeria, Schildkrout (2002) argues that the child's relative autonomy in small-scale entrepreneurship and household economics increases in accordance with his or her ability to manage work and its proceeds. Likewise in Gedeo, an implicit child–parent contract, a form of inter-generational social contract, governs the relations between children and parents. Bekelu (girl, 14 years old) told me how she covers much of her family budget from the money she earns by 'local beer-brewing, scraping and chopping *enset* and retailing food and alcoholic drinks in the market' and that without her financial contributions 'the household is not viable economically'. In this way, children's participation in family livelihoods not only helps develop their individual dispositions but also contributes to overcoming poverty and material deprivations. This participation involves multiple and often overlapping competencies: social competence (to develop interpersonal relationships), economic competence (to perform a range of household and income-generating activities), and generational competence (to care for young, elderly and sick family members, and to maintain ties with the larger network of kin).

exercising rights), potentially limits the analysis of the wider fields of power in which their lives unfold.

Individualistic readings of children's rights have many negative outcomes for working children in Ethiopia. First, in communities where collective responsibilities are vital, such a reading sets them apart and in isolation from the family and community networks on which they depend for survival, well-being and protection. Second, the emphasis on the role of state parties in safeguarding children's well-being and protection raises expectations and downplays the impact of structural economic and financial forces that sharpen poverty and inequality, particularly in the rural countryside of developing countries, and hit children disproportionately. To muster resources needed for viable livelihoods children depend critically on family collectives and social networks of support and not on the state. Family collectives are, in other words, those who shape the dominant way in which children's rights and entitlements are realised. By focusing on individual rights, contemporary discourses on rights 'throw the child out of the bath water'. Third, rights discourses have a patronising effect. This is because they not only discount the role of the families who struggle to make entitlements real for children but also ignore the meaningful roles and contributions the children themselves make to their families and the wider society.

Interdependent rights: concluding reflections

The above dissonances not only highlight how the dominant interpretations of rights are irrelevant to the children, but also reveal their standing at odds with the fundamental principle of respect and dignity on which global action is justified. Key to understanding the livelihoods of working children is the recognition of both the immediate and broader socio-cultural and politico-economic contexts in which their lives unfold and in which rights, duties and obligations are closely interrelated to those of the collectives to which they belong. As White (2007) argues, the 'universal rights of the child' do not transfer directly into the everyday contexts of working children and their families in Ethiopia. This is not to say that Gedeo children have no rights, but their rights are interdependent with those of the wider family networks with whom they collaborate and in which mutual and long-term livelihood strategies are set.

In sum, collectivist rural societies such as Ethiopia make the individualistic overtones of the CRC problematic. By failing to open up spaces for incorporating collectivistic understandings of children's rights and duties, there is a risk that policies that aim at implementing the CRC not only obscure the existing collective rights of children but also negate the very entitlements they already have in society. Recently many African countries, including Ethiopia, have begun harmonising national laws with the CRC[6] (Doek, 2007). This is a disturbing development that may hinder rather than empower children and their meaningful role in society. There is a need to move away from the vertical state–child axis to exploring the interdependent functions of children *inside* society in order to reveal the multiple responsibilities borne by children (Burr, 2002; Roche, 1999). We also need to seek out the local cultural resources that may be mobilised in the interest of empowering working children (White, 2007). This requires moving beyond a single reading of rights as a standard global benchmark against which all childhoods should be measured and engaging with how family collectives in rural societies provide enabling spaces for children to make their rights real.

Although less known than the CRC, the African Charter on the Rights and Welfare of the Child, ratified by forty-five of the fifty-three countries of the continent, is seen as a comprehensive instrument (which paradoxically enough supplements the CRC) in setting out rights and defining principles and norms for the status of African children (Chirwa, 2002). The rationale for the African Charter was the feeling of member states that the CRC 'missed important socio-cultural and economic realities of the African experience'.[7] As opposed to the CRC, which makes it generally clear that children are independent subjects, the African Charter emphasises 'the need to include African cultural values and experience in considering issues pertaining to the rights of the child in Africa' (Olowu, 2002: 128). By focusing on protection and provision, the Charter provides to the global children's rights framework a useful correction, namely to reconceptualise rights as interdependent. In addition, since it considers the obligations of children in tandem with their rights, it has important implications for placing children within the context of their families and communities as well as for exploring rights from the perspective of duties and responsibilities. Article 31 states that: 'Every child shall have responsibilities towards his [sic] family and society, the state and other legally recognised communities … the child, subject to his age and ability shall have the duty [among others] to work for the cohesion of the family, to

[6] The Ethiopian Labour Proclamation No. 377/2003 prohibits the employment of persons under the age of 14.

[7] Preamble of the African Charter.

respect his parents, superiors and elders at all times and to assist them in case of need.' By acknowledging the significance of children's responsibilities, the Article shifts attention away from the vocal, global and participating child (as articulated in the CRC) to the uniqueness of the local, dutiful and cultural child who views his or her life as being closely tied together with the lives of families and communities.

That said, it is vital to bring the perspectives and daily realities of marginal children into mainstream debates and concerns of development. There is a lot the Western world needs to learn from the views and lived experiences of children in communities like those in Gedeo regarding how collective rights, duties and responsibilities may not necessarily constrain their individual freedom. Rather than simply advancing children's rights based on the premises of current liberal ideology as being 'correct', it is important to explore how interdependent rights and relationships could inform efforts for making entitlements real for vulnerable children.

Acknowledgements

The fieldwork expenses for the study were funded by the Research Council of Norway. I am grateful to the Faculty of Social Sciences and Technology Management, Norwegian University of Sciences and Technology (NTNU) for granting me a two-year postdoctoral fellowship that gave me the opportunity to complete the written work. The chapter has benefited greatly from the insightful comments and editorial suggestions of Olga Nieuwenhuys and Karl Hanson, to whom I am grateful.

References

Abebe T (2007) Changing livelihoods, changing childhoods: patterns of children's work in rural southern Ethiopia. *Children's Geographies* 5(1–2): 77–93.

(2008) *Ethiopian Childhoods: A Case Study of the Lives of Orphans and Working Children*. Ph.D. Thesis, Trondheim: NTNU Press.

Abebe T and Kjørholt A T (2009) Social actors and victims of exploitation: working children in the cash economy of Ethiopia's south. *Childhood* 6(2): 175–94.

Aitken S, Estrada S L, Jennings J and Aguirre L M (2006) Reproducing life and labor: global processes and working children in Tijuana, Mexico. *Childhood* 13(3): 365–87.

Alanen L (1998) Children and the family order: constraints and competencies. In: Hutchby I and Moran-Ellis J (eds.) *Children and Social Competence: Arenas of Action*. RoutledgeFalmer: Taylor and Francis, pp. 29–45.

Ansell N (2005) *Children, Youth and Development*. London: Routledge.

(2009) Childhood and the politics of scale: descaling children's geographies? *Progress in Human Geography* 33(2): 190–209.

Bass L (2004) *Child Labor in Sub-Saharan Africa*. Boulder: Lynne Rienner Publishers.

Bevan P and Pankhurst A (eds.) (1996) *Ethiopian Village Studies: Adado Gedeo*. Available at: www.csae.ox.ac.uk/evstudies/pdfs/adado/adado-hiphotos.pdf (accessed 10 December 2011).

(eds.) (2007) *Power Structures and Agency in Rural Ethiopia: Development Lessons from Four Case Studies*. Report for the empowerment team in the World Bank poverty reduction group. University of Bath.

Bourdillon M (2001) *Earning a Life: Working Children in Zimbabwe*. Harare: Weaver Press.

Boyden J and Levison D (eds.) (2000) *Children as Economic and Social Actors in the Development Process*. Stockholm: Ministry of Foreign Affairs.

Brogger J (1984) *Belief and Experience among the Sidamo: A Case Study towards Anthropology of Knowledge*. Trondheim: Norwegian University Press.

Burr R (2002) Global and local approaches to children's rights in Vietnam. *Childhood* 9(1): 49–61.

CSA (2002) *Child Labour Survey in Ethiopia*. Addis Ababa: Central Statistics Authority.

Chirwa D M (2002) The merits and demerits of the African Charter on the Rights and Welfare of the Child. *The International Journal of Children's Rights* 10(2): 157–77.

Doek J (2007) *In the Best Interests of the Child: Harmonization of National Laws with the Convention on the Rights of the Child*. Addis Ababa: The African Child Policy Forum.

Ennew J, Myers W E and Plateau D P (2005) Defining child labor as if human rights really matter. In: Weston B H (ed.) *Child Labor and Human Rights: Making Children Matter*. London: Lynne Rienner Publishers.

Hamer J H (1987) *Humane Development: Participation and Change among the Sidama of Ethiopia*. University of Alabama Press.

Hamer J and Hamer I (1994) Impacts of a cash economy on complementary gender relations among the Sadama of Ethiopia. *Anthropological Quarterly* 67(4): 187–202.

Holloway S L and Valentine G (2000) *Children's Geographies: Playing, Living and Learning*. London: Routledge.

Holt L and Holloway S L (2006) Editorial: Theorizing other childhoods in a globalised world. *Children's Geographies* 4(2): 135–42.

Invernizzi A (2003) Street-working children and adolescents in Lima: work as an agent of socialization. *Childhood* 10(3): 319–41.

James A and Prout A (1997) *Constructing and Reconstructing Childhood: Contemporary Issues in the Sociological Study of Childhood*. London: Falmer Press.

James A, Jenks C and Prout A (1998) *Theorizing Childhood*. Cambridge: Polity Press.

Jennings C A (1997) *Gender, Economic Adjustment and Women's Paid and Unpaid Work in Latin America*. Master's thesis, University of Minnesota, Minneapolis.

Kabeer N, Nambissan G and Subrahmanian R (eds.) (2003) *Child Labour and the Right to Education in South Asia*. Sage: London.

Katz C (2004) *Growing up Global: Economic Restructuring and Children's Everyday Lives*. Minneapolis: The University of Minnesota Press.

Kjørholt A T (2004) *Childhood as a Social and Symbolic Space: Discourses on Children as Social Participants in Society*. Ph.D. Thesis, Trondheim: NTNU Press.

Matthews H (2003) Coming of age for children's geographies. *Children's Geographies* 1(1): 3–5.

Nieuwenhuys O (1994) *Children's Life Worlds: Gender, Welfare and Labor in the Developing World*. London: Routledge.

(1998) Global childhood and the politics of contempt. *Alternatives* 23(3): 267–89.

(2001) By the sweat of their brow? Street children, NGOs and children's rights in Addis Ababa. *Africa* 71(4): 539–57.

Olowu D (2002) Protecting children's rights in Africa: a critique of the African Charter on the Rights and Welfare of the Child. *The International Journal of Children's Rights* 10(2): 127–36.

Oxfam (2002) Mugged: poverty in your coffee cup. Available at: www.maketrade-fair.com/assets/english/mugged.pdf (accessed 12 May 2005).

Poluha E (2004) *The Power of Continuity: Ethiopia through the Eyes of its Children*. Uppsala: Nordic Africa Institute.

Porter K A (1996) The agency of children, work and social change in the south Pare mountains, Tanzania. *Anthropology of Work Review* 16(1–2): 8–19.

Punch S (2002) Youth transitions and interdependent adult-child relations in rural Bolivia. *Journal of Rural Studies* 18(2): 123–33.

(2007) Generational power relations in rural Bolivia. In: Panelli R, Punch S and Robson E (eds.) *Global Perspectives on Rural Children and Youth. Young Rural Lives*. London: Routledge, pp. 151–64.

Reynolds P (1991) *Dance Civet Cat: Child Labour in the Zambezi Valley*. London: ZED books.

Reynolds P, Nieuwenhuys O and Hanson K (2006) Refractions of children's rights in development practice: a view from anthropology. *Childhood* 13(3): 291–302.

Robson E (2003) Children at work in rural Northern Nigeria: patterns of age, space and gender. *Journal of Rural Studies* 20(2): 193–210.

Robson E, Bell S and Klocker N (2007) Conceptualising agency in the lives and actions of rural young people. In: Panelli R, Punch S and Robson E (eds.) *Global Perspectives on Rural Children and Youth. Young Rural Lives*. London: Routledge, pp. 135–48.

Roche J (1999) Children: rights, participation and citizenship. *Childhood* 6(4): 475–93.

Schildkrout E (2002) Age and gender in Hausa society: socio-economic roles of children in urban Kano. *Childhood* 9(3): 344–68.

Stephens S (1995) Children and the politics of culture in 'Late Capitalism'. In: Stephens S (ed.) *Children and the Politics of Culture*. Princeton University Press, pp. 3–44.

Tadesse K (2002) *Five Hundred Years of Sustainability? A Case Study of Gedeo Land use (Southern Ethiopia)*. Heelsum: Treemail Publishers.

Thorsen D (2006) Child migrants in transit: strategies to assert new identities in rural Burkina Faso. In: Christiansen C, Utas M and Vigh H E (eds.) *Navigating Youth, Generating Adulthood: Social Becoming in an African Context*. Uppsala: Nordic Africa Institute, pp. 88–114.

United Nations (2007) The millennium development goals. Report, UN, New York. Available at: www.un.org/millenniumgoals/pdf/mdg2007.pdf (accessed 10 December 2011).

Wells K (2009) *Childhood in a Global Perspective*. London: Polity Press.

White S C (2007) Children's rights and the imagination of community in Bangladesh. *Childhood* 14(4): 505–20.

Woodhead M (1998) *Children's Perspectives on their Working Lives: A Participatory Study in Bangladesh, Ethiopia, The Philippines, Guatemala, El Salvador and Nicaragua*. Stockholm: Save the Children Sweden.

Young L and Ansell N (2003) Fluid households, complex families: The impacts of children's migration as a response to HIV/AIDS in Southern Africa. *The Professional Geographer* 55(4): 464–76.

5

Young carpet weavers on the rights threshold: protection or practical self-determination?

TOM O'NEILL

Introduction

One of the premises of the new paradigm of the sociology and anthropology of childhood that currently inspires much contemporary research on children's lives in developing contexts is that children are autonomous social actors who have perspectives on their own lives, and livelihoods, that researchers ought to highlight in their accounts of them (James and James, 2001; James and Prout, 1997). This insight has gone a great distance towards recognizing children as more than mere subjects of development, or passive recipients of family or institutional socialization efforts. The conceptualization of working children as the powerless victims of exploitative labour forces as is assumed in children's rights discourse is difficult to sustain when research takes into account children's own perspectives on what they do (White, 1999; Woodhead, 1999).

Working children are agents, if we understand 'agency' as does Laura Ahearn (2001: 112) to be a 'socio-culturally mediated capacity to act', that is, an abstract capacity that is enabled and/or constrained by social and cultural structures and discourses. Understanding agency as such resolves the dichotomous theoretical tension between agency and structure that has long framed debates in the social sciences; it also suggests that action need not be rational, strategic or even intentional for it to be potentially transformative. As Pierre Bourdieu (1990: 66) observed, social agents act with a 'feel for the game' because they have an embodied sense of the rules of the field on which they play, rules that they may be hard pressed to articulate but by which they nevertheless negotiate the world in which they live and work. Working children share an evolving capacity of practical self-determination that develops in relation to the lived condition of their lives, rather than through global children's rights discourses and their translation into local labour policy. Though these a priori capacities exist independently from positive law, they are a form of living right that is perhaps unwittingly thwarted by international conventions that aspire to protect children from the exploitative potential of wage labour.

For many anthropologists, one of the most controversial aspects of the 1989 Convention on the Rights of the Child (CRC) is its use of a fixed age as a threshold to specify rights, protections and entitlements (Boyden, 1997; Burr, 2006; de Berry, 2004). Generally, that threshold is 18 years of age, which is commonly held as an international standard, but Article 32 of the CRC also requires states to set minimum ages for employment so that children may be protected from work that is 'hazardous' or that may be 'harmful to the child's health or physical, mental, spiritual, moral or social development'. Critics have charged that these age thresholds are arbitrary, an unreliable indicator of individual self-determining agency, and that they ignore much cultural variability in how individuals mature into adult roles (Archard, 1993). Age thresholds, because of the effect of their legal validity, lend themselves to the universal, prescriptive application of children's rights in ways that can undermine the ability of the young to act in their own best interests. It is important to note that rights of protection, as for example those granted under Article 32 of the Convention that protect children from exploitative forms of labour, also have the effect of excluding some children who are at or near the age threshold from acting in a self-determining way; David Archard (2003: 24) writes that 'this is the price paid for having to operate with such a threshold'.

In this chapter I speculate on whether this price is too high, at least in some contexts. David Archard's not unreasonable response to this problem is to refer to normal distribution; when the numbers of individuals who are unfairly penalized by an age limit becomes sufficiently large, then the threshold itself is 'poorly chosen' and requires amendment. Allison James (James and James, 2001: 34) has argued that 'law is a key mechanism that mediates between, but also preserves, the boundaries between adulthood and childhood', but legal age thresholds do not only estimate a normative division between childish vulnerability and self-determining adulthood; in some contexts they actually construct those boundaries.

A key assumption of child rights advocacy that instrumentally deploys the legal authority of the CRC is that something like a functional national rule of law exists in developing countries, and if so, that it can be relied on to protect children from the harmful effects of labour. This, arguably, was not the case in Nepal, which signed the 1989 Convention on the Rights of the Child in 1991 only a year after political upheaval overthrew the absolute power of its monarchy, ushering in a period of political instability that made social policy implementation slow and enforcement a low priority for revolving governments. At about the same time, hundreds of thousands of migrants came to the Kathmandu Valley to find work in a rapidly expanding carpet industry, most of who were young. The publication of a 1993 report by a Nepalese NGO Child Worker's in Nepal (CWIN, 1993), and the broadcast of a television documentary about child labour in Germany where most Nepalese carpets were sold, led to an international outcry against the use of child labour in the industry. Chowdhry and Beeman (2001) have argued that transnational activism over issues like child labour are taken up by local actors out of economic compulsion rather than altruistic intent. Efforts to make Nepalese labour laws consistent with the CRC and International Labour Organization standards, by designating carpet weaving as a hazardous industry and setting age restrictions, served the objectives of protecting trade, particularly for large, formal carpet exporters (O'Neill, 2005). Given these conditions, it is little wonder that the implementation of child labour policies failed to take into account the living realities of young male and female carpet weavers.

One problem with the instrumental deployment of CRC principles is the question of participation; how to adequately assess the ability of children and youth to competently act in their own best interest. Archard (1993: 65) argues that 'children should only be permitted to exercise rights to self-determination if they themselves are self-determining agents', but also admits that their seeming lack of agency may be due to the institutional and legal denial of an opportunity to exercise their autonomy because of their age. If it is assumed that children cannot act in a self-determining manner and legal thresholds are imposed based on that assumption, then it may be the law that produces child and youth incompetence, and not their own innate lack of ability. In what follows I show that many of the young Nepalese carpet weavers who became the subject of protective legislation and advocacy that culminated with the introduction of the 'Rugmark' child labour-free certification programme in 1996, were by and large fully capable of practical self-determination, that is, of acting in their own best interests through daily practice. Children's rights advocates also speak of a child's right to be heard but too often instrumentalists seeking to protect children from labour's harmful effects are deaf to theses voices. This chapter is based on interviews with carpet factory managers and weavers, as well as participant observation in a number of carpet factories amid widespread debate on child labour policies prior to the introduction of the 'Rugmark' programme.

Competent weavers, vulnerable workers

Watching a weaver at work on a carpet loom can be a bewildering experience. The weaver is usually focused to the front, plucking taught cotton warp strings like a harp, a blur of fingers, looping, thrusting and drawing tight around a steel rod tied to the warp's face. When the neat row of knots extends to the end of the rod, he picks up a makeshift hammer and drives the rod to the bottom of the warp, where he slices across the knots with a flat knife. The tools are quickly set aside, the bar lifted again, lashed to the warp, and the process repeated. His eyes lift away from his hands as he studies the plastic-covered graph paper that contains the design he is to follow. He looks down, fumbles with balls of wool that roll at his feet, and finds the one with the correct colour. In the dark weaving hall it is often difficult to see subtle colour, so there is a numbered code that is also followed. He repeats these motions minute after minute, centimetre after centimetre, for five, ten, twelve hours, sitting on a bare wooden plank at the bottom of the loom.

Carpet weaving comes down to this: supplies of raw wool obtained from Tibet and New Zealand washed and coloured, rolled into balls and supplied to the weaver, who studies a weaving diagram that renders a design often faxed to Kathmandu from Germany or the United States – all of these elements are placed in the weaver's hand and tied to the warp. The carpet weaver, usually a migrant from Nepal's hill regions to a bustling peri-urban settlement located on the threshold between city and country, is the unrecognized focal point in a global industry that employs many but enriches few. Just under one half of them were female, the rest male; most of them were young. Prior to 1994 many of them may have been, in fact, children. All of them were in Kathmandu to earn wages that were far beyond what they could have earned in their villages, even though they were a pittance compared to wages in the city (O'Neill, 2004).

For young weavers the carpet factory also provided a home, as the dusty, dark and dirty carpet factory also served as their living quarters for as long as they worked. They worked with up to six other weavers who would sit on the wooden plank beneath their loom, often surrounded by dozens of other looms. They would work, on and off, for over twelve hours a day, managing in that time to weave about 30 to 35 centimetres, or only about a third of the piece wages they would earn for one square metre of carpet. They were paid only when the carpet was finished and cut from the loom.

Industrial spokesmen often boasted that the craft of Tibetan carpet weaving revived a tradition that was in danger of being lost, and provided the Tibetan diaspora with badly needed income in Nepal. Most of the weavers, however, were young Nepalese who wove carpets intended for the European consumer market, carpets that bore little apparent similarity to traditional Tibetan carpets. These weavers were not refugees; they were migrants who followed their friends, families or labour contractors in a search for seasonal, insecure work. The work itself, the kinetic aspect of it at least, was not hard to learn or master. A child could do it.

Though the craft of weaving itself was not difficult to acquire, learning the skills necessary to negotiate piecework wages, locate, obtain and keep better paying jobs, and avoid frequent attempts by employers to short-pay, cheat and even occasionally debt-bond weavers, required a competency that few migrants, of any age, were in possession of when they arrived in Kathmandu. One encounter I had with a young carpet weaver illustrates what could and frequently did happen when they were not skilled in this regard. This occurred after we conducted a focus group with a number of unionized carpet weavers on the banks of the Bagmati River, conducted there, it should be added, because the weavers were afraid to speak inside the factory where the managers could hear them. As we were wrapping up, collecting demographic forms and labelling the tape recording of the session, a union official who assisted me noticed a man and a woman who appeared to be observing us. He approached them and asked them if they wove carpets. They said that they did and, picking up on what they had heard in our focus group discussion, related their experience of having taken a loan (*peskii*) from an employer and then discovering that they had repaid more than what the loan was worth because the employer lied about the amounts that they had repaid. They could not 'do the sums', being illiterate and unfamiliar with numbers, thus they could not independently record their repayments. The union official asked their age; the man was 18, the woman, who was nursing an infant as we spoke, was 16.

Such exploitation was often cited by children's rights advocates as a reason to protect children from this kind of labour. Even though they could do the work and needed the wages, from a rights-based perspective the potential risks to their development meant that they should be precluded from doing so as a matter of international law. Such exploitation, however, was the experience not only of child weavers; it was part of a pattern of domination frequently practised by Tibetan or Nepalese carpet manufacturers that affected weavers of all ages. These men and, occasionally, women were known by their weavers as *saahu-ji*, a Nepali word that invokes the role of hill shopkeepers as providers of credit as well as goods (Zivetz, 1992). What made this form of exploitation possible was the weaver's lack of schooling, which meant that they could not 'do the sums' and advocate for their own interests. In Nepal, as in many underdeveloped states around the world, many people who live hand-to-mouth existences in the impoverished hinterlands receive little or no education. Most adult weavers also lack formal education, rendering them essentially childlike in their negotiations with educated *saahu-ji*.

Yet it was the risks that the industry posed to vulnerable children that received the disproportionate attention of the world community. The years that followed the promulgation of the CRC were also the same years in which tens of thousands of young migrants came to Kathmandu to weave carpets. Many of them were well under 18 years of age, and this aroused the opprobrium of many international agencies that condemned the exploitation of children by the industry. Had this migration occurred in the years before the emergence of a global children's rights agenda, it may well have been unnoticed by the wider world; but in the first half of the next decade not only was the carpet industry coming under heightened global scrutiny, the children's rights agenda became a prominent and well-funded priority in many NGO and INGO development plans.

In 1994 a documentary programme about child labour in the Nepalese carpet industry on Nord Deutscher Rundfunk aired to German audiences, Germany being the largest market for Nepalese carpets. The programme had a devastating effect, tarring the entire industry as exploitative and prompting consumer boycotts. As my first fieldwork was conducted just weeks after the broadcast, its local effect was palpable; although I never viewed the programme, I did obtain a copy of the production script, which exemplified the dominant assumptions of the children's rights agenda:

> Children as disposable goods, supplies are no problem. Slave traffickers bring more and more children from the most remote villages. The parents are told that the children get trained. Most families don't know what to expect for their children in Kathmandu.
>
> Once they arrive at the carpet factory, they are at the mercy of brutal wardens. A few years ago, this exploitation of children did not yet exist in Nepal, because the carpet industry did not exist. It was the German importers who initiated mass production of Nepali carpets. They saw

> their chance to make a bigger business than elsewhere. At the expense of the children, wages were brought down to an absolute minimum.
>
> (NDR, 1994)

This narrative placed the burden of blame on Western commercial interests, as if local forms of caste discrimination and debt bondage did not exist, and constructed the child weaver as helpless, and hapless, victims of traffickers and of strangers who brutalized them in the factories. The child is presented as subordinated, passive and in need of our protection, or at least of more restrictive labour laws that would preclude this kind of exploitation. Many carpet *saahu-ji* complained that the documentary was sensational and manipulative, as for example by showing interior shots of young weavers at work through iron bar windows, commonly used in Nepalese buildings to allow air in, while the commentary described the prison-like nature of factories. Also, they claimed, the programme juxtaposed exterior shots of prominent export carpet factory signs with interior shots of child labourers that were actually filmed elsewhere, implying that specific export companies were involved in child labour.

After several hapless efforts by the Nepalese government to enforce its own child labour law, the 'Rugmark' programme, which had some success in India and elsewhere, was introduced, financed and operated by an independent international NGO. Rugmark recruited carpet factories to regularly submit to random labour inspections and issued tags that certified their carpets as child labour-free. Western consumers could be assured that the carpets they purchased had not been made by impoverished child weavers. Once the tag was viewed, any further thought about the structural injustices of global commerce, or the continuing plight of the many children who continued to labour, unnoticed, in other sectors of Nepal's economy, was extinguished.

Rugmark has been a positive programme for the industry, as it has allowed it to shake the exploitative reputation it had earlier earned, and it provided education or family reunification for a comparatively small number of rescued carpet weavers (Rugmark, 2008), but most other weavers continued to struggle to provide for themselves and their families on wages that did not even keep pace with Kathmandu's rate of inflation. Like the young couple I referred to above, many young weavers were living autonomously, away from their families in the hills or lowland *terai*; though few could articulate their rights, or even acknowledge themselves as independent social actors in a state that supposedly guaranteed those rights, they consistently showed that they were masters of practical self-determination, a form of social agency that is enacted through practice, and not through intentional strategy. Even though they often identified themselves as helpless victims of wage exploitation, their behaviour demonstrated a capacity for action that belied the childlike constructions that were assumed in global protectionist efforts.

Footloose labour

Young carpet weavers are a difficult group to study, at least directly. Where several studies of them have been mounted from local non-government organizations that work from a children's rights perspective to protect and provide for children who have been rescued from carpet factories (Baker and Hinton, 2001; Cross *et. al*, 2001), my work has always been to approach weavers in the factories where they work. Thus, where previous studies stressed the vulnerability of young weavers to the physical, social and psychological risks of their exploitation, my preference has been to focus on the weavers as active agents who negotiate their own livelihood in an industry that is itself vulnerable to the capriciousness of global export markets. Where carpet factories have been described in some reports as dark, dusty places in which young weavers are all incarcerated, in my work they appear more as spaces that enabled some forms of action while constraining others. Young weavers are not passive subjects in these spaces; carpet factories are also schools in which they acquire practical skills not only in the arts of weaving, but also in the arts of negotiation and resistance.

One formidable challenge in this research has been getting unfettered access to carpet weavers, for carpet *saahu-ji* closely protected access to their factories and monitored what their weavers said to outsiders. This was in part due to a sensitivity they had about how outsiders perceived their labour practices and also in part due to their need to protect proprietary designs from being leaked to other producers. Weavers themselves were also often guarded when speaking with researchers, because they feared the wrath of their employers for anything said out of turn and also because they could not easily articulate their own experience according the conceptual categories of the outsider. Their self-determination was best viewed in practice, as an embodied sense of the rules of their trade that they lived daily but found difficult to put into words. This made face-to-face interviews difficult, at least at first, and thus my first encounters with carpet weavers were in factories where frequent informal observation was arranged with often suspicious *saahu-ji*. It was difficult at first, moreover, to interview female weavers because of my own gender, though in time techniques were developed to include their voices. In order to establish a comparative frame for these observations, I chose carpet-weaving operations that represented the structure of the industry, including factory size, capitalization and market access. Here I sketch a comparison between three medium-sized facilities where regular observations were conducted twice weekly over a three-month period.

The first of these factories was located in a spacious, well-lit facility about 10 kilometres north-east of central Kathmandu. The *saahu-ji*, Naresh Shrestha, looked out onto the factory floor from a windowed office from where he could see most of the activity in the factory. Plexiglas panes embedded in the metal roof of the factory let available light down onto the three rows of metal looms at which the weavers worked. Each loom sat up to three weavers, who worked as team on a single carpet, seated on wooden boards cushioned with sacks of wool off-cuttings. Though the factory was sizable, the rows of looms were separated by a narrow walkway littered with balls of wool, tools and weavers sprawled out for a rest.

Naresh's weavers lived in rooms at the back of the factory. Weavers in all factories were assigned rooms when they took on work at a factory; most of the weavers were migrants from Nepal's eastern hill and *terai* regions and they slept, four to a room, in this dormitory. In most of the rooms there was a small gas stove located in the corner where weavers cooked basic meals of *dhaal bhaat*, white rice covered with a lentil sauce, accompanied by a few pieces of curried vegetable. A large open compound between the dormitory and the factory was brightly painted and clean. A painted notice, positioned prominently on the wall facing the factory, warned in English, 'child labour strictly forbidden'. There were water taps along the side that fed into concrete washbasins, and two clean Asian-style toilets for factory employees.

Naresh Shrestha was one of many Nepalese who came to invest in the carpet industry in the early 1990s, as production levels increased dramatically and it became the single largest foreign export earning industry in the country. Seeing profit in the industry, but with little practical experience, he joined his younger brother as a partner in this carpet factory, and used his considerable social charm to secure lucrative subcontracts of programme carpets – carpets pre-ordered by European exporters – that were the bread and butter of his business. Like many other *saahu-ji* at the time, Naresh had never woven a carpet of his own, and his knowledge of the craft of weaving was limited. Young carpet masters, carpet weavers who he placed in a salaried supervisory role, managed the day-to-day operations on the weaving floor. Naresh was an urban, educated Nepali, a member of the Newari community who were the traditional inhabitants of the Kathmandu Valley, and was on the board of directors of a local child rights NGO that played a prominent role in advocating against the employment of child labourers by the industry. He described his factory as a 'model' that was often visited by foreigners to see how a carpet factory could be run ethically and profitably; and indeed it was substantially different from many of the dark and dirty weaving halls in Boudha. Naresh's social position, however, placed him at some distance from the weavers he employed, as he suggests here:

> Actually I didn't know that much about the carpet business. My younger brother had opened a factory in Chabahil with his partner. He said that this work is good for us so we did it at that time. Now I also have not that much of an idea … I am not interested in it. Because the labourers give us trouble. Those people who used to work a little, most labourers are uneducated. They have not studied. If we teach them, it takes a lot of time. At least they have to take a bath one time a week. 'You have to throw the snot away.' 'You have to sit like this on the toilet.' We teach them everything. How much we teach doesn't go into their brain. Those who are involved here gave trouble for their parents, didn't want to read, didn't want to work at home, there are many.

Naresh's apparent disdain for the weavers he employed is framed in a persistent though contradictory antagonism between urban dwellers and the rural migrants who perform most of the menial tasks in the industry. The relationship between educated, 'developed' Nepalese and uneducated 'undeveloped' rural peoples implies a teleological narrative: a distinction between city and country, modernity and pre-modernity, and the future and the past. Raymond Williams has argued that this tension between the village and the city is central to our representations of the developing capitalist mode of production; it also figures in Nepalese national ideologies of development and modernization (Williams, 1973). As Stacey Pigg (1992: 507) wrote about the assimilation of Western discourses of progress in rural Nepal, 'social categories of development are not simply imposed from the outside on rural people but assimilated into the ways they see themselves and their relations to other Nepalese.' One such category of development is childhood, and the international campaign against child labour was assimilated into the prevailing class and caste structures that differentiated carpet exporters, subcontractors and weavers.

While sensitive to a need to protect children from the risks of child labour, it was clear that Naresh regarded his weavers as being little more than children, even if they met the legal minimum age of working under Nepalese law at the time. As we walked the rows between his looms talking to his weavers (and followed suspiciously by his carpet masters), it became apparent that many of them were quite young; only a handful, in fact, were over 20 years of age. Most were between 16 and 18, while a handful were as young as 14. At the time, a weaver could begin working legally at the age of 14, but only to a maximum of 36 hours a week until they were 16. Few *saahu-ji* or weavers were even aware of these restrictions, which if adhered to would have meant that a young weaver would not have been able to make a living wage from their work. Naresh's weavers worked for piece rates, which was standard practice across the industry, and most told us that it would take at least three working days to complete one square metre, for which they would be paid 350 rupees, payable only after the carpet was completed. During our first visit, we spoke to three boys at work on a multicoloured circular carpet, who told us that they were actually college students trying to earn some extra money to pay their tuition. It was extraordinary that these boys did not fit the customary profile of a young carpet weaver as a poor, uneducated migrant from Nepal's undeveloped regions, ands we made a note to continue our conversation with them during our next visit.

When we returned the following week, the boys were gone; indeed we found that only a handful of weavers we had seen the previous week remained. We asked one of the carpet masters where they had gone, and he told me that most had left having completed their orders. It was common, he said, for weavers to move on after completing only one or perhaps two carpets, as often there are no other orders to work on. Under the piece rate system, if a weaver does not work, they do not get paid, and most needed to move on to find work elsewhere. Naresh's antagonism to his weavers was grounded in their objectification as labourers: on a pattern of securing programme orders, hiring the weavers to weave them, paying them off, watching them go and then repeating the cycle. Employee loyalty was unlikely in a piece-rate wage system.

Yet loyalty, or rather subservience, was something that *saahu-ji* clearly expected. On one occasion Naresh pulled us aside as we arrived to observe the weaving, and complained that three weavers 'ran away at midnight' the previous evening, after working at his factory for one and a half years. Carpet factory *saahu-ji* and masters consistently described the departure of carpet weavers as a flight from responsibility, in this case rendered even more illicit by the fact that the departure was at night. Young weavers are free to go whenever they collect their pay and settle their accounts with the *saahu-ji*, and most of them move frequently to find other work, ideally obtaining it in a weaving hall of a large export factory where they would earn a much higher piece rate. These girls, however, had absconded without completing their orders, so the looms had to be dismantled and work started again. For a medium-sized subcontractor like Naresh, a footloose labour force is risky; he and many other small factory *saahu-ji* complained that they often received programme orders only to find it difficult to obtain good weavers to fill them.

Weaving careers

Our observations in a second medium-sized subcontracting factory showed that *saahu-ji* could adopt different strategies of labour domination to reduce these risks. This factory was selected for observation because it was the only one of close to 300 factories surveyed during my research that consistently employed children under the age of 14, or in violation to national labour laws. The factory was run by two brothers, themselves quite young, who, unlike Naresh Shrestha, began in the industry as weavers themselves. Where Naresh Shrestha was an active member of a children's rights organization and claimed to be running a 'model' enterprise, both Mingmar and Tsering Lama had been one of the few factories to have been visited by a Labour Department inspector, and had moved their factory at least once that year to avoid future inspection.

Mingmar and Tsering's factory was located near Jorpati Chowk, a dangerous intersection filled with auto rickshaws and buses idling in wait for passengers with enormous trucks filled with gravel or piles of loose, multicoloured carpet wool, blasting their horns as they pressed through. The factory itself, a recently built but already dilapidated-looking tenement, was located down a narrow alley connected to the street. Iron bars in the windows on the ground floor gave the building the appearance of a prison. Mingmar and Tsering's weaving hall was on the ground floor; inside were a number of industrial carpet looms, tightly arranged on a concrete floor. Most of the looms were occupied by young weavers, working by bare light bulbs that dangled in the dusty air. The place looked so sinister that I was initially reluctant to request that Mingmar and Tsering allow me to observe there.

They did, however; much to my surprise, though, on my first day of observations a suspicious weaver, who I later learned was the carpet master, stopped me at the door and consulted Mingmar and Tsering, who spent most of their time in their flat on the second floor, about letting me in. Afterwards, the master became an expert guide, showing me the looms, explaining the weaving process. When I pointed to a young boy at work at a loom and asked how old he was, he looked at me and shrugged. '*Chauddha laagyo*', he said, or roughly 'like 14'. It was a phrase that I commonly heard in many factories at the time that showed both that legal age limits for child labourers were widely known, and also that they were being widely flouted, as 'like 14' could mean that the weaver was only 13 or even younger, but that for the purpose of the question they were old enough.

This relaxed atmosphere was largely because at the time of my observations Mingmar and Tsering had no programme orders, thus the weavers were working on what was known as 'stock' carpets, and were working at a relaxed pace. Stock carpets were often imitations of designs from other factories that were sold to a merchant who came by from time to time to purchase quantities of these carpets at extremely low prices; at the time of my research, Mingmar and Tsering were being paid cost or even less than cost for what their weavers produced.

Gradually we came to know that most of Mingmar and Tsering's weavers were in the 12 to 17-year age range, that they were migrants from the eastern *terai* region and, in comparison to the weavers we observed in Naresh Shrestha's factory, that they were inexperienced. On one occasion I sat down with three young weavers and spoke to them about weaving carpets, and how their employment was arranged. They worked as we spoke; the young weaver in the middle was trying to drive the steel rod, bound with knotted wool, to the formed carpet below. He threw the flat headed hammer used to do this inexpertly so that it stuck the warp strings in mid stroke, causing the entire carpet to vibrate so violently that the outside weavers couldn't form their knots. At first the older weavers ignored this, but after a few minutes they told the child to stop with some irritation, and we continued to talk. The oldest boy there told me that he was *chaudda laagyo*, and that he received a piece rate of 325 rupees per square metre. This rate was 25 rupees less than the average, but like most other weavers he received his wages in full upon completion of the carpet. The youngest boy in the middle admitted to being 12 years of age, and revealed that he only received half of the piece rate, while the other half was paid to a *thekadaar*, or labour contractor, who was a woman who ran a cold store located at the end of the alley on which the factory was located.

This labour-contracting arrangement was described to me by various people, though never in quite the same way. Sometimes children were reported to receive even less of their wage, were put on a paltry salary, or received nothing at all. Alternatively, their portion of their wages was remitted to their parents in the hills, though these remittances may never arrive there. Some weavers were under a *thekadaar* for three months, others for six months, and others indefinitely. Mingmar reported that he paid the same rate for each square metre to weavers whether they worked under a *thekadaar* or on their own. Weavers who worked under a *thekadaar*, however, only received half of that wage; the *thekadaar* pocketed the rest.

Though anti-child labour NGOs have understood the *thekadaar* to be an unambiguously exploitative figure in the industry, in reality their role is far more complicated. The relationship that a child weaver would have with their *thekadaar* is one of dependency, as the *thekadaar* not only arranges for their employment and trains them in weaving skills, they also characteristically cook and care for children in their charge. The *thekadaar* is a form of 'jobber' who provides workers for the informal economies of South Asia and employment opportunities for peasants in need of wage labour to supplement agricultural earnings (see Breman, 1996). Labour contracting in the industry has been identified as a mechanism by which *saahu-ji* indirectly dominate labour, and specifically child labour, but what was interesting about Mingmar's factory was that at least one half of the weavers there were not working under one. These weavers were generally more experienced than the younger weavers who worked under a contractor. Though subject to the persistent and systematic wage exploitation of the commoditized labour market, they kept what they earned even though they ought to have earned far more than they kept. For young weavers bound, however temporarily, to a labour contractor, sitting beside a comparatively free worker provided a model for future action; and the considerable volatility in the market for weaving labour provided plenty of scope for this action.

Because many of the weavers in Mingmar and Tsering's factory were working under a labour contractor, and because they were providing work for their weavers even though they were not working on a specific subcontract, the numbers of weavers in their factory was far more consistent than in Naresh Shrestha's. But after a few months, those not working under a labour contractor also began to drift away either to work elsewhere or return to their villages. Even weavers who were under a labour contractor would leave, particularly if their apprenticeship period was over; mostly they went from place to place in the company of friends or family.

Looking beyond the carpet factory

In a third factory, weavers were employed in a full export company, owned by a second generation Tibetan refugee who occupied a factory located on land owned by a Tibetan monastery just outside of Boudhanath. The factory was clean, heated, well lit and much more spacious than elsewhere. The weavers lived in what appeared to be brick barracks that circled the factory; these were also roomier and cleaner than elsewhere. An obligatory 'no child labour' sign hung from the gate to the factory compound, and the *saahu-ji* permitted the weavers to plant a garden in the compound to supplement their food supplies; during my fieldwork, rows of maize towered in most of the open areas of the compound. Sonam, the *saahu-ji*, appeared to be an able and cosmopolitan businessman who spoke a number of languages, including Tibetan, Nepali, English and of course German, enabling him to communicate with the European carpet importers who placed orders with his company. He was able to pay his weavers a top piece rate, expected them to be highly skilled, and thus most of them were a good deal older than in the other factories. Many of them were young women, who Sonam preferred to hire because they were 'more serious'. As he stated:

> normally we don't give much (work to) boys because then we get sometimes a problem, like if we have a bad person he can create the problem by, you know, inducing the others also. And sometimes when we have a lot of boys then we have to give them advances and then these boys always make a point of running away when they have too much advance in their name.

Sonam refers here to the practice of granting salary advances (*peskii*) to weavers as a form of short-term credit. Weavers often asked for *peskii* when they start weaving and ideally repay it from their first pay packet, but some weavers would leave the factory before doing so – sometimes without even weaving a knot. With over 300 carpet factories in the immediate area, and over 1,500 in the Kathmandu valley itself, a weaver could run off and work elsewhere or return to their villages; either way the funds are lost to the *saahu-ji*. Thus the comparatively good working conditions that Sonam maintains reflect his need to retain a footloose labour force, and is also a sign that weavers had a great deal of practical power. In some cases, the *saahu-ji* needed them more than they needed the *saahu-ji*'s work.

Despite Sonam's suspicion of young male weavers, two younger weavers were frequent participants in my weekly visits to the factory. The two were brothers; I met the first boy, named Ram, during my first visit, when he told me that he had been at the factory for two years already, even though he was only 14. His brother Tashi, 16, arrived later from another factory, where he worked as a design illustrator, in which he drafted paper designs and coloured them for other weavers to follow. A shortage of work there compelled him to work as a weaver with his brother. Tashi told me that he looked forward to going back to that work, because clearly he saw carpet weaving as a less prestigious job. He complained that his hands and eyes were in pain much of the time; carpet weaving is tedious and physically demanding work, and most of the weavers I talked to spoke constantly about the physical injuries and the psychological numbing.

As I lived not far away from Sonam's factory, I frequently bumped into Ram and Tashi in the neighbourhood. The first time this happened, at mid-day, I asked if they were having a day off. No, he said, he was working, though he did not explain why he wasn't at the factory. Each time afterwards when we would meet accidentally, usually at the Boudhanath stupa square, I would ask if he was on a day off, and he would say no – I eventually found out that he tended to wander in the afternoon heat, as it was too hot inside the weaving hall to work. After the sun went down, the factory would get busy again, as Ram and the other weavers tried to make up for lost time.

I saw Ram again one last time, on the bustling main road outside of the stupa gate. I asked him if he was on a day off, and he told me, 'yes'. He then explained that he left Sonam's factory, quit carpet weaving altogether and that he was now training as a *thanka* painter. He wanted eventually to make a living by painting and selling Tibetan religious art to tourists. I was impressed by his aspiration; at 14, Ram had made a mid-life career change, abandoning what he and many weavers regard as the menial work of weaving carpets.

Conclusion

I conclude with the story of Ram's brief career as a carpet weaver because it is a story that contradicts dominant conceptions of the child carpet weaver as vulnerable, dependent and subject to the exploitative control of their employers. In this chapter I have argued that at least some carpet weavers demonstrated an evolving capacity of practical self-determination that developed in relation to the lived condition of their lives, rather than through global children's rights discourses and their translation into local labour policy. Carpet merchants, capitalists and labour contractors were adept at dominating weaving labour, but there was considerable scope for weavers to resist that domination; young carpet weavers not only learned weaving skills as they worked, they also learned these methods. What they learned is that they belonged to no one but themselves and that they could change jobs, evade credit payments or even return to other aspects of their lives without being subject to unreasonable authority. For young weavers at the critical threshold between dependency and self-determination this was particularly the case; and instrumental efforts to protect them often contradict their own efforts to live autonomously.

In 2000 the Nepal Child Labour (Prohibition and Regulation) Act ruled that children under the age of 16 are prohibited from working in risky occupations such as in manufacturing industries, including carpet factories. The Act did not extend to agricultural or informal labour, where it was estimated in 2008 that 2.9 million children between the ages of 14 and 17 worked; thus it left them to toil in obscurity (ILO, 2012: 35). Where in the past a small number of these children and youth migrated to Kathmandu to weave carpets for a comparatively higher yet still meagre wage, this possibility was closed by the new law. A decade after I concluded my fieldwork with Nepali carpet weavers, Rugmark inspectors pay unannounced inspection visits to up to 65 per cent of all carpet factories in Nepal, effectively ensuring that young people like Ram are excluded from working in carpet factories. The opportunities for self-determination that I observed ten years earlier are now only a matter for historical reflection, as international opprobrium over child labour exploitation in concert with local economic self-interest ended them.

Setting age thresholds to protect children is a pragmatic necessity. However, one of the consequences of the legal age or work threshold is that it imposes on youth forms of institutional dependency, either in schools or in families. Legal thresholds actively demarcate the boundary between childhood and adulthood by prescribing limits to individual action on either side of the threshold. This demarcation is a result of a powerful global process to establish universal labour and industrial standards over a wide variety of local economic and cultural contexts. In the case of the young Nepalese carpet workers, children's protection rights ultimately restricted their living right to participate in the construction of their own futures.

References

Ahearn E (2001) Language and agency. *Annual Review of Anthropology* 30: 109–37.

Archard D (1993) *Children: Rights and Childhood.* London: Routledge.
(2003) *Children, the Family and the State.* Aldershot: Ashgate.
Baker R and Hinton R (2001) Approaches to children's work and rights in Nepal. *Annals of the American Academy of Political and Social Science* 575(1): 176–93.
Bourdieu P (1990) *The Logic of Practice.* Stanford University Press.
Boyden J (1997) Childhood and policy makers: A comparative perspective on the globalization of childhood. In: James A and Prout A (eds.) *Constructing and Reconstructing Childhood: Contemporary Issues in the Sociological Study of Childhood.* London: Falmer Press, pp. 190–229.
Breman J (1996) *Footloose Labour: Working in India's Informal Economy.* Cambridge University Press.
Burr R (2006) *Vietnam's Children in a Changing World.* New Brunswick: Rutgers University Press.
Chowdhry G and Beeman M (2001) Challenging child labor: transnational activism and India's carpet industry. *Annals of the American Academy of Political and Social Science* 575(1): 58–175.
Cross J J, Sharma M and Shrestha S (2001) Weaving carpets, weaving lives: childhood and ethnicity in downtown Kathmandu. *International Journal of Anthropology* 16(2–3): 153–9.
CWIN (1993) *Misery Behind the Looms.* Kathmandu: Child Workers in Nepal Concerned Centre.
de Berry J (2004) The sexual vulnerability of adolescent girls during civil war in Teso, Uganda. In: Boyden J and de Berry J (eds.) *Children and Youth on the Front Line: Ethnography, Armed Conflict and Displacement.* New York: Berghahn Books, pp. 45–62.
ILO (Central Bureau of Statistics, Government of Nepal) (2012) *Nepal Child Labour Report: Based on Data Drawn from the Nepal Labour Force Survey 2008* International Labour Organization, International Programme on the Elimination of Child Labour (IPEC), Central Bureau of Statistics of Nepal Kathmandu: ILO, 2012–1v.
James A and James A (2001) Childhood: toward a theory of continuity and change. *The Annals of the American Academy of Political and Social Science* 575(1): 25–37.
James A and Prout A (1997) A new paradigm for the sociology of childhood? Provenance, promise and problems. In: James A and Prout A (eds.) *Constructing and Reconstructing Childhood: Contemporary Issues in the Sociological Study of Childhood.* London: Falmer Press, pp. 7–33.
NDR (Nord Deutscher Rundfunk) (1994) Nepal – teppiche: Deutsche kaufhauser profiteren von kinderarbeit. *Panorama* programme script in author's possession.

O'Neill T (2004) Weaving wages, indebtedness and remittances in the Nepalese carpet industry. *Human Organization* 62(2): 211–20.

(2005) Labour standard regulation and the modernization of small-scale carpet production in Kathmandu Nepal. In: Smart A and Smart J (eds.) *Petty Capitalists and Globalization: Flexibility, Entrepreneurship, and Economic Development*. Albany: State University of New York Press, pp. 201–25.

Pigg S (1992) Inventing social categories through place: social representations and development in Nepal. *Comparative Studies in Society and History* 34(3): 491–513.

Rugmark (2008) Annual Report. Available at: www.goodweave.org/uploads/2008%20Annual%20Report.pdf (accessed 12 June 2012).

White B (1999) Defining the intolerable: child work, global standards and cultural relativism. *Childhood* 6(1): 133–44.

Williams R (1973) *The Country and the City*. New York: Oxford University Press.

Woodhead M (1999) Combatting child labour: listen to what the children say. *Childhood* 6(1): 27–49.

Zivetz L (1992) *Private Enterprise and the State in Modern Nepal*. Madras (Chennai): Oxford University Press.

PART II

Social justice

6

Conflicting realities: the Kikuyu childhood ethos and the ethic of the CRC

YVAN DROZ

> Children are a wealth because a person with no children is not important in this world; even if he dies, he will not be called a deceased because he did not leave anything behind.
>
> (Kikuyu man, 20 years old, Laikipia, 1995)[1]

During one of my last visits to Nairobi I was surprised by the many Western-funded NGOs campaigning for children's rights that had sprung up since the earlier days of my fieldwork among the Kikuyu: in 2005, for example, there were more than 100 NGOs helping street children. My feeling of surprise came from an uneasiness I felt about the avowed aim of the NGOs to make Kenyans 'aware' of children's rights and what I came to understand during my fieldwork among Kikuyu peasants about the ethos of the accomplished person (Droz, 2000b). I was puzzled about the kind of articulation between this ethos and how NGOs interpreted and sought to disseminate children's rights. In this chapter I attempt to give voice to the Kikuyu peasants of my study to tease out the challenge that NGOs must address in seeking to make people such as the Kikuyu 'aware' of children's rights. My argument is that though the Kikuyu conception of children is continuously translated to meet the challenges of new situations and contexts brought about by education, urbanization and evangelism, the underlying ethos of the accomplished person remains somehow constant; in other words, it does not converge towards the conception held out by such human rights instruments as the CRC. I argue that, in spite of its claim to universality, the conception held out by the CRC is no more universal than the Kikuyu ethos and that children's rights should be seen as work in progress where no conception of childhood is a priori defined as the only valid one.

[1] I collected the quotations used in this chapter during my fieldwork between 1993 and 1995 among peasants in Laikipia plateau.

The Kikuyu[2] conception of childhood is broadly consistent with a representation of children that is widespread throughout Africa. Though there are countless variations, subversions and manipulations, this conception seems to be based on a few common principles. First, a child is not a full person until he or she has completed the necessary rites of passage – especially male and female circumcision – which give him/her a status within the group. Second, a child does not exist in a vacuum, but belongs to a family and has to give back the 'present of life' s/he received from his/her parents: his/her main duty is to bear children for his/her parents and to devolve the 'traditional' family names. Third, s/he has to pay respect to her/his relatives and must obey them. In short, a child is not born with innate, individual rights, but is an evolving person embedded in a web of social relations informed by both rights *and* duties.[3]

The Convention on the Rights of the Child (CRC) articulates a universalistic catalogue of rights that originates in a culturally specific conception of children: the 'precious child' of twentieth-century neo-liberal thought about the self-governing individual (see also the introduction to this volume). The explicit politico-philosophical system on which the claim to universality is based articulates what I shall call an 'ethic' to distinguish it from the implicit system of values (ethos) of conceptions such as the Kikuyu's. Does the ethic of the CRC, as politicians, policy-makers, NGO staff and donors interpret it in order to make the Kikuyus aware of children's rights, make sense when set against the Kikuyu childhood ethos? In what follows, I will begin by shortly describing how this ethos informs ideas about the child's rights and duties and showing how they relate to the Kikuyu ideal of the 'accomplished person'. Next, I contend that the ethic of the CRC is in fact nothing more than a very specific and localized Western ethos. I finally discuss possible links between the childhood ethic behind the CRC and the Kikuyu childhood ethos and argue that before one may envisage a dialogue between the two, the Kikuyu childhood ethos needs to be acknowledged and treated on an equal

[2] As I argue elsewhere (Droz, 1998), the 'ethnic' labelling of people was a colonial invention in Kenya. Local politicians later reappropriated this identity register in order to reach out to a 'national' political audience. This historical process led to the local imaginary of ethnic groups (see Lonsdale, 1992). I do not use the word 'Kikuyu' in a culturalist perspective, but to refer to the identity register of ethnicity and its related ethos.

[3] I thank Olga Nieuwenhuys, Fenneke Reysoo and Yonatan Gez for their comments and help. However, the responsibility for the potential shortcomings and misinterpretations of this text is – unfortunately – solely mine.

footing with the Western ethic, which is – ultimately – a rationalized ethos articulating the governance of childhood in the new world order.

I follow the Weberian path and infer an ideal-type of the Kikuyu – as well as Western – ethos of childhood. It does not need to be said that this Kikuyu ideal – or the CRC ethic – does not exist in the social reality, but, in spite of constant adaptations, continues to represent the core values commonly shared by people claiming to be Kikuyu. In order to benefit from the heuristic development of the ideal-type, I take the risk of essentializing the Kikuyu conception of children, as well as the CRC ethic. Of course, in everyday life Kikuyu people and the promoters of children's rights formulate these two ideal-types in a whole range of discourses and practices. Theses depend on the identity register the actors mobilize in an actual social setting. Be they man or woman, old or young, rich or poor, and so on, people will express the Kikuyu ethos of childhood or the CRC ethic in a vast number of social practices. Being an anthropologist I, however, feel that from this chaotic catalogue of practices some principles governing the behaviour of social actors can be inferred. To avoid the trap of reification, I will give voice to 'real' Kikuyu people in order to illustrate in vivo how the Kikuyu ethos of childhood is expressed in a specific setting, namely among the peasants living on the Laikipia plateau among whom I carried out fieldwork in the early 1990s (see Droz, 1999).

Kikuyu parents' views of children: a Weberian perspective

> You cannot work for nothing! When I am working now, I know that I am working for my children. If I don't have them, I will not be able to work and I will also not be happy, I will be lonely.
>
> (Kikuyu Woman, 40 years old, Laikipia, 1995)

Having children is one of the conditions of becoming an 'accomplished person', the Kikuyu ideal of the self. Childless men and women cannot achieve this sense of accomplishment, and consequently their lives appear socially meaningless. Children being the bearers of lineage names, it is the duty of every Kikuyu to name his or her children after his or her parents or bear the consequence of being cursed. That is what a respondent told me:

> To have a child means a lot according to my understanding. One, it means that you have a helper, that is if you are sick, you can have someone to give you water, cook for you, weed and plant and also harvest for you … It also means that you are not barren and you will have somebody to bury

> you when you die, especially when you have boys. Because girls will leave you and get married … It also means that when one dies he/she will be remembered because his/her children will be left, but if you don't have a child and you die, your name will be lost and forgotten forever
>
> (Kikuyu Woman, 40 years old, Laikipia, 1994)

A young man added to this representation of the importance of having children:

> To have a child means that you have been declared to be a parent or a caretaker or have reached the stage of motherhood, or if you have a child that you named after your father or mother, then they will know you have given their name to a first born. Others will say that now you are strong. Also you will know that you are not barren. A child is also a present from God. To have a child means that now you have somebody to help you because even if you die there will be somebody to hold your head … although these days are not as those of the past … If you see a person who doesn't like children, he is not an honest person.
>
> (Kikuyu Man, ~20 years old, Laikipia, 1995)

As in most peasant societies, Kikuyu people consider children as helpers whose duty it is to work in their parents' fields or household. Nevertheless, parents also have their duties. First, they must rear their children according to the Kikuyu ethos. Second – since the 1930s – they have to send them to school to learn the ins and outs of 'White men's power' or, nowadays, to get a degree and – hopefully – secure a job in the public administration or the private sector. In 1983 Jean Davison summarized elderly women's views of childhood as follows:

> Children are highly regarded by the Gikûyû[4] and are included in all aspects of life – whether it is a circumcision or a clan meeting. Childcare is the responsibility of the entire extended family, not just the mother. Though the father is absent much of the time, when he is at home he shows great affection for small children in particular. Children are in close contact with their mothers' bodies for the first year and are held often by various members of the family. From then on, older siblings are responsible for much of the childcare, and grandmothers are as important as mothers once a child is weaned.
>
> (Davison, 1989: 27)

Common as it may seem, it is the symbolic importance of children for Kikuyu people that informs this style of upbringing. After the birth of the firstborn, people no longer address the new parents by their Kikuyu

[4] There are several written forms for the Kikuyu ethnonyme.

names, but as father or mother of the newborn. The new mother ceases to be a *mûirîtu* (circumcised girl) or a *mûhiki* (married woman with no child) and becomes a *mûtumia*;[5] likewise, the father passes from the status of *mwanake* (circumcised man) to the one of a *mûthuri*, that is head of a household. Both are now closer to becoming accomplished persons and will from now on behave in accordance with this new status.

> There is a saying *mûndu ûri mwana ndakuaga*: whoever has a child will never be forgotten; since this child will be named after him/her.
>
> (Kikuyu Man, ~20 years old, Laikipia, 1995)

In pre-colonial times, beside kinship and age-class, the generational principle was used to organize Kikuyu society.[6] This principle prescribed a degree of resemblance between grandparents and grandchildren. They belonged either to the Maina or to the Mwangi generation. The two generations took turns in symbolically possessing the land and presiding over rites of passage. Their symbolic power was supposed to protect the land against drought, pests and sorcery. Every thirty years or so, a major ritual mobilized the entire society, cleansed the land of curses, settled disputes or vendetta between lineages and marked the handing over of power to the other generation.

In spite of major political and socioeconomic changes, Kikuyu people still give great importance to personal names within the family and name their children after their parents following a specific order: the first male baby receives the name of his father's father, the second his mother's father, and so on (Leakey, 1977: 515–17). The same applies to baby girls. Though still considering the passing down of forbears' names[7] imperative, most people are no longer able to explain the practice and do not consider it as in older times indicative of the respect of their ancestors' spirit. They rather believe that one must name children after their forbears so as not to lose the family names and in order to preserve the memory of the deceased. That remembrance – often mentioned to explain concern for inscribing the family lineage on the tombs of family members – is synonymous with respect for parents and, by extension, for the spirits of the defunct:

[5] 'Nevertheless, children determine a woman's social status to a great extent, and a woman is usually called by the name of her firstborn child' (Davison, 1989: 27).

[6] See Peatrik (1995) for a complete description of the pre-colonial Kikuyu social organisation.

[7] The names in question here concern only the Kikuyu name. The Christian name depends on the parents' choice.

> The main reason for naming children after deceased family members is to make sure that even after death they remain alive due to the names and physical appearance of the kids. Another reason … is to show gratitude for the ways in which your parents nurtured you. In this way you show that you suffer just like your parents suffered in bringing you up and that you really appreciate that.
>
> (Kikuyu Man, ~18 years old, Laikipia, 1995)

Custom, remembrance and communion with parents beyond death would explain this deep attachment to family names. The supposedly similar physical appearance between grandparents and grandchildren is meant to recall for the living the memory of deceased ancestors. Furthermore, naming children after grandparents demonstrates respect for parents because it is a way of having their own parents symbolically 'reborn' and of paying the 'debt of life' that is owed to them. This naming practice is mandatory and no one dares neglect it for fear of an ominous curse from a dying parent. The possible sanctions incurred when a parent, usually the mother, does not follow this custom demonstrate the importance that is still attached to this practice:

> For Kikuyu parents, if you do not name your children after your parent, you will be hated and humiliated by the community. That is they will be talking evil about you thinking that your relationship with your parents is bad. They will also regard you as an outcast, who has been disowned by her own parents.
>
> (Kikuyu Woman ~40 years old, Laikipia, 1994)

> The spirits of those who have been denied this respect may start haunting the members of the family in question, either by diseases or to point of death. The family may remain in problems for a long time and these will continue to their children and to the children of their children. The children may die and the parents may be denied the right of giving birth again.
>
> (Kikuyu Man, ~20 years old, Laikipia, 1994)

Failing to name children after grandparents endangers the immemorial generational bond and brings the risk that ancestors will be condemned to oblivion. It is therefore the worst of insults and may attract a curse on the offspring resulting in collapse and sudden death. It is thought that the spirits of the dead will intervene to punish the culprit by taking the life of the newborn, just as the child's parents tried to remove the dead from collective memory.

If people do not follow the practice, the consequences reach far beyond the realm of the domestic unit, the entire neighbourhood being likely to vilify the couple for having thus insulted their parents and, by extension, all of their ancestors. Everyone will try to fathom the hidden reasons for such a despicable action. Refusing this fundamental right to grandparents is equated with repudiating one's parents:

> If a man has a child that he has not called after his father or mother, it is not good because it is something he owes them … he should also call his children father or mother … if you don't do that you are going to be cursed as those people who are denied offspring. Other children you can name them after other relatives, but if you don't name them after other relatives, then, it's a curse. The parents will be useless in future as they will be cursed and also the child will look as if he is not blessed in this world.
>
> (Kikuyu man, ~25 years old, Laikipia, 1994)

> The spirits of those to whom this respect has been denied may start haunting the members of the family in question and cause diseases or death. The family may remain in problems for a long time and these will be passed on to their children and their children's children. The children may die and the parents may be denied the right of giving birth.
>
> (Kikuyu man, ~20 years old, Laikipia, 1994)

Apart from death and sickness, there is also a risk that the spirits of the deceased will remove the guilty couple's generative powers. This is regarded as a terrible vengeance because sterility condemns its victims into remaining as an incomplete being (*thaka*).

There is another aspect of name-giving that must be emphasized here. Like the death-bed curse, it offers parents a powerful means to pressurize their children. Living grandparents of a newborn child who feel that their children disrespected them may actually refuse to have their names transferred to the baby. This refusal is equivalent to a curse and constitutes a terrible sanction, for the death of the newborn must inevitably follow:

> There are some parents who say that they should not be named after by anybody, this is a punishment to the person to be named because if he is not named appropriately, he has no other option than die … If the grandparents of the newborn or any other relative refuses to pass on their name then the children may be named after animals … that's why we have names like Wangombe, Njogu, etc. … Nothing happens to the parent apart from losing the child.
>
> (Kikuyu man, ~20 years old, Laikipia, 1994)

Thus, sons or daughters who reject their parents will see their lineage jeopardized because of parental sanctions. The foundation of the values that guide daily life and inform respect for elders is to be found in a cluster in which soul, death and offspring are intimately linked and in which children take a central position.

Although destabilized, parental authority is still strongly in place. Children are obliged to name their own children after their parents under pain of losing their reputation, their offspring and their ability to propagate, hence relinquishing any hope of becoming an 'accomplished person' on the one hand, and on the other, they need the consent of their parents to name their children after them. As young parents feel that the 'souls' of the family always roam in their vicinity and can put those who do not respect their parents in harm's way, the seemingly innocent name-giving practice is turned into a powerful means to assure the authority of elders over their grown-up children.

Let me now summarize the Kikuyu conception of childhood. First, a child is considered as a gift of God, for a child is a 'blessing' for the parents, who may then reach the full adult status, that of the 'accomplished person'. Having proven their reproductive power and having paid back the 'gift of life' received from their own parents, they can now accede to the status of *mûtumia* (for the mother) and *mûthuri* (for the father). Second, when having a child, the parents gain the social recognition of their extended family. Indeed, to have a child secures the land and the names of the family: the (male) newborn will inherit the land, avoiding the possibility of it being abandoned to 'foreigners', and the child will – once adult – perpetuate the names of the family and guarantee the lineage's immortality.

As everywhere in Africa, the child's role is not only symbolical; he or she also has a very pragmatic role to fulfil in the life of the household. In everyday life a child is a helper both in the domestic sphere and on the land. Kenya lacks a social security system for unsalaried people so that a child is also the provider for his or her parents in their old age. Of course, a child is also considered a burden financially (school fees and medical care) and psychologically (source of worry about his or her future). But beyond that, as the child contributes to transform the new parents into accomplished persons, he or she also provides them with access to membership of rotating credit associations. These important institutions offer a kind of social security through a combination of savings and mutual help and are reserved to people who, having borne children, have proved capable in the eyes of the community of facing up to the harshness of day-to-day life in Kikuyu country.

I now move on to argue that, in spite of constant adaptations to changed situations, there is a continuity in the discourses and social practices of Kikuyu parents and children that reach back to pre-colonial times. Life in pre-colonial Kikuyu society was seen as a succession of rites of passage: birth, 'second birth' ritual, circumcision, marriage, parenthood, death (Leakey, 1977). Adulthood was reached after marriage, and – particularly – after having had at least one child. As the treatment of the dead body of childless individuals demonstrated, a person was not considered 'normal' unless s/he had had a child. No one dying without offspring received respectful treatment. His or her spirit was not supposed to join the ancestors' souls, and was deemed to roam and haunt the living (Droz, 2011). The name of the ill-fortuned deceased was lost for the family, for it was perilous to name an infant after one who did not succeed in having children. Hence, the Kikuyu conception of children – up to parenthood – as unachieved persons, as said, is still a widespread idea in Africa.

The actual frontier between childhood and adults-to-be was the ritual of male and female circumcision. Before this ceremony, a child was not considered to be a social person. He or she could behave irresponsibly without being reprimanded. His or her death concerned only the nuclear family for the deceased was 'just' a child and – at best – an adult-to-be. This did not mean that parents did not love and cherish their children; quite to the contrary. Children were not only fully embedded in the social networks of the family, they participated in the day-to-day activities and helped in the household duties or work in the fields. One might also say that children stood at the very centre of society.

Today, the same conception is still the rule, with the addendum of formal education. As said, early in the twentieth century schooling became increasingly imperative for Kikuyu children.[8] Children went to school while continuing to work for their family, but parents had to meet the costs of education. Kikuyu people are known to be the best-educated group in Kenya. Every year a competition takes place between districts and provinces to obtain the first places in the national exams.[9] Kikuyu

[8] See Droz (1999) or Peterson (1996) for the history and representation of school among Kikuyu people.

[9] In Kenya, every pupil has to pass an exam every year and the aggregated results are used to rank the school.

people eagerly await the results and are particularly proud of their position at the top of the grading. Concerned parents struggle to pay school fees for their children, hoping they will find a job in the administration or the private sector. Moreover, school achievement increases the amount of bride wealth parents may demand for their daughter. Thus, parents consider schooling as an investment in children, for both boys and girls. Educated boys will secure their parents' subsistence in old age and will ensure that their land is not lost, while educated girls will contribute their bride wealth to help their brothers to marry. Consequently, sisters make it possible for their brothers to have children, and their parents to fulfil their moral duties.

The fascination with school is consistent with the ethos of the accomplished person that every Kikuyu strives to achieve. The Kikuyu pre-colonial moral order was already informed by this ideal (Droz, 2000b). An 'accomplished man' would become the founder of a new lineage after having cleared the land, winning it from the forest by the sweat of his brow. In a society where corpses were usually exposed to the hyenas, burial in the hard-won land was a sign that one had fulfilled one's individual and social mission. Burial symbolized the highest possible attainment for a man and his spouse and was a sign that the living owed them deep respect (Droz, 2011). In order to obtain the honour of being buried, they both had to respect the etiquette during their entire life, the man and the woman having to participate in the different councils of elders. The man had to marry one or several women and have children. Sons were important, for they were destined to carry their father's corpse and lay it in the tomb. Women could only be buried if their husband had already had this honour bestowed on him. Conversely, a man could only respect the etiquette thanks to the social competences of his spouse(s). The ideal wife would rear many children, cultivate fertile fields, brew a delightful beer, roast exquisite meat, entertain her husband's friends, educate her children and maintain peaceful relationships with her co-spouses. In order to fulfil this ideal, a man had not only to work hard and surround himself with women, children, relatives and clients but also receive the help of God – or be lucky, for in order to be buried he had to die peacefully. The core of this ethos was an ideology of self-made people, who, thanks to their hard work and abundant children, were able to obtain land and attract clients to extend their social network and gain prestige. As I have argued, the trans-generational bond – conveyed by the reuse of the family names – lies at the core of the Kikuyu childhood ethos. The familial phylum (Neckebrouck, 1978) has to be perpetuated by having children, the holders of the family names. They warranted to the lineage symbolic immortality and the remembrance of deceased members of the family.

To summarize the Kikuyu childhood ethos, a child is not considered in terms of having universal rights, but as one link in the chain of generations. Both parents and children are indebted to their ancestors. They have to pay back the debt of life to keep alive the names of the lineage. For men and women, to have children is part of a path to social accomplishment that they have to follow. The Kikuyu conception of children is thus entangled in a holistic worldview, in which children are the means to complete a 'good life'. They are cared for in order to achieve this ideal and will in due time follow the same path, be it in their own way. Indeed, this ideal of the accomplished person is continually in dialogue with the changing social reality. Education has for instance changed the age at which children used to be circumcised. While it used to be carried out at the age of 16 to 18, now the ritual is more likely to take place at 14 to 16, before children leave their parental home to attend secondary schools in nearby towns. Following their religious denomination or in keeping with modern ideas about possible damaging effects, at least half of girls are no longer being circumcised. Though it is difficult to say how these girls will fare in the future, they may have to deal with the difficulty of claiming an adult status in a situation where male and female circumcision is widely considered the essential *rite de passage* for the end of childhood. There is a danger that they will remain suspected of being irresponsible persons unable to control their sexuality. There are also more boys whose circumcision is carried out in clinics while they are still very young, a possibility that is not open to girls since the law prohibits female circumcision (Droz, 2000a, 2009). Hence, both the discourse and the practices associated with the ideal of the accomplished person are in constant mutation. However, these mutations do not seem to bring its underlying logic nearer to the logic animating those who work to promote the CRC among such peasant communities as the Kikuyu. I briefly discuss why this is so below.

The CRC ethic of childhood

I turn now briefly to the conception of childhood that inspires the NGOs that work to promote the CRC in order to show how it contrasts with the Kikuyu childhood ethos.[10] I am well aware of the approach to the CRC

[10] See for example Nieuwenhuys (2007) for a detailed analysis of the 'global child' conception.

currently adopted by many legal scholars: 'While some elements of the CRC may certainly have roots in purely western concepts, as arguably is the case for the general principle of the "best interests of the child", on the whole the Convention is deliberately accommodating of diverse implementation contexts and relatively flexible' (Arts, 2010: 13; see also Brems in Chapter 10 of this volume). My aim here is therefore not to reject the CRC as an instrument of Western dominance, but rather to highlight the tension arising from the encounter between CRC promoters and peasant communities such as the Kikuyu. My point is that while both the promoters of the CRC and the Kikuyu adhere to a distinct and enduring ethos, only the former claim that their ethos has the legitimate right to dispel and replace the ethos of the latter by presenting it as an ethic, or an explicit system of values. What, then, are the underlying concepts that make this ethic difficult to articulate to the Kikuyu ethos? These concepts are, I claim, premised on the twentieth-century liberal idea of the 'precious child' as a person endowed with inalienable rights. The CRC lists these rights in the bureaucratic style typical of UN declarations.[11] The idea that a child is born with inalienable rights is rooted in a Western conception of the human person, where humankind is conceived as made up of rational individuals (Panikkar, 1999). This also applies to the Western ethos of the child: the duty of parents being to care and protect him or her in order that s/he becomes a free and autonomous individual. The historical invention of childhood in bourgeois Europe during the Enlightenment has been thoroughly documented by Philippe Ariès (Ariès, 1960; Ariès and Baldick, 1962). Here, it suffices to underline its historical, local and class embeddedness in order to question its universal validity. By presenting this local morality as an ethic – an explicit system of values – that attributes universal rights to children, CRC promoters such as child rights NGOs in Kenya attempt to exercise hegemonic power over other ethos of childhood.

The 'precious child' is believed to be an individual with specific needs and rights, a potential adult to whom proper material and emotional conditions must be offered for his or her physical and psychological development. The liberal notion of the precious child has important consequences for the parents and their worldview:

> From now on enterprising parents earning money to spend on their children's good quality food, education, health, housing and recreation, in other words, on the realization of their children's rights, were to be set as

[11] See Rist (2002) for a critique of UN declarative style.

> examples. The failure to realize rights became a 'failure of parental altruism' and put on the account of poor parents' lack of initiative, ignorance, laziness, insensibility or, worse, religious and political fanaticism. A failure to offer constant care and supervision, to buy private education, to provide children with expensive medicines, vitamin-rich food, electronic toys and mobile phones and so on, was no longer the outcome of some structural injustice in the global system of distribution.
>
> (Nieuwenhuys, 2007: 158)

This implicit understanding of childhood intimates compulsory duties for parents. Parents who fail to live up to the duty to realize children's rights have to be educated to learn how to raise their children.

NGOs and international organizations have used this – supposedly universal – representation of children to develop strong advocacy activities to marginalize the local conception of children:

> The 'model' NGO-child is preferably sufficiently small in size to appear much younger, has a heart-rending personal story of extreme abuse that refracts negatively on both his or her own society and parents, has the determination and intelligence of an autonomous adult yet nourishes only one dream: be restored to a lost childhood … Local conceptions, culture and practices are treated as the Oriental Other, the 'before' on which the child actors are invited to dwell in extenso to contrast its hellish inhumanity with the 'after', where children attain both their rights and their salvation.
>
> (Nieuwenhuys, 2007: 156–7; see also Cheney, Chapter 8 of this volume)

This model of childhood also pervades the activities of local and international NGOs in Nairobi, where it has increasingly been embraced by the upper class.

In Kenya a whole range of discourses dwell on the CRC ethic, such as the precious child conception of the upper class, the 'child-in-danger' conception of international NGOs working with children or the conception of childhood exploited by local NGOs in order to gain support from the donor community. At the turn of the millennium, as I showed elsewhere, the Kenyan Government also used this ethic for political purposes. In 2003 Kibaki's new regime, which came to power after Moi's had been displaced, sought to build a brand new image, trying to rehabilitate street children as a signal that a new era had been born. The appearance of street children in Nairobi's business centre was represented as a sign of the troubled era of the previous regime. Begging for money without working and struggling to survive in grinding poverty, they were to become the living proof that Moi's government did not care for its citizens. As a sign that a new era had begun, the police force swept the city of Nairobi. Street dwellers were brought to sorting camps within the city where children, men and women were separated. This broke up the social ties that wove the street gangs together. And when 'father', 'mother' and children were taken to different rehabilitation projects far out in the countryside, this process effectively tore street families apart. The government offered an institutional setting for each category: children were directed towards orphanages; women and men were taken to separate camps. As the call of some street mothers crying for their lost children echoed in Nairobi newspapers, NGO representatives took up the issue with the government, who agreed to allow mothers to keep younger children with them in the camp. The camps were the heritage of the previous government, who had used them to train private militias. Dressed in paramilitary uniforms, ex-street children were first disciplined through military drills and hard work under the hot sun, where they had to grow their own food to learn how to earn a living by the sweat of their brow. Professional skills, for example carpentry or sewing, as well as how to read and to write, were imparted in their spare time. The internment of street dwellers was presented as a children's rights issue and tagged onto the intervention policies of NGOs and the development community; the rehabilitation process itself, by contrast, echoed moral ethnicity and treated street children as strays in need of disciplining into an ethos of work that would turn them into accomplished men and women. The worrying implication of this situation was that the children coming back to the streets after having been 'rehabilitated' would be seen by the public as antisocial, immoral elements that refuse to work.

Producing a peculiar assemblage with the Kikuyu ethos, Kibaki's regime then promoted a new policy said to be protective of street children's rights by putting them 'to work to bring them back to the Kikuyu community'. In doing so, the government tried – successfully at that time – to transform the political setting, breaking with the previous corrupt political class and whitewashing its (Kikuyu) nationalist image while at the same time paying lip service to the donor community's insistence on the promotion of children's rights (Droz, 2006). This is but just one of the innovative expressions of the dialogue between two conceptions of childhood. What it demonstrates is that to be effective, interventions for children must not only articulate the local ethos of childhood, but that, in spite of the support of child rights NGOs, this articulation does not necessarily result in a treatment of children that is respectful of the ways in which they may conceive of their rights.

This said, the NGO discourse on children's rights hardly reaches the majority of Nairobi's inhabitants, not to speak of the small towns and rural areas where the local childhood ethos still governs day-to-day activities. For most Kikuyu people – rural and urban – the NGO discourse appears alien to their conception of childhood.

Kikuyu ethos and CRC universal ethic

The distinction between ethic and ethos as two distinguished systems of values – the former politico-philosophical and the latter implicit and embodied – helps us to understand the difficulties of articulating living rights and the universal ethic of human rights. Ethos – or local morality – is a system of values incorporated, implicit and potentially contradictory. Ethos is expressed in practices or in interaction and is informed by a structured pool of principles for action, felt to be legitimate and recognized as just. These implicit systems of values belong to what Bourdieu has termed *habitus*, an embodied and adaptive system of perceptions, representations and dispositions socially acquired during one's life history (Bourdieu, 1980, 1997). Every human being develops and transforms a local ethos during his lifetime. But only a minority adhere to an ethic, a rationalized system of values.

An ethic is a rationally structured set of explicit and argued values. It is often used as a hegemonic rhetoric to legitimize specific – in this case Western – standpoints. In other words, arguments belonging to an ethic are used in a struggle to impose a localized ethos as a dominant system of values. An ethic's universalistic claims collide with local moralities, which are dismissed as irrational worldviews based on traditions and naïve or inadequate representations. The self-assigned duty of ethic, then, is to enlighten an irrational deemed ethos, in this case to bring the light of the CRC to Kenyan local societies in order to instigate a change in behaviour or social practices. At issue is whether this actually happens.

The Kikuyu ethos of childhood does not regard children as endowed with rights in isolation from their social surrounding. Children are unachieved persons and can only exercise or be entitled full rights as they gradually acquire personhood in a network of relationships. It is true that the Kikuyu parents also have to take care of their children, to educate and prepare them to struggle for life and to set up a family, and children have an implicit right to live and to be cherished by their relatives. But not for their own sake: children are 'merely' the temporary holders of the names of the lineage. Their duties are to become responsible adults and to have children of their own in their turn. This fate will keep alive the familial phylum and give their parents their full adult status. Thus, children are inscribed in a specific worldview, where they occupy a transitive place in a symbolic chain of generations.

Children, as any other person among the Kikuyus, are not considered autonomous individuals entitled to a list of specific rights irrespective of their personal merits. Of course, as other children in the world, they develop their own specific individual identity, but this they can only do if they fulfil their duties towards their lineage and respect the ethos of the 'accomplished person'. To uncover the implicit components of the Kikuyu childhood ethos and the underlying elements of the Western conception of children as promoted by Western-funded NGOs might help to open a dialogue between the heralds of CRC ethic and this specific Kenyan childhood ethos. Exposing these two local moralities and understanding the CRC ethic as merely a rationalized conception of a specific ethos may be conducive to countering the latter's claim to be a hegemonic system of values that overruns localized childhood ethos. Once one highlights and acknowledges the specific components of each local morality of children, then – and only then – may a fruitful conversation develop between the stakeholders of children's rights and the children who grow up embedded in their local morality, be they Kikuyu or Western.[12] This process could help prevent the current misunderstanding about the imposition in the Kenyan setting of a supposed universalistic child ethic, which is, in fact, nothing more than a rationalized twentieth-century Western ethos of childhood. At issue is that rights are what people say they are, so that all ethos also include rights even if they are not necessarily cast in a liberal, individualist idiom and that, as the example of street children in Nairobi highlights, these interpretations are loci of struggle.

References

Ariès P (1960) *L'enfant et la vie familiale sous l'ancien régime*. Paris: Plon.

Ariès P and Baldick R (1962) *Centuries of Childhood : A Social History of Family Life*. New York: Vintage Books.

[12] See Droz and Lavigne (2006) for an introduction to a dialogical ethic applied to the development setting and for an example of a dialogical ethic applied to the clitoridectomy among Kikuyu people.

Arts K (2010) *Coming of Age in a World of Diversity? An Assessment of the UN Convention on the Rights of the Child*. Rotterdam: International Institute of Social Studies, Erasmus University Rotterdam.

Bourdieu P (1980) *Le sens pratique*. Paris: Minuit.

(1997) *Méditations pascaliennes*. Paris: Seuil.

Davison J (1989) *Voices from Mutira: Lives of Rural Gikuyu Women*. Boulder: Lynne Rienner.

Droz Y (1998) Genèse d'une 'ethnie': le cas des Kikuyus du Kenya central. *Canadian Journal of African Studies/Revue canadienne des études africaines* 32(2): 261–84.

(1999) *Migrations kikuyus: des pratiques sociales à l'imaginaire; Ethos, réalisation de soi et millénarisme*. Neuchâtel and Paris: Institut d'ethnologie and Maison des sciences de l'homme.

(2000a) Circoncision féminine et masculine en pays kikuyus: rite d'institution, division sociale et droits de l'homme. *Cahiers d'études Africaines* 158: 215–40.

(2000b) L'ethos du mûramati kikuyu: schème migratoire, différenciation sociale et individualisation au Kenya. *Anthropos* 95: 87–98.

(2006) Street children and the ethic of work. New policy for an old morale, Nairobi (Kenya). *Childhood* 13(3): 349–63.

(2009) La morale de l'interdiction de la clitoridectomie en pays kikuyu. *Anthropologie et Société* 33(3): 118–37.

(2011) Transformations of death among the Kikuyu of Kenya: from hyenas to tombs. In: Jindra M and Noret J (eds.) *Funerals in Africa: Exploration of a Social Phenomenon*. New York: Berghahn, pp. 69–87.

Droz Y and Lavigne J-C (2006) *Éthique et développement durable*. Paris: Karthala and IUED.

Leakey L S B (1977) *The Southern Kikuyu Before 1903*. London, New York and San Francisco: Academic Press.

Lonsdale J (1992) The moral economy of Mau Mau: wealth, poverty, and civic virtue in Kikuyu political thought. In: Berman B and Lonsdale J (eds.) *Unhappy Valley: Conflict in Kenya and Africa. Violence and Ethnicity*. London, Nairobi, Kampala and Athens, GA: James Currey, Heinemann Kenya and Ohio University, pp. 315–504.

Neckebrouck V (1978) *Le onzième commandement. Étiologie d'une église indépendante au pied du mont Kenya*. Immensee: Nouvelle revue de science missionnaire.

Nieuwenhuys O (2007) Embedding the global womb: global child labour and the new policy agenda. *Children's Geography* 5(1–2): 149–53.

Panikkar R (1999) La notion des droits de l'homme est-elle un concept occidental? *La Revue du MAUSS* 13(1): 211 35.

Peatrik A-M (1995) La règle et le nombre: les systèmes d'âge et de génération d'Afrique orientale. *L'Homme* 134: 13–49.

Peterson D (1996) *Dancing and Schooling: Missionaries, Athomi and the Outschool in Late Colonial Kenya*. University of Minnesota.

Rist G (ed.) (2002) *Les mots du pouvoir. Sens et non-sens de la rhétorique internationale*. Paris and Geneva: PUF and IUED.

7

The politics of failure: street children and the circulation of rights discourses in Kolkata (Calcutta), India

SARADA BALAGOPALAN

This chapter explores the emerging discourse of children's rights amongst a group of street children in Kolkata (Calcutta), India. Through a focus on three different narrative incidents it attempts to expand reflection around children's rights from its current focus on efforts of nation states to 'implement' the Convention on the Rights of the Child (CRC) to the contingent sphere of subjectivities and meanings that children make of 'rights'. This meaning-making, or the processes of translation that the universal undergoes, brings to the fore local webs of signification that reveal disjunctions in these children's understanding of rights. These disjunctions, I argue, represent the cultural workings of historically constituted subjectivities and the ways in which these produce an ambivalent reading of 'rights' and the state. This ambivalence forms part of what this chapter characterizes as an absence of 'rights-based subjectivities'. This is namely the post-Enlightenment concept of the autonomous (sovereign) individual from which the notions of rights and citizenship are derived. The particular historical insertion of former colonies into these processes of Enlightenment through colonial rule, during which a large majority of the population were not recognized as citizens but governed through modern technologies of the colonial state, has produced a different understanding of rights and citizenship amongst them. This absence of the hegemony of liberal practices that underlie the creation of a modern self does not mean that marginal populations neither understand the language of rights nor take state entitlements seriously. Rather, I contend that street children locate a reading of rights less in terms of an individuated sense of entitlement and more within a larger understanding of community. Disruptions produced in the *everydayness of rights*, including how children interpret rights, make them their own and weave their desires into them to reveal processes of translation of assumed universals. In other words, processes of translation are disclosed in the tensions between the normative (and always) pedagogic imperative that marks state and civil–social interventions on children's rights and children's interpretation of these. I suggest that the open-ended and contingent nature of these processes should not be read as a failure to reproduce the universal, and therefore as a 'lack' or an imperfect modernity. Contingency should rather be interpreted through a historical lens and read as a political moment (Chatterjee, 2004), a disruption that requires the existing paradigm of children's rights to include the meanings that different populations of children make of rights.

The chapter is organized into four sections, the first of which uses broad-brush strokes to discuss existing academic writing on children's rights. This is not an attempt at a literature review but rather helps to establish a context for the argument. The second section provides three narrative incidents culled from my ethnographic research that represent examples of dissonance with the ways children's rights have been discussed thus far. While aware that the politics of everyday experience always exceeds the neatness usually attributed to historically constituted selves, in the third section I interpret these examples to discuss the formation of subjectivities in modern India. The fourth section concludes the conceptual argument being made in this chapter through putting forward the idea of a double-sided politicization of children's rights.

Existing research on children's rights

The idea of children's rights has gained increasing acceptance around the world in conjunction with transnational, governmental and NGO efforts to protect those represented as vulnerable and promote their rights. An impressive amount of research and writing on children's rights, including a scholarly journal devoted to this (*The International Journal of Children's Rights*, which began in 1993), is a reflection of the growing recognition of the impact of this new discourse in framing global understandings of young people's lives. Current writing on children's rights can be tentatively classified into three broadly separate though interrelated domains of enquiry. The first and earliest of these (which precedes the CRC) is a more philosophical query about whether children have rights and if so, what it would mean for children to have rights (Archard, 1993a, 1993b, 2002). These two questions were usually taken together and the ontological nature of the deliberations meant that the category 'child' was constructed primarily through a universal biology of physical age. However, in more recent debates centred around the CRC, there is increased recognition of the child as a culturally mediated subject, and therefore a willingness to recognize and critique the CRC as having idealized a Western-bourgeois childhood as the norm (Boyden, 1997; Nieuwenhuys, 1998). However, this recognition has failed to exercise the desired critical effect and research continues to document the ways in which traditional child-rearing and socialization practices in different societies impinge upon the implementation of the CRC (Parry-Williams, 1993) taking an 'enlightenment universalism' as a normative ideal (Freeman, 2002).

Authors working in the second domain of enquiry are interested in gauging the extent to which processes of implementation and the resultant realization of children's rights is being achieved. Revealing structural and bureaucratic roadblocks, these authors understand them primarily in terms of poor governance, inadequate mechanisms and faulty procedures. This includes authors who have focused on the processes of drafting the Convention (Grover, 2004), the effectiveness of mechanisms for annual reporting by states (Scherer and Hart, 1999), its inadequacy in addressing the needs of specific populations of children (Pare, 2003), and so on.

The third domain of enquiry focuses on the child itself and is concerned with giving children a 'voice', an active capacity to speak and narrate their lives as a way of facilitating a more participative implementation of the various provisions of the Convention and its promise of equality (Kufeldt, 1993). Having different children speak acknowledges to some extent cultural difference. But while this has produced a vast amount of methodological writing on how to do research with children in ways that take cognizance of the differentials of power and hierarchy, the ways in which language shapes, delimits and always already mediates the child's interaction with the adult are seldom questioned (Rose, 1984).

The above three domains of enquiry in the emerging field of childhood studies and the growing multidisciplinary interest in children provide a moment of 'conjuncture' (Balibar, 2005), or an event that changes the ways in which the issue is discussed. The emergence of a new understanding of children and childhood has made it difficult to continue discussing the category of the child in the singular and as impeded by biological incapacity. Particularly marginal children's issues have been articulated through a rights discourse with its attendant understandings of entitlement and agency. The substance of an international treaty such as the CRC is to assert the equality of all children globally to certain basic and agreed upon entitlements or rights. However, the reverse side of this equality is the underlying assumption that these rights will be uniformly comprehensible locally. Thus far local difference has been analysed in terms of the cultural acceptability of certain articles in the CRC. Central to these analyses has been whether the entitlements of particular provisions are sensitive enough to local difference in their insistence on promoting only a particular way of dealing with the issue at hand. The idea of all children being rights-bearing subjects is hereby universally assumed and is considered to have a similar indexical valence for the culturally diverse population of children the CRC seeks to bring within its purview. On a very commonsensical note, this does not preclude the intense pedagogic activities required to familiarize children with the idea of rights, particularly around the specific contents of the CRC. The point about the universal assumption around all children being 'rights-bearing subjects' has more to do with historical processes through which ideas around rights, citizenship and so on get distilled. This does not erase the need for pedagogic processes around the specific articulation of 'children's rights' but rather highlights the different subjectivities with which these pedagogic processes work and which, more importantly, mediate the formation of identities. Even though discussions around the contents of the CRC took into consideration several 'cultural' concerns of different nation states, the underlying assumption was that childhood is primarily a biological given, thus allowing for a universal calibration around children's assumed dispositions, capabilities, understandings and so on. This explains to some extent the implicit assumption that the idea of possessing rights is equally intelligible to all children worldwide. This assumption rests on a binary between the normative, transcendental universal principle and the particular within which it circulates. The ways in which children in various parts of the globe experience the rights they have been guaranteed then becomes less relevant. My approach is very different. My starting position is that the creation of individuals into rights-bearing subjects is neither natural nor inevitable since this has been interrupted by differing processes of modernity.

Three narrative incidents

My aim here is not to oppose the universal enlightenment language of rights with a local example that speaks to the inappropriateness of universal moral judgements that have been so often heard in human rights debates.[1] Positing the hegemony of particular constructions of a Western society versus the cultural specificity of the rest of the world is an ineffective way of situating the argument. Both these constructions should be seen, I argue, as products of a colonial knowledge that sought to legitimate the superiority of the West against its Others (Tsing, 2005). The claim to the universality of rights and all of what it embodies is closely intertwined with the complex history of modernity and colonialism that produced, legitimated and put into circulation certain ways of thinking about the self and the world. This is not to deny that the idea of the universality of rights already had a certain materiality among the local populations that preceded and framed the ways in which documents such as the CRC have been interpreted and put into practice.

The following narratives are based on fieldwork conducted for a period of approximately fifteen months between 1992 and 1995 at a street children's shelter in Calcutta, India. Calcutta is infamously reputed to have the largest numbers of street children, which include both children living on the street as well as those who work on the street and live at home. Street children emerged as a major object of concern from the mid 1980s onwards and the city saw the rise of several NGOs that began to work with this population of children, offering them a range of services. My ethnography was based at an NGO shelter located on a station platform in the second busiest station in the city, namely Sealdah Station. Begun by Cini-Asha in 1989, this shelter for boys consisted of two sheds at the end of Platform 10 and the children who lived on the station were mostly Bengali-speaking and were either from the poorer south-eastern districts of the state, particularly South 24 Parganas, or from neighbouring Bangladesh. For most of the boys from Bangladesh their 'illegal' crossing was not particularly difficult (the border not being subject to as much surveillance as it is now) provided they had adequate finances to bribe the guards on both sides. Although the official register had over seventy names written in it, the shelter usually housed around forty boys on

[1] The critique on the cultural relativism of human rights has moved beyond interrogating its non-coherence for particular cultures to understanding 'human rights' itself as culturally and historically inflected rather than a normative universal. Alisdaire MacIntyre puts this well in his discussion of the idea of 'emotivism' to highlight that all moral judgements are 'expressions of preference, expressions of attitude or feeling'. He states that 'rights' implies an underlying set of socially established rules that come into existence under particular social circumstances in particular historical periods (see MacIntyre, 1981). For an overview of contemporaneous human rights literature on diversity and the universal aspirations of human rights, see Brems in Chapter 10 of the present volume.

average. In addition to providing these children with a roof above their heads, this shelter was also equipped with lockers, a bathroom, some utensils and a stove for cooking, ran an informal banking system, as well as provided daily literacy classes and weekly counselling sessions. The boys who lived at this shelter chose it voluntarily and they often came and left as they pleased. The main reasons for leaving were either because they had taken up some temporary labouring job in the city to earn more money at short notice, or had decided to lay low for a while because of a fight with another child or a staff member. I spent a large part of the day observing these children in everyday negotiations with each other, the staff and the routine of activities provided.[2] What began as an initial focus on their literacy experiences widened into an ethnographic study of their lived worlds. I conducted two sets of unstructured interviews with about seventy boys at different points during my time at the station. In addition to this, I conducted unstructured interviews with the field staff at the station shelter and staff who worked at the main office and coordinated work at various other shelters that the organization ran in addition to working towards city-based coalition efforts. I also conducted interviews with the parents of fifteen boys, because these parents had visited the shelter during the time that I was there. Members of these children's extended kinship networks at the station and its vicinity were also interviewed as part of the research's effort to map the material realities of these boys lives and the ways in which these affected their sense of self.

First Narrative: By the mid 1990s, largely due to transnational discursive and funding regimes intent on promoting the CRC, the idea of children's rights was gaining ground amongst NGOs in Calcutta and began to frame their programmes of reform with street children. One of the popular forms this took was involving street children in a pedagogic exercise around scripting skits concerning children's rights issues that the children then performed for a larger public during city-wide events such

[2] This routine included three hours of literacy instruction in the morning before lunch, followed by a couple of hours of recreation after which a few boys were assigned to cook the evening meal while the remaining hung around the shelter or the platform. Weekends were devoted to rag-picking. This NGO, like several of its partners in the city-wide coalition, functioned on an understanding that it was 'important' that these boys not lose touch with their income-earning activities like rag-picking, their daily foraging for fruits and vegetables from Kole Market, the nearby wholesale vegetable market, and so on. The rationale for allowing the boys to continue with these activities (which the staff explicitly characterized as stealing while the boys used this term more selectively) was because they worked with the assumption that the NGO presence in these lives should only be viewed as temporary and should not radically disrupt the past lives of these children.

as the Calcutta Book Fair. Scripting sessions usually began with the staff person leading the discussions. During one such session in which twenty boys were present, the staff person began: 'This skit is to show the audience that all children including all of you have rights. You have a right to food, to education, to sleeping under a mosquito net.' Shankar, an older boy and a consummate actor, piped in authoritatively: 'We are doing this skit so people really understand the way we live, the way we stay.' Liton, a younger boy who, because he was shy, was seldom included in the cast, asked quietly: 'Will they give us money when we tell them that we have rights?' This immediately had all of the boys chattering wondering how much might be made. The staff person loudly replied: 'No, all we want is their understanding.' Liton, keen not to lose out on the humour his statement had generated, said: 'I know the perfect first line for the play. I can open the dialogue saying to the rest of the boys as if my character is not one of them, "Why should the *babus* [middle class] listen to you? After all they make money from people like you."'

Second Narrative: I had accidentally taken Raju, a 13-year-old street child's, new second-hand shirt. He had left it with me for safekeeping, reminding me to be sure to give it to him when I left for home, but I had forgotten. The next day was a scheduled rally that various NGOs were jointly holding under the umbrella of the newly formed coalition CLPOA (Calcutta Level Programme of Action) to sensitize the city to the rights of child labourers. All the boys from the shelter at Sealdah Station were expected to attend. When I reached the Maidan in the early hours of the morning I saw several hundred children already assembled and animated by the presence of so many of their peers who had gathered together. Almost all children were street children and child labourers who were now members of one of the organizations that were part of this coalition. I rushed to where the Sealdah children were standing and asked where Raju was. One of the staff remarked that Raju had severely resisted coming to the rally because he did not have proper clothes. She added that it was only after a lot of convincing on her part that he had decided to come and that she had told him that what he wore really did not matter, because after all they were going on a rally to alert the city to the plight of poor children like him. When I found Raju he was wearing a torn red T-shirt that he always wore at the station and was sulking against a tree. I quickly handed him his shirt. He smiled shyly, changed immediately and went and joined the group. His face bore no trace of his earlier moodiness. Relieved, I began to look around and saw that all the boys from Sealdah were dressed in the clothes that they usually reserved for special occasions and in addition all of them had shoes instead of the slippers they usually wore.

Since it was a Saturday and this was a commercial area of the city, the rally took off through large empty roads. The older boys carried the banners and initiated the chanting of slogans. They appeared serious in the task assigned to them and were not easily distracted for about the first fifteen minutes of the rally. After this they began to lose interest because the rally had not attracted much attention. They passed the banners on to younger children and began talking amongst themselves complaining about the lack of drinking water. As the long line of children wormed its way through residential areas some men, women and children stared curious out of windows and doors of homes, buses and shops. The older boys appeared unfazed by the attention and teased each other for being tempted to pick up pieces of metal that they found on the road (to recycle later), which they refrained from doing under the watchful eyes of the staff. They remarked on passers-by commenting on them, and occasionally joined in the chanting of slogans, at times competing at raising their voices as loudly as possible. Some of the young heads that peered out from the apartment windows seemed to be those of children who were employed in these households as domestic workers, and one of the older boys commented on their lack of freedom compared to his own. The staff pointed out that these domestic workers were also child labourers but this did not spark any response. The rally ended in an upper-middle-class school in the city where there was a stage set up for government and NGO officials to deliver speeches against child labour. Coke had been poured out into plastic cups for the thirsty children, who gulped as many glasses as they could.

Having drunk their fill, the children from Sealdah decided to pick up the plastic glasses and empty Coke bottles and sell them to a recycle merchant to make some money to hire a TV and VCR to watch a video in the shelter that evening. The rally having concluded, the children quickly started picking up as much plastic as they could, collecting these into bags that they hauled on their back on their way to the recycling shop. Not wanting to get their clothes dirty, the older boys supervised the work, which the younger ones, lured by the prospect of seeing a free movie in the evening, swiftly performed. Raju, being one of the younger boys assigned the task of carrying a bag filled with plastic cups to the shop, handed me his shirt and his shoes for safekeeping. Since the crowd of children brought together by the rally was still present in the school grounds and some of the speeches by the organizers had just begun, I asked Raju why he did not want to wear his new shirt anymore. He replied: 'Aunty, my new shirt will get dirty carrying this *bosta* [bag]. No one is going to give me a look when I roam the streets ragpicking. In the morning it was different; we were out walking as part of a procession which usually attracts attention and so I wanted to look my best.'

Third Narrative: The boys routinely awoke at 3 a.m. in order to earn a living at the nearby wholesale vegetable and fish market. Set up during the colonial period as one of the major markets in the city, Kole Market continues to attract farmers from the southern part of the state who travel by train to Sealdah Station to sell their produce. These small farmers sell their vegetables and fish to wholesale vendors, who in turn resell them to several local vegetable and fish markets around the city. The market is hectic with activity from about 3 a.m., with vegetables being unloaded from trucks, farmers arriving in droves from Sealdah Station and vendors busy setting up their stalls and haggling for the best price. The boys often walk together to the market, but once there a quick movement of the eye by one of them signals that it is time to split up.

Once inside the market they make their way through the narrow lanes between baskets that have vegetables piled high on top of each other. These baskets rest on a concrete platform about 3 feet from the floor with the vendor often sitting on this platform surrounded by a variety of vegetables. The tall piles of vegetables provide enough cover for the boys, who make their way through the various vendors who sit facing each other. The boys usually begin by picking the vegetables that have fallen on the floor during the morning's rush at the market. They know that this clearing up will meet little resistance from the vendors. But the vegetables acquired this way are few and often not in the best shape. Usually it is the novices, the boys who have recently arrived at the Sealdah shelter, who engage in this foraging from the market floor. They are often advised by the older street kids to begin with this until they acquire greater confidence, skills and a sense of the rhythm of the market. The more experienced kids carry umbrella spokes inside their shirts to delicately poke and take out vegetables from the expansive piles. The skill lies in knowing which vegetables to poke so that the entire pile is not upset and to do this quickly enough to avoid being caught. Lingering in front of a pile raises immediate suspicion and so they have to walk, poke, pull out and deposit into their shirts in one steady motion, making the choice of vegetable appear less calculated and more instinctual. Their shirts, of which the first three buttons are open and the rest tucked in to their shorts, serve as a hiding place. From time to time they leave the market to empty their shirts into a companion's bag and then begin again. When they feel that they have an adequate amount of vegetables, the boys set up their own small vegetable stall outside the market, arranging these on the floor, and then begin selling at discounted prices. If caught they risk getting yelled at or at worst beaten by the vendor. Often, however, the mundaneness of their daily forays have also meant that some vendors have learnt to accept their presence and turn a blind eye. Getting caught at the nearby wholesale fish market usually exacts the most severe punishment with the vendors at times calling in the police. But the children are often willing to risk this because the margins of profit that they can get by selling fish are far greater compared to gathering vegetables, which they view as more time-consuming. There is also the added pleasure of transgression because of the level of difficulty entailed in getting the fish.

One morning the children rushed into the shelter with an injured Jehangir. He had been beaten up by the local policeman at the fish market. He was bleeding quite profusely in his arm, and the staff immediately provided him first aid and checked that no bones were broken. All of the boys began narrating what had happened and asked me to make a note of it in my blue book. Jehangir had been caught taking the fish, and the shop-owner had tied him upside down and had started beating him. A local policeman called to attend to the matter convinced the shop-owner that an arrest was less effective than a public thrashing, which would serve to deter similar boys from stealing. The policeman then took over beating Jehangir from the shop-owner, continuing for at least another five minutes before untying him and asking the boys to take him back to the shelter. The boys also added that during the entire duration of the beating the policeman and the shop-owner loudly cursed the boys, discussing how nothing would ever come of them because they were born to be on the streets and steal. Later that afternoon, when Jehangir had recovered, we talked about what had happened that morning. I told him that there were certain procedures associated with what a policeman should do when he caught a child stealing. Jehangir listened to me patiently, utterly unconvinced, and when I finished he said that he felt that the policeman had really done him a favour. He said the policeman was a friend of his and that was why he had chosen to beat him up publicly. Looking at my expression of surprise he added: 'It would have been much worse if he had arrested me. They would have put me in the lock-up until I got bail and over there worse things happen. He was both doing his job and helping me by beating me at the market itself. I know him because when I sleep on the station platform he often asks me to run small errands and gives me a blanket to cover myself at night.'

Living rights as frictions

The pedagogic project of teaching street children their rights is central to the work of NGOs, and the skit, rally and so on represent the material form through which these discourses operate to try and secure, in an Althusserian sense, points of identification for the production of new subjectivities. However, this production circulates within existing cultural systems of meaning-making and always undergoes a translation. The idea of cultural translation is borrowed from Judith Butler's (2000) essay 'Restaging the universal', in which she uses Hegel to discuss the 'particular' as always already part of the 'universal' rather than just its supplement. Contending with a static understanding of the world in which subjects are viewed as being formed through certain pre-existing, fixed categories, Hegel argues that the categories through which the world becomes available to us are shaped by our experience and are continually being remade by this encounter. Using this line of reasoning, Butler contends that there is never one 'constitutive' moment to which the idea of the universal can be reduced. Rather, this continuous shaping of categories means that the universal is realized through the work of cultural translation. The stubborn trace of the particular taints the claims that the universal formally makes about transcending particulars.

Anna Tsing in her book *Friction* (2005) further develops the idea of the universal through discussing global connections, the aspiration for these and the ways in which these materialize in people's everyday lives through 'friction' or the grip of this encounter. Rejecting the terms of the earlier debate that tended to juxtapose the universal against a particular, Tsing says that it is important to bring into our understanding the ways in which the universal works in a 'practical sense'. Her idea of 'practically engaged universality' includes an understanding of the universal as an 'aspiration', an 'unfinished achievement' and therefore invested with desire, rather than as the imposition of a pre-formed law. The resultant object of study, or the ethnographic object, is then neither the universal nor the culturally specific but rather the 'travel' that this universal aspiration is required to undertake both across distances and differences. Friction is not an allegory for resistance to the universal by virtue of one's cultural location. Rather, it recognizes that friction can both sustain as well as dismantle the hegemony of the universal. The attempt is to understand the working of the universal as an aspiration that produces the desire for global connections. These aspirations result in friction because the process of realizing the universal is never the same everywhere.[3]

Both Butler's and Tsing's work is relevant to my understanding of children's rights as always already involved within certain processes of translation, whether at the level of states, civil society organizations or individuals. This enables me to recognize the historically specific cultural assumptions that disrupt the stability of universal categories, and thereby interrogate 'implementation' as part of a hegemonic reading of children's rights.

Each of the narratives discussed above speak to a complicated everydayness that pervades these children's understanding of rights. This focus on the everyday as a way of understanding the workings of the universal requires a tracing of the complex ways in which marginal communities experience and relate to the normative sphere of the legal as well as its subtending historical processes. In the first instance, Liton believes that talking about rights to a general public is a ploy that will allow him to raise money. While this could be interpreted as Liton's inability to imagine himself as a citizen-subject possessing rights, his reading of the situation contains a canny reading of exploitation as an integral part of his life. Liton's last line, 'Why should the *babus* listen to you? After all they make money from people like you', reveals lived realities within which power hierarchies and its attendant webs of exploitation persist despite liberal discourses to the contrary. His comment on the *babus* needs to be read in terms of what it helps establish, that is his awareness of everyday workings of power, rather than be viewed as his inability to grasp the idea of rights. Even though he does not fully understand this new discourse of rights, when corrected by the staff worker he is quick to grasp that it contains the promise of certain entitlements. But its irony is immediately apparent to him, that is the realization of these rights is dependent upon persons who currently exploit him accepting his status as an equal. Liton's scepticism about rights contains within it an incisive ability to interrogate its liberal veneer through juxtaposing this with his intimate knowledge of the *babus* that at once rids the discourse of the innocence of the entitlements that it promises.

[3] On a connected note Annelise Riles (2006) discusses the discursive engagement between anthropology and human rights. She shows how, while lawyers point to anthropology's fixation on culture, anthropologists are at pains to highlight that human rights law can also be viewed as a set of cultural practices available for ethnographic enquiry.

This absence of belief in liberal equality is not cynicism but rather a reflection of a more general everyday experience of hierarchies of caste, region, religion, wealth and gender that continue to frame people's lives in India. Even though the country's liberal Constitution provides recourse to challenge and there exists a surfeit of progressive legislation that guarantees and works affirmatively to engender equality, this does not produce the kind of individuated understandings of citizenship and equality circulating as the norm in Western liberal democracies. Why this difference persists despite the Indian Constitution and the various laws reflecting the necessary liberal guarantees of equal and individuated citizenship is best understood historically. From the institution of civic rights in civil society to political rights in the nation state, in the West citizenship has developed chronologically. In former colonies the formation of independent nation states was preceded by colonial rule with its technologies of governmentality that administered colonial subjects not recognized as citizens (Chatterjee, 2004). With independence India adopted a democratic form of government with universal adult franchise, and this meant that all Indians received the right to vote without necessarily being inserted in ideas of citizenship and the self that this form of government assumed. The absence of hegemonic bourgeois and liberal practices, which Ranajit Guha (Guha and Spivak, 1988) has famously characterized as 'dominance without bourgeois hegemony', does not mean that India is non-modern, but rather that modernity took a different form in former colonies. Guha has discussed the ways in which the formation of modernity and citizenship in former colonial countries constructed the domain of the political as split into two distinct though interwoven sensibilities. The first is the formal–legal and secular network of governance; the second is that of relationships of direct domination and subordination that derive their legitimacy from day-to-day practices. The modern self and citizen in India is then substantially different from the Enlightenment citizen-subject who can desire rights, reason and freedom.

Street children such as Liton contend on a daily basis with the politics of direct domination and subordination in which the state and its liberal guarantees are largely missing, thereby rendering ambivalent and distant citizenship's promise of individuated equality. The available register through which the state is present in these subaltern lives is instead largely conveyed through various welfare measures, and these technologies of governmentality coexist with the sphere of the legal that is experienced most often as coercive. Spivak's (1991) distinction between time and timing, in which the former refers to the state's capacity to speak to master concepts such as liberty, freedom in terms of an abstract monumental time that sustains its transcendental continuity, while timing, on the other hand, refers to processes through which subalterns deal with the law as it manifests itself in their lives in terms of surveillance, scrutiny and a continuing pedagogic project, is useful in this respect. The domain of rights gets framed at the intersection between the benign sphere of welfare and the coercive realm of the law and produces diffident negotiations with the state that rely more on the identities of the 'community' than individuated discourses of citizenship. Getting the *babu*, a word that is often used as a colloquial metaphor for a state functionary, to accept street children as having 'rights' appears facile precisely because subaltern processes of survival necessitate a certain scepticism towards the state. This ambivalence does not mean that the children do not wrest certain recognitions and rights from the state. In fact, more recent theorization has drawn attention to Indian democracy and 'political society' as a realm that allows for an expansion of freedoms of people whose claims might be viewed as illegitimate in the West. Partha Chaterjee's (2004) discussion on 'political society' examines claims on the state often grounded in violations of the law, for example by illegal squatters making demands for electricity and water. These claims, often directed at expanding governmental activities in their favour, are seldom for individual selves but are viewed as gains for the community, the moral community that is an empirical object to be acted upon by the state and a locus of identity that binds people together. Given the 'illegal' status of these communities, these claims, argues Chatterjee, are those that would have been difficult to realize through civil society. It is the ability of postcolonial states to deal with these claims that Chatterjee characterizes as the expansion of freedoms.[4] The reason I dwell on this expansion of freedoms is to move away from a transition narrative that often frames the reading of subaltern negotiations with the sphere of rights. The discourse of transition assumes a future moment of complete understanding, one that mimics

[4] For more on the idea of 'political society' read Chatterjee (2004). A critique of this idea of 'political society' includes the fact that potential displacement and the precarious resettlement of 'illegal' squatter communities largely comprise Chatterjee's imagination of populations who gain in freedoms through political society. He fails to interrogate the ironic nature of the settlement, which most often is an endorsement of the state's conditionalities. Moreover, its working understanding of governmentality in a postcolonial context does not include an analysis of biopolitics, nor does it aid an analysis of shifting understandings of state and economy. Nevertheless the idea of 'political society' is a productive frame within which to imagine the workings of Indian democracy outside of a formal focus on elections as a dominant sign of the mobilization of marginalized communities.

the West, and which can be gained through pedagogic efforts. I suggest that the ambivalence of subaltern claims reflects a deep awareness of the state's functioning and the ways in which it may be manipulated. Liton's statement on the *babu* is indicative of the hyper-awareness that frames subaltern knowledge of the state and the rationale of community that predominates does not easily allow for a conceptual separation between child and adult, or more importantly for the child to be understood as a significant and distinct actor vis-à-vis the state.

This absence of an individuated understanding of rights and entitlements is also present in Raju's sartorial self-absorption. The rally appeared unsettling because of the inconsistency between the official identities assigned to the boys as 'child labourers' and their continual attempts to exceed this reading of their lives. At issue is not that the boys were unable to identify with the purpose of the rally. Their enthusiastic chanting of slogans indicated their willingness to perform the identities (as child labourers aware of their rights) that the rally required them to assume. But what they continually also appeared to resist was the uncomplicated reading of their lives that assuming these identities contained. Their wearing of their best clothes was meant to signal a performative break between this 'public' event and their daily forays into the street as ragpickers. Their gesturing to the difference between them and the young domestic help revealed their identification as the better placed amongst their working peers because of the independence they exercised, as street children, in the choice of how to earn an income as well as how to spend it. The break was most prominent at the point when the rally ended and the children returned to the street as ragpickers. Their identity as ragpickers was what the rally had paradoxically wanted to freeze, but for the children it was something they wanted to reassume only when formally finished with the gazing public. The self-evidence of the public gaze that characterized their lives on the street as ragpickers functioned, quite naturally, as the only trope through which they could be effectively re-presented to the middle class. But this was not the way in which these children desired to be seen. The material practices through which children's rights are being translated in the lives of poor children – namely rallies, skits, drawing competitions and so on – are viewed by the children as 'events' that seek to simultaneously engage them and the gazing public in a pedagogic exercise around children's rights. The breaks with the event, however, cannot be too easily interpreted as 'resistance' because not only do these very articulate children not employ this language to frame their actions, but it is also precisely the absence of formal deliberation around their actions that reveals their everyday insertion within more enduring identities and communities. Rather than the officially produced category of 'child labour', it is these that provide meaning to their lives.

While these enduring identities or the sphere of 'community' usually works to strengthen their lives, the conflict that they may create is apparent in Jehangir's inability to characterize the policeman's beating as a violation of his rights. The policeman's disregard for procedure, which Jehangir views as a favour, is what the law attempts to protect children against, namely arbitrary acts of violence by persons who are in a position of power. Jehangir, however, evokes the history of a prior relationship to argue that the policeman's actions were done in good faith, revealing hereby the importance of affective ties in his self-constructions. The absence of malice is based on his refusal to view the policeman as an anonymous and powerful state functionary against whom he may take legal action on the basis of an individuated discourse of rights. Jehangir is more than familiar with this discourse and aware that the NGO would have aided him in taking all the necessary action to file a case. The incident is then not a reflection of the inadequacy or incompetency of pedagogic instruction but rather intimates the durability of contending family and community identities. While ideas around 'protection' in children's rights discourses affirm affective ties, they cannot include the capriciousness of community, particularly since the young age of those it seeks to protect requires a strict surveillance of violence and other forms of exploitation. When it comes to lives steeped in the density of kinship networks, the absence of a shared reading of what constitutes violations – and the apparent elasticity in interpreting these within subaltern communities – makes a pedagogic project relying on an instrumental reading of the law falter.

Politicizing rights

Although each of the three narratives discussed above point to an absence of easy identifications and smooth transitions with respect to the children's rights discourse, my aim has not been to argue that rights are insignificant. I do not wish to condone the arbitrary dispensation of justice by police officials, nor censure the use of public rallies because children's understandings exceed their particular portrayal of their lives. I argue against the logic of 'transition' that frames current understandings on 'implementation' to gesture to the complexities that frame the creation of new rights-based subjectivities. The gap between an instrumental reading of legal provisions and children's lived realities highlights the complicated translation that rights discourses undergo. What is needed, I feel, is a politicized analysis that works both with the state to secure necessary entitlements while simultaneously allowing for a more open-ended articulation of rights. Using the CRC as the ethical register with which to critique the state for the gap between the rhetoric of new laws and its more reluctant implementation is a challenge already taken up by NGOs and various other civil–social actors. What is needed in addition, however, is a politicized dissonance that does not resist the idea of rights but rather uses the sense of agency and entitlement it signifies to fill it with a different content. A good example of this is the work of the Bhima Sangha,[5] an organization of children in Bangalore, who have been working with the NGO Concerned for Working Children (CWC) to reduce the economic need for children to work while recognizing that currently children do need to combine school and work. Refraining from valorizing any side of this equation, Bhima Sangha quite successfully rejects the prevailing binary between formal education and child labour. Bhima Sangha sets up schools in villages that offer both formal and informal education, the latter for children who must continue to work and need flexible hours to attend school. The organization also helps individual children secure a place in school and negotiates with employers to allow the children time for their education. While seeking to raise awareness about children's rights including all aspects of child protection, the organization is against the boycott of products made by children. Bhima Sangha wants good health care for working children as well as security and respect for the work they do. In the first international meeting of working children that they organized in 1996 they listed ten points or demands (also referred to as the Kundapur Declaration), which included the need to tackle poverty, greater economic activities in rural areas and decentralization in decision-making so that children will not be forced to migrate, an educational system that takes their lifeworlds seriously and for work with dignity in which the hours are adapted so that there is time for education and leisure (see also Liebel in Chapter 11 of this volume). In addition Mayall

[5] Bhima Sangha is active mainly in Bangalore and in six districts of Karnataka and its current outreach is a few tens of thousands of young people between the ages of 6 and 18 years. In Bangalore there is a near equal division of members across sex but in the rural areas girls predominate as boys migrate to look for work. More recently Bhima Sangha has been working along with Concerned for Working Children to reach out to organizations throughout India to form children's unions. But this is still in large part an isolated initiative. For more read Milne (2007). Also see the website: www.workingchild.org (accessed 11 November 2011).

(2000) argues in favour of recognizing childhoods as political spaces and through this to rethink the 'protection, provision and participation' that dominates current agendas, but fails to detail what this rethinking would entail. The double-sided politicization I argue for is more complex than either 'implementation' or 'resistance' when understood (as they currently are) as mutually exclusive renditions of marginal children's experiences with rights. Neither of these renditions sufficiently locates the idea of children's rights within a historical understanding of how local communities are inserted into modern life. They also fail to map the material processes that produce new subjectivities. My argument in favour of a double-sided politicization attends to the multiple ways in which children's rights as an emerging discourse is continually subject to processes of translation and meaning-making. While there is certainly a certain fixity of meaning attributed to the content of particular rights, the ways in which this meaning then circulates and is understood by communities is always less self-evident. This contingency is not a moment of transition into something that will gradually be fixed and secured within the certitudes of a normative rights discourse. Recognizing this meaning-making as constitutive of what rights are, while simultaneously translating the CRC into national laws that protect children and provide them with certain guarantees, is the shift that I have been arguing for.

References

Archard D (1993a) *Children: Rights and Childhood*. London: Routledge.

(1993b) Do parents own their children? *The International Journal of Children's Rights* 1(3–4): 293–301.

(ed.) (2002) *The Moral and Political Status of Children*. Oxford University Press.

Balibar E (2005) Difference, otherness, exclusion. *Parallax* 11(1): 19–34.

Boyden J (1997) Childhood and policy makers: a comparative perspective on the globalization of childhood. In: James A and Prout A (eds.) *Constructing and Reconstructing Childhood*, 2nd edn. London: Falmer Press, pp. 190–229.

Butler J (2000) Restaging the universal: hegemony and the limits of formalism. In: Butler J, Laclau E and Zizek S (eds.) *Contingency, Hegemony, Universality: Contemporary Dialogues on the Left*. New York: Verso, pp. 11–43.

Chatterjee P (2004) *The Politics of the Governed: Popular Politics in Most of the World*. New York: Columbia University Press.

Freeman M (2002) Human rights, children's rights and judgment: some thoughts on reconciling universality and pluralism. *The International Journal of Children's Rights* 10(4): 345–54.

Grover S (2004) On recognizing children's universal rights: what needs to change in the Convention on the Rights of the Child. *The International Journal of Children's Rights* 12(3): 259–71.

Guha R and Spivak G (eds.) (1988) *Selected Subaltern Studies*. Oxford University Press.

Kufeldt K (1993) Listening to children: an essential for justice. *The International Journal of Children's Rights* 1(2): 155–64.

MacIntyre A (1981) *After Virtue: A Study in Moral Theory*. London: Duckworth.

Mayall B (2000) The sociology of childhood in relation to children's rights. *The International Journal of Children's Rights* 8(3): 243–59.

Milne B (2007) Responsible citizenship or delinquency: the case of working children in India. In: Behera D (ed.) *Childhoods in South Asia*. Delhi: Pearson.

Nieuwenhuys O (1998) Global childhoods and the politics of contempt. *Alternatives* 23(3): 267–89.

Pare M (2003) Why have street children disappeared? The role of international human rights law in protecting vulnerable groups. *The International Journal of Children's Rights* 11(1): 1–32.

Parry-Williams J (1993) Legal reform and children's rights in Uganda – some critical issues. *The International Journal of Children's Rights* 1(1): 49–69.

Riles A (2006) Anthropology, human rights, and legal knowledge: culture in the iron cage. *American Anthropologist* 108(1): 52–65.

Rose J (1984) *The Case of Peter Pan: The Impossibility of Children's Fiction*. London: Macmillan.

Scherer L and Hart S (eds.) (1999) Reporting to the UN Committee on the Rights of the Child – analysis of the first 49 State Party Reports on the education articles of the Convention on the Rights of the Child and a proposition for an experimental reporting system on education. *The International Journal of Children's Rights* 7(4): 349–63.

Spivak G (1991) Time and timing: law and history. In: Bender J and Wellberry D (eds.) *Chronotypes: The Construction of Time*. Stanford University Press, pp. 99–117.

Tsing A (2005) *Friction: An Ethnography of Global Connection*. Princeton University Press.

8

Malik and his three mothers: AIDS orphans' survival strategies and how children's rights translations hinder them

KRISTEN E. CHENEY

While I was on a short research visit to Uganda in December 2007, Malik (whom I describe in my book, *Pillars of the Nation* (Cheney, 2007)) invited me to his older brother's wedding reception. Malik, 19 at the time, was raised by his maternal grandmother after both of his parents died of AIDS when he was 7 years old. He often writes emails to me calling me 'mum', because, he says, 'I lost my mother when I was very young, but you do all those things that a mother would do for me.' I provided for his schooling, but he had also become a talented musician who was living with a traditional dance troupe that got high-profile gigs, such as dancing for Queen Elizabeth during the 2007 Commonwealth Heads of Government Meeting in Kampala.

Malik's dance troupe was also hired to perform at his brother's wedding reception, so I arrived early with him while they were still setting up. He led me over to where two of his aunts were tying ribbons and attaching them to the floral arrangements. He introduced me to them, and while I sat with them making bows, Malik continued to set up the band. Imagine his embarrassment when he rushed over shouting, 'Mum! Mum!' and both myself and his two aunts turned around! My jaw dropped in disbelief: I had thought I was the only person he called 'Mum' and was momentarily shocked that I was not the only one to have earned what I held to be quite an honorific title. As I got over my own (mild) sense of betrayal, I realized that the cultivation of relationships with several different 'mums' was actually a brilliant strategy on Malik's part that hinged on the recognition of both affective and material elements that are essential to local constructions of kinship (aunties are routinely referred to as 'mums'), and which international development's approaches to the AIDS orphan crisis tend to gloss over, or even subvert. Despite his participation in numerous music, dance and drama festivals designed to familiarize children with their rights by cultivating a culture of constitutionalism (Cheney, 2005), Malik had learned that, rather than awaiting the full realization of the Convention on the Rights of the Child (CRC) – ratified by Uganda and enshrined in the 1995 Constitution – he had to rely on his own situationally appropriate strategies.

African AIDS orphans are typically institutionally framed as particularly vulnerable children (Meintjes and Giese, 2006; Sloth-Nielsen and Mezmur, 2008; The Joint Learning Initiative on Children and HIV/AIDS, 2009), and thus are even less endowed with agency than 'normal' children. There has been ample research on governmental and non-governmental responses to the Africa orphan crisis (Foster *et al.*, 2005; Guest, 2003; Singhal and Howard, 2003), but – though it is apparent that their needs are not being met (UNICEF, 2008) – little work has been done to document children's own responses to orphanhood and their agency in ameliorating its circumstances. Yet in my research with orphans, I have noted that children are very active in securing their perceived needs. Ironically, particular translations of children's rights may in fact hurt their efforts more than it helps them: the current historical convergence of children's rights dissemination and the global aid industry's attention toward the AIDS orphan crisis in Africa has led to a paradox of social justice for orphans, in which children's rights are pitted against their needs.

In this chapter I first outline the global and local dynamics, including various rights translations, that influence the construction of orphan identities in Uganda. This describes the parameters within which orphans must operate so as to secure their needs. In the process, I reveal how top-down translations of children's rights discourses can make rights largely irrelevant to – and may even jeopardize – AIDS orphans' everyday survival. I then discuss children's alternative strategies, noting that in this context both children and adults come to see orphan identification with victimhood as necessary to secure their needs, thus paradoxically reinforcing NGO and government actions that reinforce a protectionist reading of children's rights. Attention to multiple actors' interpretations of rights and their consequences for Orphans and Vulnerable Children (OVC) reveals the complexities with which OVC must grapple and the compromises they must make – including deferment of their own understandings of their rights – in order to further their quest for social justice.

The dynamics of orphan policy

Recent scholarship on the institutional entanglements of transnational development regimes with local African AIDS orphans suggests a profound reification of the category 'orphan' (Chirwa, 2002; Henderson, 2006; Meintjes and Giese, 2006). The Convention on the Rights of the Child (CRC) makes no specific mention – and therefore sets no definition – of orphans.[1] UNICEF defines an orphan as 'a child under 18 years of age whose mother, father, or both parents have died' (UNICEF, 2006: 4). An estimated 48 million orphans under 17 years of age live in sub-Saharan Africa today (UNICEF, 2006), and despite declining HIV prevalence rates and availability of antiretroviral drugs, about 14.8 million of them have been orphaned by AIDS (UNICEF, 2010). Uganda's orphan population is about 2.5 million, or 14 per cent of all children in the country – and as in most African countries, almost half of those children were made orphans due to AIDS (UNICEF, 2006).

UNICEF's definition of an orphan as any child whose mother or father has died puts the emphasis on static, biological definitions of kinship and orphanhood where, traditionally, orphans are socially defined. Wiseman Chirwa (2002) points out that, due to strong extended family networks, local definitions of orphanhood in Malawi have historically been based on social delineations in which situations of actual care are emphasized: most vernacular translations of orphan mean 'left behind or abandoned'. '*Mlanda*, an orphan', he writes, 'is conceptualized as a person who has gone astray, has lost his/her bearings because he/she is no longer in the protection of the family system' (Chirwa, 2002: 96). As with many African countries with a strong ethos of caring for orphans, Ugandan vernacular languages use similar terminology to describe orphans; children typically have to lose not only their mother and father but most of their aunts and uncles, and become essentially homeless to be considered orphans. In Luganda the use of vernacular terms for orphans such as *mulekwa* and *enfunzi* are so rare that my 23-year-old research assistant, whose first language is Luganda, had never heard some of them. The UN definition therefore distorts these definitions and inflates local orphan numbers, as it singles out the orphaned child as particularly vulnerable (Meintjes and Giese, 2006). In efforts to raise their visibility, international NGOs highlight the plight of Africa's AIDS orphans, lifting them out of the family context that – rather than emphasizing their social resilience – creates

[1] The CRC's Articles 20 and 21 deal with fosterage and adoption of any child 'deprived of his or her family environment'.

an orphan identity that is both pathologized (Henderson, 2006: 304) and made a site for benevolent humanitarian intervention (Ferguson and Freidus, 2007). While children's rights are often used to appeal for assistance, these constructions of orphans tend to emphasize protectionist aspects of children's rights discourse rather than children's empowerment through rights, particularly by requiring that any claims to rights or services be initiated by an adult caregiver (see Margaret's story, next section, for an illustration). NGO interventions can thus reproduce the status quo between children and adults. This trend will become even more problematic for the actualization of rights as more and more orphans are left to fend for themselves.

As if to exacerbate the overwhelming statistics generated by the UN definition of 'orphan', the aid industry has also cultivated the terms 'Orphans and Vulnerable Children' (OVC) and 'Children Affected by AIDS' (CABA) to emphasize the concept of childhood vulnerability. These terms were created to help recognize that it is not only orphans who are in need of assistance; even before being orphaned, children experience adversity due to their AIDS-infected parents' failing health. According to Sofia Gruskin and Daniel Tarantola, 'Children are affected when their close or extended family, their community, and, more broadly, the structures and services that exist for their benefit are strained by the consequences of the HIV/AIDS pandemic' (Gruskin and Tarantola, 2005: 138). By this definition, however, *every* child in sub-Saharan Africa is now a CABA. Similarly, the Uganda government recently drafted a national OVC policy that defines childhood vulnerability as:

> vulnerable because of any or all of the following factors that result from HIV/AIDS
>
> Is HIV-positive
> Lives without adequate adult support (e.g., in a household with chronically ill parents, a household that has experienced a recent death from chronic illness, a household headed by a grandparent, and/or a household headed by a child)
> Lives outside of family care (e.g., in residential care or on the streets), or
> Is marginalized, stigmatized, or discriminated against
>
> (Uganda Ministry of Gender Labor and Social Development, 2004: 2)

In the spirit of decentralization, it goes on to state that 'each community will need to prioritize those children most vulnerable and in need of further care' (Uganda Ministry of Gender Labor and Social Development, 2004: 2). While recognition of children's multiple vulnerabilities is important, it again inflates the population of children targeted for (largely non-existent) services. UNICEF Uganda's HIV specialist for OVC Prevention, Dorothy Oulanyan, estimates that this describes approximately 70 per cent of the nation's children.[2] Though such a model of child vulnerability is not inaccurate for many of Africa's children, the Ugandan government's growing acknowledgement of child vulnerability is in itself seen as an achievement by children's rights advocates, even while it creates an untenable demand for OVC services (Cheney, 2010).

The inflation of these numbers, in combination with emphasis on the vulnerability of OVC, presents an obstacle to the actualization of children's rights for orphans. Despite the acknowledgement of a full-blown orphan 'crisis', little is being done to empower 'the next generation of orphans, who will likely have fewer older adults left to care for them, thus the number of older children caring for their younger brothers and sisters will only increase' (Gruskin and Tarantola, 2005: 138). We must consider the implications of this trend when I argue that the international development community's intervention in traditional extended family systems of orphan support disenfranchise orphaned children through constant reinstatement of their vulnerability rather than emphasis on their rights. Further, attention to the way in which AIDS is made the culprit conceals the vulnerabilities of children (not only orphans) created by the devastation of neoliberal, postcolonial state restructuring and Africa's destabilization by the global free-market economy (Englund, 2006). Children are deprived daily of food security, health care, housing and education by the vagaries of the free market and Uganda's crippling foreign debt, even as privatized NGO interventions that 'invest in children' (Mahon, 2010) supplant the responsibility of the state to its citizens. Children's rights cannot be made meaningful without full acknowledgement of their very violation, especially economically and socially. INGOs' efforts to address this vulnerability through a discourse of benevolent humanitarianism, without directly addressing broader issues of structural poverty and child empowerment, thus hinders orphans' survival. Due to the situation produced by this inherent contradiction, rather than argue for their rights, children necessarily reproduce tropes of orphan victimhood. In what follows, I address this dynamic and its implications for children's social justice.

Local dynamics of orphan support

During my 2001 dissertation fieldwork at a primary school in Kampala, Uganda, I met many children living with extended family after their

[2] Personal communication, 2007.

parents had died, often of AIDS. Margaret was one of them. She was the tallest girl in the fifth grade, with bright eyes and a gracious smile. She lived with her uncle because both her parents had already passed away. One Monday morning at school, she accosted me. Her uncle had also passed away from AIDS complications the previous Friday. Her aunt was not her blood relative, and if Margaret stayed with her, her aunt could not guarantee that she could afford to pay Margaret's school fees. Three days after her uncle's death, Margaret was already soliciting alternative sources of support. Might I be able to find someone to sponsor her education, she asked?

In addition to requests like Margaret's, I also regularly received written requests from guardians and children for sponsorship. Education is seen as a panacea for orphans' problems by making of them modern citizens in a market-based system of human capital (Bloch *et al.*, 2006). Despite its failure to deliver on that promise, education remains African children's and their families' greatest hope for escape from poverty. Seeking individual sponsorship was just one of many tactics that children employed to compensate for the loss of a parent.

These experiences led me to this ethnographic project, conducted with a team of youth research assistants over several trips to Uganda totalling seven months of fieldwork from 2007 to 2009. I conducted fieldwork in an area outside of the capital city Kampala where I have long-standing ties with the community, having supported OVC initiatives there since 1993. I had suspected that the community's proximity to the city, about eight miles outside of Kampala, would help members gain easier access to the NGO and government assistance concentrated there. Yet we found that the forty orphans and their guardians in the study group had seldom had direct interaction with government institutions or NGOs dedicated to orphan aid intervention. Orphans are reared instead by relatives, who rarely receive material assistance from sources outside the family. In the absence of aunts and uncles – due mainly to death or labour migration – who would typically take responsibility for orphan care, grandmothers are increasingly beset with this task.

When they do have a little help, it is usually through a combination of working family members' remittances and local women's cooperatives – not government or NGOs.[3] The international development community has shifted to supporting more community-based organizations (CBOs) because

[3] The one notable exception was guardians with HIV-positive children who are in a free anti-retroviral drug programme through Mulago Hospital and The AIDS Support Organization (TASO).

of government graft. In 2005, for example, Teddy Seezi Cheeye, the Uganda Director of Economic Affairs in the Office of the President, embezzled 120 million shillings from the Global Fund to Fight AIDS, Tuberculosis and Malaria – an incident which, despite Cheeye's conviction in 2009, has caused Uganda to lose billions more in funding (Wandera, 2009). With CBOs, locals supposedly have more ownership over projects such as community gardens and income-generating activities. However, the basis of rewards for voluntary work in CBOs recognizes only people's collective effort within the project and not whatever else they do for OVC. People therefore end up leaving the projects because they see no benefit in them. Even savings and loans groups can quickly become exclusionary. One grandmother in our study had joined a women's cooperative in hopes of receiving benefits that would help her to provide for the fourteen grandchildren for whom she was the primary caregiver. They established a rotating credit scheme based on dues, but with the immigration of more wealthy city-dwellers to the area, the cooperative's dues, which loan recipients used to purchase cars and refrigerators, soon outpriced her modest means. At the same time, land was being parcelled off and sold to urban families for home construction, leaving indigenous families with too little land on which to cultivate food for their growing families, even as they took in more orphans.[4]

Education is often also out of reach for OVC, at least at a consistent level. Children may start the term, but rarely do they finish it without being 'chased away' for failure to pay the fees. In any case, children typically learn about their rights in school. Children not attending school therefore do not always learn of their rights, and it does not occur to them to fight for them, whereas children regularly in school already have that fundamental right met and can then start to tackle other rights issues. The focus, however, is still on access to education, rather than its quality.

This lack of accessiblity does not stop children like Margaret from trying to secure NGO resources, though. Children who learn about their rights – through schools or government/NGO 'sensitization' campaigns – may utilize rights language to try to operationalize them in their own interest, but they are quickly disavowed of the tactic by the very organizations that promote children's rights, as they often stress obedience to adults over assertion of rights (Cheney, 2007). In Margaret's instance, I suggested that she seek assistance from one of the NGOs whose offices were ubiquitous in the city of Kampala. In a 2008 survey, VIVA International found

[4] Food security was one area where I saw rural families as relatively better off; they often had ample land and so did not require cash in order to eat.

more than 500 organizations in Kampala working on children's issues,[5] so there was certainly no shortage. Margaret replied that she had already been to Christian Children's Fund (CCF), a charity whose commercials in the USA describe what wonders your coffee money can do for an individually sponsored child and her community in the developing world, conveniently reducing daunting issues of structural violence to 'doable' monthly remittances (Bornstein, 2003: 95). But they had essentially slammed the door in Margaret's face and told her she would have to come back with an adult to vouch for her if she wanted to be considered for CCF sponsorship. Despite general INGO recognition of increasing numbers of guardian-less children, instances like this demonstrate how children's ability to act on their own behalf is still thwarted by systems of power that emphasize protectionist translations of children's rights instead of participatory ones, thereby touting children's rights in theory much more than in practice. If all rights claims necessarily require access to a public sphere that is not so much a space of rational deliberation as a site of power (Asad, 2003: 184), orphans' vulnerabilities in particular reveal how little access children actually have to their rights. Advocacy groups turn out to be a necessary intermediary in the process to claiming rights, yet children cannot even access those groups on their own.

The politics of NGO intervention

Chirwa (2002) notes that international NGOs allocating assistance on the basis of a 'social rupture' model of intervention, in which aid organizations falsely assume the total breakdown of traditional social safety nets for orphaned children, masks the plasticity of those systems. When we examine prevailing attitudes about child obedience, we see how adults are responding more in their own best interests than in children's. In such conditions, children's rights then become a front rather than the motivation from which people act. Despite the increase in orphans and child-headed households, we can also see how NGOs arrive at the necessity of adult interlocutors for children seeking their services, as they cannot effectively be separated from their family context. Many NGOs, who were the first line of response to the orphan crisis, started out by targeting orphans individually, but they reverted to a family model of care both in response to calls for strengthening local social safety nets, and because of the ways in which targeting orphans individually upset family

[5] Personal communication from VIVA officers.

and community dynamics. Uganda Women's Effort to Save Orphans (UWESO), one of the first organizations to assist orphans in post-war Uganda, started out by providing school tuition for orphans. Baker Waiswa, Projects Coordinator for UWESO, noted that 'it got to a point where NGOs actually raised the status of the orphan *above* that of other children'. But, Waiswa told me:

> The families were so poor ... that the orphans went to school and the biological children sometimes failed to go to school. So it even posed a challenge to the parents. You cannot explain to a child and say, 'Yes, I love you, though I am not able to take you to school.' They say, 'But what about this one?' However much you explain, 'Well, they brought money, etc.' they kind of can't believe it, so it was a problem.
>
> (personal communication)

UNICEF's Oulanyan also said, 'We got kids who would actually say, "Well, if my mom and dad died, I could get schoolbooks"' (personal communication). As a result, organizations realized they had to shift their focus from direct assistance for individual orphans to supporting families in their efforts to raise them.

While this is appropriate in a local context, it necessarily reinforces protectionist aspects of children's rights by recognizing the need to address children as part of nuclear households as well as extended family networks. Leaving out entirely the question of child-headed households, this changing ethos of caring for orphans becomes ever more closely linked to provision of resources earmarked for orphans within traditional family care systems; aid is usually used by guardians to take care of their own biological children before – and sometimes in place of – the orphans in their homes. Some children, including many in our study, have reported attempts by aunts and uncles to lay claim to their deceased relative's land by claiming responsibility for the orphaned children (Rose, 2005). They eventually chase the orphans off their parents' land and keep it for themselves.

While Chirwa may be right in criticizing social rupture models, the family-focused INGO intervention itself has led to a transformation of the processes by which orphan care is determined in extended family networks. In an era of ever more pervasive NGO interventions, even extended families' decisions to provide orphan care increasingly hinge on the extent to which it may help them secure already needed resources through either government or NGO interventions. Care-giving decisions amongst extended families are therefore increasingly made based on family members' connections to NGO networks as much as these

'traditional' systems, and their claims to have a 'love' for orphaned children is alternately pitted against their own poverty or made a measure of their worthiness to receive assistance within aid industry discourses. Again, the 'orphan' is reified from family in such a way that her sentimentalization becomes necessary.

Though research has shown that building orphanages in poor communities can produce more orphans by inadvertently encouraging people to abandon the children they cannot feed (Phiri and Webb, 2007: 324) – and thus rightly turned much of NGO response to the orphan crisis against institutionalization – the existence of any perceived humanitarian assistance for orphans in the community also produces, if not the actual orphans, at least the demand for more orphan services. Aside from its impact on orphaned children's lives, this expectation can inhibit the growth of community-led initiatives (The Joint Learning Initiative on Children and HIV/AIDS, 2009). Even in my own research project, one of the greatest challenges was appeasing the guardians who jostled to get their children into the study on the assumption that material assistance would follow; despite my fervent denial of it, they had assumed that a *mzungu* like myself represents an aid organization, and that the purpose of my study must have been to figure out how I would spend the millions of dollars I had to unload before the end of the fiscal year. They maintain this hope despite consistent disappointment: 'Many NGOs come here promising us something', they complained, 'but we receive no assistance.' Yet guardians were clearly aware that OVC have become NGO targets. They therefore cultivated an OVC identity in children, coaching them to emphasize their deprivation in order to solicit handouts. This was ironically what we kept hearing from children in initial interviews, not necessarily because children experienced their circumstances as lacking, but because their guardians had encouraged them to reiterate that point as a subtle solicitation. Indeed, many guardians had incorrectly assumed, through my fifteen-year association with the local community school, that I sponsored many of the children there. At the same time, NGO initiatives have let government off the hook for addressing broader issues of poverty and have left guardians in the even more precarious situation of deepening poverty and heightened false hope.

Whose 'best interests?'

The 'best interests' principle is mainly what distinguishes children's rights from other human rights. This central tenet of the CRC is often translated in NGO service delivery in such a way that NGOs require an adult interlocutor for children like Margaret who are seeking support. For this reason, children's rights as they are currently implemented by many aid organizations are not generally transformative of orphans' circumstances because they tend to maintain adult power already prevalent in cultural norms. Reynolds *et al.* point out that 'taking the child's best interests as the leading principle of the United Nations' Convention on the Rights of the Child (CRC) clashes with priorities that children themselves may set' (Reynolds *et al.*, 2006: 291–2). Further, while the CRC allows for children's participation in defining their own interests, children are rarely meaningfully consulted in top-down organizational approaches to CRC implementation (Invernizzi and Milne, 2002; West, 2007). This is because they tend to be based on rather essentialized developmental models of children as lacking the competency to set their own priorities (James, 2011), thereby justifying adult decision-making in children's best interests.

In *Prisoners of Freedom* (2006), Harri Englund describes how the ideograph 'freedom' is used in the dissemination of human rights such that it belies the actual social and economic conditions that constrain one's freedom. Children orphaned in today's HIV/AIDS pandemic likewise become prisoners of the purported childhood innocence that protective translations of children's rights preserve, even as it too claims to 'free' children from harm. As in Englund's critique, rights become a detriment to children when NGOs' translations emphasize political and civil rights about 'hearing children's voices' (which rarely includes meaningful participation) while simultaneously eluding the debate about everyday violations of social and economic rights. On the other hand, aid industry appeals using children's vulnerability reinforce dynamics of power and authority that reduce children to objects of charity. While orphans' identification with vulnerability discourses acquiesces to the postcolonial position of subservient object of Western charity, James Ferguson has suggested that Africans' appeals for 'help' from the international community can be read as 'implicit claims to the rights of a common membership in a global society' (Ferguson, 2006: 173). Further, Gruskin and Tarantola state that 'From a child rights perspective, HIV/AIDS illuminates how cultural norms and legal precepts facilitate or constrain the capacity of children to decide on issues central to their health and well-being' (Gruskin and Tarantola, 2005: 136). But they assume the effectiveness of children's rights discourses, when ethnographic research tends to reveal their ineffectiveness. Children thus have more trouble claiming their rights either way, and the notion of rights fails to be transformative of their circumstances. Rather than invoke children's rights, orphans and their caregivers may claim a vulnerable status as an avenue to educational and economic mobility: first acquiescence to an economic hierarchy of Western humanitarianism, *then* empowerment through membership in aid programmes.

Regardless of the extent to which children may call on government and NGOs – and the rights discourses proliferated by them – to secure their needs, children are rarely successful due to their inferior status as children. This produces a paradox in which children's rights cannot be fully actuated. The problem of implementation, I argue, does not lie in the children's lack of morality and agency supposed by transnational children's rights discourses that emphasize a protectionist, 'best interests' approach to the fulfilment of the CRC over an empowering one. Rather, the problem lies in adults' use of children's rights for their own self-interest. This should not be seen as a simple act of postcolonial parody, as orphans' caregivers and NGOs alike may invoke the children's best interests principle to further their own agendas. This is seen, for example, in the ways in which families make decisions about how to allocate care-giving responsibilities for orphans after their parents have died. While several scholars have detailed a long African tradition of child circulation and fosterage for adult self-interest (Bledsoe and Isiugo-Abanihe, 1989; Notermans, 2004), Oleke *et al.* note 'a transition over the past 30 years from a situation dominated by "purposeful" voluntary exchange of non-orphaned children to one dominated by "crisis fostering" of orphans' (Oleke *et al.*, 2005: 2628). In most Ugandan ethnic groups, responsibility for the care of orphans traditionally falls with the patrilineal clan, 'a domain in which women, who are the prime carers of children', Oleke *et al.* point out, 'commonly have little or no say' (Oleke *et al.*, 2006: 271) – resulting in poorer care for children forced on affinal female kin. In an age of economic decline, however, paternal kin are refuting their obligations in this regard, claiming that children are better off with maternal kin ('it's in the child's best interests') while it also relieves them of their familial obligation (their own best interests). Children are also increasingly being born out of wedlock, so that their fathers can refute their paternity, giving them no access to clan resources. As a result, more and more orphans are residing with maternal clan members. In my 2007–09 study group among Baganda near Kampala, we found slightly more than half the children living with maternal kin. In a 2005 study by Oleke *et al.*, 'Sixty-three percent of the households caring for orphans were found to be no longer headed by resourceful paternal kin in a manner deemed culturally appropriate by the patrilineal Langi society, but rather by marginalised widows, grandmothers or other single women receiving little support from the paternal clan' (Oleke *et al.*, 2005: 2628).

Caregivers exploiting orphan care obligations for personal gain are driven not so much by 'African traditional culture' as they are by global economic and social trends and their local implications. Once again, we see that we cannot separate children's rights from broader issues of social justice. Indeed, moves toward cultural modernization that condemn and abolish traditional practices such as widow inheritance and bridewealth can serve to disadvantage women and the children for whom they care (Kilbride and Kilbride, 1990).

Assistance or no, orphans have become commodified in a chain of local and global support that makes them both potential burdens and opportunities for kin. Abebe and Aase point out that 'The fact that orphans, in many instances, contribute substantially to the livelihoods of extended families questions normative, one-dimensional notions of care whereby adults provide resources to children' (Abebe and Aase, 2007: 2068). Many children in our study described overhearing (but rarely participating in) family conversations about who would take care of them in the wake of a parent's death. Those conversations often circulated around which child would be of the most use to the adult concerned. 'I'll take Prossy because she's quiet and a hard worker', an aunt or uncle may say, 'but I don't want her brother; he's disobedient.' A relative's willingness to host an orphan is a conditional agreement; orphans must ingratiate themselves to caregivers, usually through daily exercise of obedience (*mpisa).* When asked about the texture of their daily lives, most children rattled off an extensive list of the chores they were expected to do both before and after school, including farming, laundry, cooking, washing dishes and caring for younger children in the household. At times, completing chores meant being late to school or missing it altogether. Children who do not conform to such adult expectations risk being cast out, especially once the benefits of enrolment in an orphan care programme have been received and/or ended. Obedience thus becomes a condition for care, reinforcing the usefulness of children for their guardians. In one case, two children had been taken from a rural area to the home of a woman who claimed to be their grandmother but who was not actually related at all. She wanted some assistance with chores in her home and had assured a family in her home village that she could secure free schooling for the orphans from the community school near the city. When they refused to do chores, however, she kept them home from school. Their high rate of absenteeism alerted the head teacher, who investigated. She found that the woman had finally returned them to their home after they kept running away and sleeping at a neighbour's house.

NGOs may also invoke the best interests principle to justify certain policy stances that may in fact diminish children's dignity by relegating them to the role of 'target group'. For example, aid organizations routinely pathologize children through the use of images of poor or traumatized 'poster children' to generate support for their activities (Kleinman and Kleinman, 1997).

Children's approaches to resource provision

Children have to respond within the constraints of the complex local and global dynamics of orphanhood described above in order to fashion their survival. Orphans' perceptions of organizational and familial intervention tend to be more humble and less assuming, perhaps because of the ways in which, as seen in the last section, both local notions of childhood and children's rights are translated such that they serve to maintain the status quo of adult control. Part of this has to do with the history of children's rights implementation in Uganda. UNICEF's Oulanyan readily admitted that they may have erred in their initial efforts to promote children's rights:

> We started by telling people what children's rights were, and children quickly picked up on it ... but then we got to a point where the children were running ahead of the parents and the rest of the community. Now, when you mention child rights in a community, they will say, 'You are spoiling our children! Now we can't even discipline our children. We can't tell them what to do because you've come with this child rights message.' So now we're trying to reverse that and say that children also have a right to parental guidance and put it in context so that it is not that children rule over you. But it's something so hard to reverse because we had such a big drive in the early 90s, really pushing the issue.
>
> (personal communication)

The resulting backlash against children's rights can have particularly adverse effects for vulnerable children such as orphans. Children have a keen sense of justice, but those who are schooled are also urged by the things teachers and other adults tell them to defer to adult authority, rather than defend their rights in ways that might challenge adult authority, which will administer their 'best interests' – a supposition reproduced in aid agency agendas (Cheney, 2007). Learning about their rights can be very emboldening, yet this acceptance of adult resistance to children's rights claims is in itself a kind of agency: they have learned that they must work within the constraints of contradictory global/local discourses about children and their rights, as well as within global/local power relations. It might be tempting to see this as simple mimicry of adult and/or Western discourses, but Ferguson notes, 'an anthropological insistence on interpreting gestures of similitude in terms of parody and magic has the effect of obscuring the continuing claims of Africans and others [e.g. children] to full membership rights in a world society' (Ferguson, 2006: 167). Orphans may thus be appropriating and participating in the construction of child victimhood in order to enact living rights by claiming some form of social justice-based membership in the global humanitarian community.

Children's innovative survival strategies therefore tend to capitalize more, not necessarily on their rights as children, but instead on the 'vulnerable child' discourse described above and propagated by international NGOs working in Africa under a children's rights mandate. I definitely saw this in my work with former child soldiers, who strategically utilized the trope of the traumatized child perpetrated by INGOs to gain protection from prosecution for their actions as soldiers (Cheney, 2004). In this study we see orphans using similar tactics, always using the English word 'orphan' to describe themselves in ways that only a few years ago might have been highly stigmatizing. This is because presenting as an 'orphan', in international aid parlance, may now literally pay.

From a young age, children also tend to seek resources at the local level through identification of social networks most likely to render assistance. Children build networks in ways that circumnavigate the limitations posed by the joining of children's rights discourses with AIDS orphanhood and adult conceptions of children's obedience. Often this entails embracing an OVC identity in subtle ways that will ensure their survival based on assessment of resources in their immediate environments and social networks (Nyambedha and Aagaard-Hansen, 2003: 174). For example, children often make friends with peers who are better off than them, but who are also generous and willing to share their bounty. A first-grade girl in our study told us how she loved her 'best friend' because she had given her an old pair of shoes, and she always shared the snacks she brought to school. In this way, she was able to leverage her vulnerability by raising the social status of another child who showed her generosity. The maintenance of the 'best friend' title encouraged the friend's continued generosity toward her.

A clever 9-year-old boy proudly told us about his modus operandi: on weekends, he roamed from 10 a.m. to 4 p.m. (after his chores and before his grandmother required him to be home), keeping close tabs on all the local celebrations, from birthdays to funerals. He had even ranked which families tended to have the best food at their gatherings so he could make the rounds and get fed by charming his neighbours. Few chased him away, knowing that his elderly grandmother cared for thirteen more grandchildren in a dilapidated brick house with a dirt floor, no windows and little food. The boy savvily drew on his family's known vulnerability so neighbours – many of whom did not have much themselves – would be charitable toward him in light of his public admission of vulnerability.[6] Yet this very act reveals his strategic innovation in manipulating the powerful social categories placed upon him by both local and global discourses about orphans in order to procure resources in a resource-strapped environment. So while the codifying of orphans' identities recreates children as sites for both local and global humanitarian intervention, children learn as well as adults how to 'work it'. Rather than a simple act of postcolonial mimicry (Young, 2003: 141), African AIDS orphans are translating the disempowering language of development in hopes of gaining entitlement to basic human rights and social justice through the back door: 'I am vulnerable, and I therefore deserve assistance.'

Older children (10 years old and up), by contrast, may draw on rights discourses learned in school to appeal to NGOs and/or seek individual sponsorship, but they meet with the same resistance that younger children do. Elsewhere, I have detailed the conundrums of local translations of children's rights, in which children learn about their rights only to be disappointed by how inactionable they are in their own lives (Cheney, 2007). This is further seen in countless cases like Margaret's, where children who have no adult caregiver encounter barriers of access to vital assistance unless they can find an adult interlocutor to vouch for them. While in Zambia in 2008 I spoke with the directors of a Catholic Relief Services (CRS) orphan outreach programme specifically targeting child-headed households in the Mansa District. They told me that they had children come to them seeking assistance almost daily, but because they had found rampant fraud where children commonly lied about their circumstances (often because their impoverished caregivers put them up

[6] This may be easier for children in Uganda, where AIDS carries less stigma than in other sub-Saharan African countries, where fear of infection by HIV-positive and AIDS-orphaned children still runs high.

to it), they had developed an extensive verification system that involved home visits and adult references to determine whether the children were 'legitimately' orphaned and the most needy according to the UN definition – again, usually at odds with local definitions (Meintjes and Giese, 2006). The directors talked about this as an annoyance, but they acknowledged that children and families did this out of poverty, in an attempt to subvert the disproportionate entitlements granted to orphans as opposed to other needy children by these programmes (Henderson, 2006).

When children learn about their rights, they are reminded that their fulfilment is largely as conditional as the obligation to behave for kin caregivers. At the community school handmade posters reminding children of their rights hang side by side with others reminding them of their responsibilities. So while they may occasionally talk of orphan entitlements in terms of rights, orphaned children continue to work on gaining access to resources through strategies such as cultivating fictive/selective kinships – as Malik did by claiming three surrogate 'mums'. This example of deliberate assignation of kinship terms raises the possibility of transformative relationships: by calling someone 'mum', a child elicits 'discourse expectations' of appropriate care and support. With the influx of INGOs in many areas, targeting perceived cultural representatives of international humanitarianism (usually white foreigners, including anthropologists) for educational sponsorship, as did Margaret, becomes a viable and often successful strategy. We can also discern in these actions examples of their resilience and decision-making skills in navigating the adverse conditions of their existence as orphans. The drawback is that their own strategies tend to play into the delay of a transformative understanding of children's rights.

Conclusion: translating victims into citizens

These are just some brief examples of how orphans employ their own creative survival strategies; instead of citing their rights, orphans often find it more effective to revert to a discourse of vulnerability, despite the fact that it reinstates their victimhood rather than furthering rights claims. But this in itself can be interpreted as an agentive act, as it acknowledges that protectionist interpretations of children's 'best interests' give them few opportunities to lay claim to their own rights. The norms of reciprocity and charity on which orphans base their survival strategies can therefore be seen as what Karl Hanson and Olga Nieuwenhuys (Chapter 1 of this volume) call 'living rights'.

Much of the institutional intervention on behalf of AIDS orphans in Africa is driven by a discourse of humanitarianism that compels Westerners to 'save the children' of Africa through their generosity. At the heart of the paradox of children's rights for orphans is a conflict between needs-based and rights-based approaches. Rights-based approaches, in contrast to humanitarian intervention, make no heroes out of donors; though adhering to a rights-based approach has more transformative potential, many individual and private donors find the idea of facilitating the procurement of what people are already entitled to dull compared to the promise of 'saving' a life with their spare change. At the same time as this approach depoliticizes the roots of poverty that have precipitated both the AIDS epidemic and its consequent 'orphan crisis', it strips children and families of their agency and rights-based arguments. Yet we cannot deny that in most cases basic needs must be met before rights can be adequately addressed. These two approaches are contradictorily wedded by OVC/CABA constructions as children who are *both* victims *and* denied rights, yet in need of *care* more than *empowerment* to act for themselves. The result is a failure to achieve an environment of living rights, in which the rights discourses circulating make a substantive difference in ameliorating the adverse circumstances of orphanhood.

Building more productive models for family, government and NGO intervention on behalf of AIDS orphans lies not only in local and transnational discourses *about* orphans, but in deepening our understanding of AIDS-affected children's own perceptions of their circumstances. Doing so may shift the discourse of humanitarian intervention toward augmenting children's agency, rather than emphasizing – and thereby sometimes deepening – their vulnerability. To be effective, then, children's rights translating must move from a legalistic discursive device to an everyday, indigenous language that holds its own weight in social practice. Adults must therefore come to see children's rights as beneficial to the entire community rather than a tool that can either be manipulated or implemented at the expense of adults. As UNICEF notes, they have to first undo the damage done by the way in which they introduced children's rights to Uganda in the first place. This shift may help bridge the subjective gaps between these different actors' strategies and yield a greater sense of social justice for children, but it will rely on adults and adult institutions – whether local or global, rights-based or humanitarian-based – relinquishing their power over children and recognizing children's citizenship through more transformative models of assistance (Invernizzi and Milne, 2005; James, 2011). This lies not only in emphasizing social and economic rights to alleviate the widespread poverty that drives both local adult self-interest and the global aid industry, but in recognizing children's capacity to act, legally and socially, on their own behalf to secure the resources necessary for survival – a point that ethnographic research with children is well poised to illustrate. As long as the promise of children's rights is deferred, however, children like Malik and Margaret will continue to creatively seek care in whatever ways they find effective, even as they keep struggling to give living meaning to their rights.

References

Abebe T and Aase A (2007) Children, AIDS and the politics of orphan care in Ethiopia: the extended family revisited. *Social Science & Medicine* 64(10): 2058–69.

Asad T (2003) *Formations of the Secular: Christianity, Islam, Modernity.* Stanford University Press.

Bledsoe C and Isiugo-Abanihe U (1989) Strategies of Child-Fosterage among Mende Grannies in Sierra Leone. In: Lesthaeghe R J (ed.), *Reproduction and Social Organization in Sub-Saharan Africa.* Berkeley: University of California, pp. 442–74.

Bloch M, Kennedy D, Lightfoot T and Weyenberg D (eds.) (2006) *The Child in the World/The World in the Child: Education and the Configuration of a Universal, Modern, and Globalized Childhood.* London: Palgrave MacMillan.

Bornstein E (2003) *The Spirit of Development: Protestant NGOs, Morality, and Economics in Zimbabwe.* London: Routledge.

Cheney K E (2004) 'Our children have only known war:' children's experiences and the uses of childhood in northern Uganda. *Children's Geographies* 3(1): 23–45.

(2005) Claiming children's rights: children and the 'culture of constitutionalism' in Uganda's primary school music festivals, *Image & Narrative.* Available at: www.imageandnarrative.be/inarchive/worldmusicb_advertising/kristenecheney.htm (accessed 14 June 2012).

(2007) *Pillars of the Nation: Child Citizens and Ugandan National Development.* The University of Chicago Press.

(2010) Expanding vulnerability, dwindling resources: implications for orphaned futures in Uganda. *Childhood in Africa* 2(1): 8–15.

Chirwa W (2002) Social exclusion and inclusion: challenges to orphan care in Malawi. *Nordic Journal of African Studies* 11: 93–113.

Englund H (2006) *Prisoners of Freedom: Human Rights and the African Poor.* Berkeley: University of California Press.

Ferguson A and Freidus A (2007) Orphan care in Malawi: examining the transnational images and discourses of humanitarianism. In: *American*

Anthropological Association Meetings, Washington DC, 28 November–2 December 2007, pp. 1–10.

Ferguson J (2006) *Global Shadows: Africa in the Neoliberal World Order.* Durham, NC: Duke University Press.

Foster G, Levine C and Williamson J (eds.) (2005) *A Generation at Risk: The Global Impact of HIV/AIDS on Orphans and Vulnerable Children.* New York: Cambridge University Press.

Gruskin S and Tarantola D (2005) Human rights and children affected by HIV/AIDS. In: Foster G, Levine C and Williamson J (eds.) *A Generation at Risk: The Global Impact of HIV/AIDS on Orphans and Vulnerable Children.* New York: Cambridge University Press, pp. 134–58.

Guest E (2003) *Children of AIDS: Africa's Orphan Crisis*, 2nd edn. London: Pluto Press.

Henderson P C (2006) South African AIDS orphans: examining assumptions around vulnerability from the perspective of rural children and youth. *Childhood* 13(3): 303–27.

Invernizzi A and Milne B (2002) Are children entitled to contribute to international policy making? A critical view of children's participation in the international campaign for the elimination of child labour. *The International Journal of Children's Rights* 10(4): 403–31.

(2005) Introduction: Children's citizenship: a new discourse? *Journal of Social Sciences* 9: 1–6.

James A (2011) To be (come) or not to be (come): understanding children's citizenship. *The Annals of the American Academy of Political and Social Science* 633(1): 167–79.

Kilbride P L and Kilbride J C (1990) *Changing Family Life in East Africa: Women and Children at Risk.* The Pennsylvania State University Press.

Kleinman A and Kleinman J (1997) The appeal of experience; the dismay of images: cultural appropriations of suffering in our times. In: Kleinman A, Das V and Lock M (eds.) *Social Suffering.* Berkeley: University of California Press, pp. 1–23.

Mahon R (2010) After neo-liberalism? The OECD, the World Bank and the child. *Global Social Policy* 10(2): 172–92.

Meintjes H and Giese S (2006) Spinning the epidemic: the making of mythologies of orphanhood in the context of AIDS. *Childhood* 13(3): 407–30.

Notermans C (2004) Fosterage and the politics of marriage and kinship in East Cameroon. In: Bowie F (ed.) *Cross-Cultural Approaches to Adoption.* New York: Routledge, pp. 48–63.

Nyambedha E O and Aagaard-Hansen J (2003) Changing place, changing position: orphans' movements in a community with high HIV/AIDS prevalence in Western Kenya. In: Olwig K F and Gullov E (eds.) *Children's Places: Cross-Cultural Perspectives.* New York: Routledge, pp. 162–76.

Oleke C, Blystad A and Rekdal O B (2005) 'When the obvious brother is not there': political and cultural contexts of the orphan challenge in northern Uganda. *Social Science & Medicine* 61(12): 2628–38.

Oleke C, Blystad A, Moland K M, Rekdal O B and Heggenhougen K (2006) The varying vulnerability of African orphans: the case of the Langi, northern Uganda. *Childhood* 13(2): 267–84.

Phiri S N and Webb D (2007) Programme and policy responses to the impact of HIV and AIDS on children. In: Cornia G A (ed.) *AIDS, Public Policy and Child Well-Being*. Florence: UNICEF Innocenti Research Centre, pp. 317–42.

Reynolds P, Nieuwenhuys O and Hanson K (2006) Refractions of children's rights in development practice: a view from anthropology. *Childhood* 13(3): 291–302.

Rose L R (2005) Orphans' land rights in post-war Rwanda: the problem of guardianship. *Development and Change* 36(5): 911–36.

Singhal A and Howard W S (eds.) (2003) *The Children of Africa Confront AIDS: From Vulnerability to Possibility*. Athens, OH: Ohio University Press.

Sloth-Nielsen J and Mezmur B D (2008) HIV/Aids and children's rights in law and policy in Africa: confronting Hydra head on. In: Sloth-Nielsen J (ed.) *Children's Rights in Africa: A Legal Perspective*. Aldershot: Ashgate Publishing, pp. 279–98.

The Joint Learning Initiative on Children and HIV/AIDS (2009) *Home Truths: Facing the Facts on Children, AIDS, and Poverty*. Report, Association François-Xavier Bagnoud – FXB International, Geneva.

Uganda Ministry of Gender Labor and Social Development (2004) *National Orphans and Vulnerable Children Policy*. Report, Ministry of Gender, Labor and Social Development, Kampala.

UNICEF (2006) *Africa's Orphaned and Vulnerable Generations: Children Affected by AIDS*. UNICEF, UNAIDS and PEPFAR.

(2008) *Uganda Annual Report 2007*. Report, UNICEF Uganda, Kampala.

(2010) Info by Country – Uganda. Available at: www.unicef.org/infobycountry/uganda_statistics.html (accessed 14 June 2012).

Wandera A N (2009). Global Fund hails Cheeye's conviction. *Monitor*. Available at: www.monitor.co.ug (accessed 14 April 2009).

West A (2007) Power relationships and adult resistance to children's participation. *Children, Youth and Environments* 17(1): 123–35.

Young R J C (2003) *Postcolonialism: A Very Short Introduction*. Oxford University Press.

PART III

Translations

PART III

Translations

9

Living history by youth in post-war situations

COLETTE DAIUTE

Introduction

As one among many activities for youth participation in community centres across four countries of the former Yugoslavia, Fadil and his peers wrote letters to public officials with information about how their societies could ease young people's transitions to a better future. In such activities 12- to 27-year-olds express living history, as they recognize current circumstances that challenge or support their own needs and goals. Acknowledging living history is important for each new generation but especially so for children growing up during and after political violence. Living history is, moreover, a living right, especially where armed conflict has seriously threatened childhood. In the following letter, for example, 19-year-old Fadil, whose life has been defined by the wars in the former Yugoslavia during the 1990s, 'demands' rights to an alternative history than those in power have offered:

> My letter would address the demand to give rights to youth, so we do not make obstacles to their progress disagreeing with my claim. Youth should have equal rights in everything. Our 'beautiful' country should be changed, so young people participate in politics in order to reduce corruption and bribery. Most importantly, we should provide for youth an opportunity to prove their capabilities. Otherwise, young people will continue to leave the country as long as this kind of situation is sustained.

Fadil's analysis is neither complete nor literary, but it is urgent and consistent with others across the region (Daiute, 2010). The letter identifies specific problems, solutions and consequences affecting the broader community as well as his generation: 'young people will continue to leave the country as long as this kind of situation is sustained.' Motivated by a desire to continue developing, young people focused intensely on the circumstances of their everyday lives, which Fadil identified as 'rights' to 'progress', concerns about 'obstacles', like not being able to 'participate in politics', and discontentment about not having opportunities to 'prove their capabilities', all the time feeling that adults are 'disagreeing' with young people's claims to participate in politics. Fadil's letter reveals dynamic implicit conversations among the numerous alternative narratives that justify one position or another about causes, consequences and future directions in situations defined by political violence. Some of those histories are spoken by the powerful in society, some by adults who suffered, some by organizations trying to support youth development, and, ideally, by children themselves who are rarely consulted about history. Such 'living history' that young people craft as they make sense of what is going on around them and how they fit in is influenced in relevant ways by the past while orienting to a possible future. As subjects of histories made by others, young people tend to respond strongly to obstacles, injustices and what they perceive as senselessness in the world around them. In this chapter, I argue that an astute focus on living history is a youthful capacity and that young people's participation in community organizations can be contexts supporting their use of such capacities. To build that argument, I offer theory and research interventions as illustrative not only of living rights (with living history as especially important in conflict-affected situations) but also of translations (with the letter-writing activity and comparison of letters by more and less (non) active community organization participants).

When we acknowledge that children are, from birth, social and sentient beings, we pay attention to how they manage multiple and sometimes contradictory versions of history. I draw on several theories of child development to explain the concept 'living history' as a case of 'living rights' and offer evidence of the nature and importance of living history by young people growing up in the Yugoslav wars. Drawing on data from a study with 137 youth aged 12 to 27 in four countries (Bosnia, Croatia, Serbia, refugees to the United States) resulting from the violent wars in former Yugoslavia during the 1990s, I explain that children growing up in the context of political violence and transition are especially sensitive to circumstances threatening their survival and development, thereby creating a need to recount living history in relation to their experiences. Living histories occur with oppressive histories (rigid ideological accounts) characteristic of such contexts. Given the power of official versions of history, young people benefit, moreover, from participation in transitional spaces that allow them to negotiate multiple perspectives or to make demands, as Fadil does. A skill developed by young people growing up in changing and diverse environments may, in fact, be the translation of rights from the perspectives of various stakeholders.

This argument integrates the concepts 'living rights', 'translations' and 'social justice' with the analysis of young people's letters advising public officials about how they could improve the future for the wartime child generation. Youth evaluations of the problems and possible solutions across four post-war contexts express and imply their living rights. Letters such as Fadil's translate youth perspectives for those in power. In addition, the comparison of letters by young community organization activists with those of peers who were not active in organizations offers insights about how youth can mediate discourses of community organizations with their experiences as addressed to adults in power.

Questions guiding the inquiry include: What is living history and how does it contribute to interdisciplinary theory on children's rights? How can we apply developmental theory to design research that identifies child/youth claims for living rights in situations of political conflict and transition? How do activities designed to support young people's living histories entail their translations of multiple circumstances (diverse local realities) and discourses (community centre, public officials) in their environments?

In the first part of the chapter, I provide a justification for studying children's and young people's perspectives in transitional spaces offered by non-governmental organizations (NGOs) and civil society organizations (CSOs), where their understandings can be integrated into community activities. The subsequent section presents results of a practice-based study held during a research workshop *Dynamic Story-telling by Youth*, in particular the views of young people as evidence of the concept of living history and its relation with this book's central concept, living rights. The analysis of letters by youth who are and are not active participants in community centres offers insights about how young people mediate their perceptions of societal problems in relation to involvement in organized activities. The concluding sections consider implications of children's living history as a way to create more socially just spaces for ongoing research and practice toward their expression and translations of living rights.

Research in community organizations

Before presenting our results of a practice-based study, this section briefly explains the merits of a cultural–historical approach to studying living history in community organizations that aim to provide transitional spaces for mutual child–society development in the aftermath of war.

Knowledge and thought about one's experiences and one's rights do not occur in a vacuum but evolve in material and symbolic interactions, so we contribute to understandings of living history by studying contexts where children enact these understandings. Childhood is, after all, a culture that interacts with other socially constructed groups. The cultural–historical approach, somewhat like object relations theory (Winnicott, 2005), offers principles for an analysis that integrates the person in context. Cultural–historical principles imply a notion of development that is not a linear unfolding of predictable skills but a complex interplay of capacities in diverse, real-time, goal-oriented social relationships. Young people develop goals based on their personal experience and in relation to (and sometimes in reaction to) experiences reported by others. One major developmental dynamic is what happens when different voices collide (Bakhtin, 1986), as they do in contemporary societies, especially during times of major political–economic change. Activities that are collaborative and mediated by cultural tools, like language, should, in principle, allow for discursive diversity and flexibility not only by people across settings but also, and even more importantly, by individuals engaging in different ways with events, other people and institutions where they live. Children have the right to such engagement, although those who determine what can and cannot be said in public tend to ignore or silence children's (potential) contributions to public discourse.

Originally, the concept of transitional space explained children's emotional and cognitive development as parents allowed them to explore spatially within a safe range (Winnicott, 2005). While a safe exploration space for babies is within visible and auditory proximity to their familiar caretakers, scholars have extended the concept to thinking spaces as:

> the frontier of freedom in the psychic activity in which the individual elaborates the perceived reality in order to represent or symbolize it and to become able to reflect on it … Thinking has its roots in collective activities that permit or even provoke it [as] the child and later the adolescent are called upon as co-thinkers or challenged with issues on which they have to take a stance.
>
> (Perret-Clermont, 2004: 3).

Children's participation in dramatically changing political–economic situations must thus also provide opportunities 'to generate new flows of information and debate, and narratives based on children's own perceptions' (Taylor and Percy-Smith, 2008: 389).

Since children do not develop in a social or political vacuum, 'participation needs to involve collaboration and dialogue between young people and adults and between communities and agencies, to enable joint projects for exploring, understanding, and responding to community problems as part of a community development process' (Taylor and Percy-Smith, 2008: 389, citing Percy-Smith, 2006). Organizations committed to including children's decision-making can be such transitional spaces where children interact critically and creatively with the range of rigid ideologies of school, home, government media and programmes. In these transitional spaces the past and other powerful discourses enter through young people's living histories. Instead of ignoring or thwarting this process, adults can support it by interacting with children flexibly in spaces open to the learning and developing of all involved based, at least in part, on child and youth decision-making (Hart, 2008; Thomas, 2007).

Community organizations, whether non-governmental organizations (NGOs), civil society organizations (CSOs) or grass-roots movements, have a major presence in the lives of young people worldwide, especially in situations of political violence and transition where state-run organizations such as public schools are in disarray. For millions of young people growing up during and after major political disruption, youth organizations are worth exploring as potentially developmental (Daiute, 2010) or third spaces (Gutiérrez *et. al.*, 1997). Although there are increasing debates about the nature and value of non-governmental organizations as intruders or developers, their uses by young people remain open to inquiry (de Berry, 2008). Some scholars argue that international aid workers represent the cultural values, interests and power of their funders, such as the World Bank and the United Nations, thereby imposing values and practices that undermine traditional culture (McMahon, 2009). However, when these contexts are flexible enough to allow children's living histories, we observe the mutual influence of individuals and groups relative to contemporary circumstances. Children growing up in societies undergoing dramatic political–economic change can use alternative spaces to engage diverse discourses from a variety of perspectives in the environment from their own lived experience, as we read in Fadil's letter. Through meaningful activities, transitional organizations may allow for the development of context-sensitive perspectives alternative to those of the state and family. Socio-political development may depend, at least in part, on children's abilities to integrate across such diverse perspectives.

To be developmental, those spaces must allow for the collaborative expression of multiple perspectives, debate, critique, decision-making and transformation, from the perspective of young people as living historians focused on their present situations. The appeal of activities by the numerous NGO and CSO community centres in conflict and post-conflict situations is not surprising, given their focus on issues such as human rights and social inclusion. In dramatically changing political situations we cannot take for granted the socialization from one generation to the next (if we ever can), so politically alternative spaces might allow, at least to some extent, for substantive influence by the generation growing up in the new system. Because non-state organizations typically lack the infrastructure, reach or power of state-governed spaces, they are likely to be relatively open to children's realizations of living rights, especially when their mission is to involve child and youth decision-making.

Research designs sensitive to the 'complexity, circularity, and interrelations' (Hanson and Nieuwenhuys, Chapter 1 of this volume) of rights discourses can usefully allow young people multiple opportunities to engage with diverse influences they perceive as they make sense of their everyday lives and their role in the circumstances in which they find themselves. Practice-based research, in particular, can engage young people in realistic, purposeful activities where they express, share and transform their perspectives, in this case on history shaping their daily lives, as they interact with other individual and institutional voices that are salient to obstacles and opportunities for thriving. In the terms considered in this volume, young people are, thus, translating as well as expressing living rights.

If cultural tools serve as 'conductor[s] of human influence on the object of activity' (Vygotsky, 1978: 55), a community organization supporting youth activism and critique could, ideally, be a context where young people engage in activities to identify goals ('object') and draw on a range of resources to participate in achieving these goals. When political violence disrupts cultural routines, relationships and institutions, we ask, 'How do young people use these spaces to figure out what is going on around them and how they fit in?' More specifically, we design research addressing the question, 'How do young people use innovative activities in community centres to mediate the political chaos and controversy where they live?'

A practice-based study offers theory and analysis of young people's uses of community centres as transitional socio-political spaces. If public education is designed to socialize youth to the values and practices of mainstream society, then informal education in non-state organizations is transitional when open to asking questions about mainstream systems, possible alternatives and relevant youth roles. This enterprise requires purposeful communication, such as narrating (self-societal connection), inquiring (observing what is going on and how one fits in) (Nelson, 2003) and advising (identifying and advocating for personal and collective needs and goals) (Daiute, 2010).

Study of interacting developments in the aftermath of war

In this section we now discuss the results of a practice-based study where young people interacted in organizations for community and self-development in the aftermath of war. To ensure that youth growing up in extremely challenging contexts have ample opportunity to engage substantively in individual and collective reflection, we included a full range of discursive activities not only to learn from young people but also to encourage their development. The research workshop *Dynamic Story-telling by Youth* (DSTY) involved story-telling embedded in community development activities to create social histories from the perspective of young people living with the manifestations of war and political economic transition. The curriculum and research in this project are built, in brief, on the hypothesis that rigid ideological stories ignite and maintain conflict, so positive development must, in contrast, provide young people with supportive opportunities for engaging diverse perspectives, to diverse audiences, and for a range of diverse purposes. It is this dynamic story-telling that becomes living history to transform oppressive history in the context of child and youth participation. I draw on one particular strand of data from the DSTY workshop to illustrate youth perspectives on history and their orientations for societal determination: writing letters to public officials.[1]

Inviting an explicitly authoritative youth stance, we asked participants to write letters to public officials, suggesting how they might better support youth development. We now turn to a discussion of this activity as evidence of the complexity of youth living histories in the context of community organizations.

[1] To allow for different social–relational expressions, the research workshop involves three genres: inquiry, narrative and advisory. Inquiry activities elicit and share information, focusing in this case on how people perceive their societies. Narrative activities emphasize youth experiences, relationships and self-determination. Advisory activities emphasize youth determination of society. Although these genres may differ generally as described herein, each activity involves diverse social configurations of the speaker/writer–audience–goal, allowing for diverse youth stances. In particular, youth stances across the activities in the research workshop vary for explicit and implicit relational qualities of connection, interpretation and power.

As part of the DSTY research workshop, 103 participants distributed relatively evenly across countries, age groups and activist groups wrote letters to a range of public officials, including prime ministers, presidents, mayors, university deans and school principals, among others. These youth, positioned by the activity as expert advocates, organized their letters around a range of discursive functions, including complaints, explanations of causes, thwarted goals, suggestions of how to address those complaints, explanations of why/how those solutions would work and various personal appeals. After reading the 103 letters, I identified a list of elements in each letter, including statement of a problem (explicit or implicit), the domain of life addressed (education, politics, environment, community/family, media, social/personal, work), the scope of issues (national, international, technical, systemic), suggested strategy and values stated or implied in the letter (such as human rights, peace, social order/politics, morality/religion, praxis/relevance, quality of life/fun, and so on). Beyond this taxonomy, I identified the problem–solution structure within and across the letters. I then applied a discourse analysis to identify the nature of each solution and the context of its application (a direct solution of the problem or a solution via socio-political mechanisms). To explore relationships between youth critique and their participation in community organizations, I then analysed the connection of problem-solution patterns in the young people's letters to their participation in community organizations. The complexity of youth critique in relation to their participation in community organizations would, I hypothesized, offer insights about the nature of living history and young people's abilities to transform collective activities into a socio-political analysis of their environments.

Preliminary analysis revealed six categories of solutions (provide relief, expand or reduce existing traditions, change systems, create new institutions, create new systems, avoid negative cases). When examined for the context of application, the solutions grouped into two patterns: functional solutions and mediational solutions.

Functional solutions seek relief from current circumstances, directly address specific needs and appeal for alternatives to the past (in the absence of proposing new systems to do so). The following letter, for example, offers a concrete proposal for improved education:

> Dear Minister of Education, I hope you will pay attention to my suggestions. First, schooling should be made interesting. We don't expect teachers to sing & dance but they should modernize, such as by using

> technology ... We also need less theory & more practical activity to have modern skills.

This letter-writer offers concrete suggestions, albeit to an implied problem, but does not state or explain mechanisms or outcomes in societal terms. Although appeal to modernization implies a need to address a new world order, the letter does not define the solution as a means to a societal end as well as to individual skill-building. This solution, thus, applies directly to the problem in its stated context.

Mediational solutions, in contrast, suggest new systems or institutions as means to resolution. As in the following letter, mediational solutions introduce and explain new or changed systems and institutions:

> Dear Prime Minister, It is really important to improve education in subjects such as tolerance and sexual education in schools. Tolerance is important ... [for] communication between people and to raise their self-esteem. Self-esteem motivates people, especially the young to advance in their lives. Sexual education is important because there are 100,000 abortions in Serbia each year. Youth should be better educated regarding this matter so that they don't harm themselves and their future. Youth should be better informed so that they could lead peaceful lives without too much sorrow! At the end the world stays with the young!

This young letter-writer introduces a concrete addition to the curriculum and specific outcomes for society and humanity beyond interpersonal relations.

Interestingly, these different types of solutions are connected with participation in community organizations. In particular, young people who participated in community organizations proposed meditational solutions more (61.5%) than they proposed functional solutions (38.5%), while, in contrast, their peers who did not participate in community organizations did the reverse, proposing functional solutions more (87.3%) than meditational solutions (12.7%). This analysis indicates that in addition to focusing in detailed ways on extant circumstances, young people developed strategic understandings about how to deal with problems by participating in community organizations.

The finding that all young people identified specific problems and solutions indicates their interest and capacity for engaging with rights-based issues. Even more compelling is the finding that youth involved in community organizations use those organizations to increase the sophistication of their reasoning about political processes – that is the need and processes for mediating systems to improve environments for young people via social change and, as we discuss below, living history.

Living history

Living history focuses on present circumstances in a way that orients to the future, while also considering the past, in particular as past events inhibit or support forward movement. Living history tends to be a youthful orientation because young people want to develop into adults as defined in their culture, which could also mean being different from past norms, such as those that created war. From the perspective of socio-historical developmental theory (Vygotsky, 1978), we can interpret that young people's letters to public officials and the specific sensitivity of community-oriented young people illustrate the interaction of individuals in society. Living history assumes that as soon as children can interact with those around them verbally or through other symbolic means, they learn what to focus on, such as that bullets may come through the window, that they need to help the family, such as by fetching water at a central source in town when the supply at home is blocked, that they should align with supportive forces, that some people rely on bribery rather than jobs as a means of survival, and that their fate may be like that of adults with no means of providing for themselves or their families. Fadil's letter, like those of younger children and older youth, is evidence of such context-sensitive thought processes, rarely mentioned in policy or research with children growing up during and after armed conflict.

Young people's claims of living history are especially poignant in situations of war and the aftermath where the stakes are high and desires to present certain versions of history become oppressive in several ways. Most obviously, wars damage society. Political violence causes death, abuse, displacement, coercion, discrimination, environmental devastation and the interruption of political and civic institutions. Periods of material destruction can be protracted, with consequences lasting at least seven years (Collier, 2003). In addition to ongoing material consequences, symbolic circumstances persist in post-war periods.

History is also oppressive as nations try to forge new policies and identities during political transitions. In addition to physical reminders of wartime, such as bullet-pocked buildings, collapsed bridges, abandoned factories and incapacitated adults, myriad symbolic reminders circulate in society, such as rigid justifications for the past war and new narratives for future membership in the European Union. Historical accounts by powerful actors such as the government and mainstream media focus on the past, either to justify violence or to distance themselves from it aggressively. Requirements for political change, such as practising democracy and reforming institutions are, for example, imposed without local precedents, a situation that is especially acute in the post-war Western Balkan nations aspiring to European Union membership. When not aggressively pursuing one alternative or another, governments may flounder in instability, in part when subject to international control, as with the UN Protectorate in post-war Bosnia. At the time when Fadil wrote his letter, his country Bosnia and Herzegovina was, for example, stalled by territorial division based on separation of formerly warring ethnic groups (Parish, 2010), a situation described by another local youth as untenable:

> Politicians are corrupted and they are not doing anything for our well-being. With two entities, how can we have a normal country which will have laws that can benefit youth?

The image of the child in contexts of political violence and transition is then reduced to potential victim or villain. Some young people suffer war-related trauma (Barber, 2009) and some internalize past hatreds (Edelstein, 2006), but a past focus on war events and their continuation tells a smaller part of the story than once assumed (Bonanno, 2004; Summerfield, 1999). Actual trauma and social reproduction must be addressed, but we must also consider when images of youth serve the interests of the state, church or other powers (Boyden, 2003). Governments emphasize breaking with the past, yet relying on resources such as humanitarian aid for their survival may maintain a posture of helplessness. Like children and youth born during and after the recent armed conflicts in the former Yugoslavia and Rwanda, post-war generations are often perceived as traumatized, as potential ethnic cleansers, as requiring violence prevention or citizenship education. At the same time as such deficits are imposed on children and youth, adults in their societies express the need to protect them from the horrors of the past, which often results in reducing formal and informal conversations about recent history (Freedman and Abazovic, 2006). Such oppressions wrought of focusing on the past undermine claims for youth participation and self-determination, because they imply that young people do not have their own sensible interpretations of the situation.

Although young people may be persuaded by some versions of oppressive history, a quality of developing thought is to make active sense of what is going on in the environment and one's own role in it (Nelson, 2003). In this process youth integrate accounts of the past, whether rigid ideological accounts or negotiated agreements about basic facts,[2] in terms of their own experiences of everyday life. The post-war generation whose parents grew up and were educated in Yugoslavia now live in separate countries differing in political and economic stability, reconstruction of infrastructures, relationships with the European Union and other factors (Goehring, 2007). Differences centre around the redevelopment of economic institutions that can employ people, and create daily activities for the adult population and a sense of future trajectory for young people.

Examining youth perceptions of these diverse circumstances offers insights about how age and national and cultural origin may matter less than interaction with the circumstances of daily life (Daiute, 2010; Daiute and Lucic, 2010). Consider, for example, 16-year-old Margareta's narrative about conflicts among adults in her country of Croatia:

> I can't think of anything except the Homeland war. Yugoslavia fell apart. Then the Serbs, aggressors, destroyed Croatia and my hometown as well. I don't know how the participants felt. I do know that in my family there was optimism and hope for [a] better future. The Serbs had a plan to become a huge and a powerful nation. Conflict was solved with Croatia's victory in the war. Today we have an independent country. These hopes came true. But the life in Croatia is not even close to the one we expected it would be (bad privatization, corrupted politicians, low life standards, etc.).

Margareta's account is consistent with the general outline of events from the perspective of her country. After referring to the 'Homeland war', based on a script that blames the Serbs for destroying Croatia, Margareta comments on the unfulfilled expectations of her family, who had hoped the war would lead to a 'better future'. Although obviously occurring within Margareta's subjective perspective, as well as within those of her countrymen, the script of the homeland war is permeable to a reality she perceives in her everyday life: 'bad privatization, corrupted politicians, low life standards, etc.' Because Margareta wrote this narrative in a community centre teaching coexistence, the critical reflection about the war and other elements of her narrative certainly echo voices therein as well.

[2] Yugoslavia existed as a socialist federation of six republics from 1945 to 1991, when nations furthest west declared independence, resulting in a sequence of events that led to the catastrophe of geo-political fragmentation based on ethnicity (Silber and Little, 1995). The resulting expulsions, ethnic cleansing, bombing and physical violence left from 250,000 to 400,000 dead across the area, hundreds of thousands wounded physically and/or emotionally, millions displaced within the region or beyond, many emigrating several times, and many eventually returning to their pre-war areas (www.unhcr.org, accessed 9 June 2012).

Margareta integrates such diverse perspectives in a coherent voice, perhaps because she perceived the freedom to do so. She narrates her family's hopes for the war sympathetically ('I do know that in my family there was optimism and hope for a better future') and in contrast to her family's adversaries ('The Serbs had a plan to become a huge and powerful nation'), but then offers her perspective in stark contrast to the results of the hopes: 'But the life in Croatia is not even close to the one we expected it would be.'

In a similar process Ljubicica interacts with various very different issues in Serbia. In this commentary about problems in her country, Ljubicica expresses intolerance for passivity in the face of political challenges.

> Problems include: the lack of motivation and awareness that one can direct his or her own destiny, i.e. that some things do depend on us; war, consequences of the war, poverty; the influence of the church interfering with the state affairs, which must not be so.

Interjecting herself as co-responsible, 'some things do depend on us', Ljubicica connects with the fact of war and its numerous consequences, from poverty to intrusions of the church in politics. Since Serbia is widely recognized as having caused much of the destruction during the war, such living histories by Ljubicica and her peers express self-reflection and distancing from their elders quite unique to their circumstances (Daiute, 2010). Like many of her peers, this young Serbian woman is not only intolerant of past violence committed in the name of Yugoslav unity but also rejecting what she perceives to be a lack of engagement by some youth based on their complaint that *they* did not commit the atrocities. We learn from these narratives, as we did from youth letters to public officials discussed above, that young people exposed to the oppressive circumstances of war perceive their living circumstances – opportunities as well as obstacles. While implying a past reality that created the current problems, these children and youth are not passive in the face of these challenges.

In summary, living history is the expression of living rights – young people's perspectives on the current political–economic situation as they focus on obstacles, sometimes wrought of the past, and strategies for seizing opportunities toward a good life immediately and in the future. The past, thus, does not exclusively define how young people perceive their present or future lives, as is typically assumed in research and practice on armed conflict. So, we must acknowledge spaces for young people's critical and creative thinking, in part because the best means of dealing with the past has not yet been clearly defined (Freedman *et al.*, 2008). If oppressive history is a focus on the past, we can define living history as the understandings, questions and goals of young people in their present and future as they draw on the past in ways relevant to daily problems and goals. As numerous societies experience political violence at the beginning of the twenty-first century, inviting living histories in contentious contexts becomes an increasingly important living right.

Living rights to living history

We focus in this section on how recognizing young people's development of living histories connects with rights as defined by elites through the concept of living rights.

During the twentieth century international institutions drew on human rights instruments as the basis for children's rights. The awareness of childhood as a unique and valuable culture deserving of rights is a major advance. As with the creation of official historical accounts, children's rights have been defined from the perspective of those in power, in particular in the 1989 United Nations Convention on the Rights of the Child (CRC). In that and other instruments, children's rights have primarily been approached and studied as forming part of global governance whereby principles and rights enshrined in international human rights documents must be implemented at the national and local levels. In this view, implementation is considered as the 'translation' of international norms into practice, from top to bottom. However, as Hanson and Nieuwenhuys develop in the introduction to this volume, a concurring dynamic is possible that starts from children's own conceptualizations of their rights or 'living rights', defined as what children themselves actively identify or treat as a child right (Hanson and Nieuwenhuys, Chapter 1 of the present volume) and continues with the negotiation of rights among diverse actors. NGOs and CSOs in conflict-affected areas provide their own translations of international norms, sometimes in ways that are formulaic but at other times in ways that invite children's interpretations of those norms (Daiute and Turniski, 2005).

Research has also begun to offer insights about the experiences of children whose rights have been blatantly violated during and after war (Daiute, 2008). There is much more to learn about how children view such specific circumstances related to socio-political aspects of social justice, inclusion and developmental opportunities. The CRC is used extensively as a tool for teaching children about rights and promoting their participation in achieving rights (Hart, 1997), and when broadening our examination to how children make sense of rights beyond the literal treaty to the system of implementation and monitoring, we can identify children's understandings of rights in action. One illustrative example of the need to examine the dynamics between top-down and bottom-up definitions of rights is child labour (Nieuwenhuys, 1994; see also Liebel, Chapter 11 of the present volume). A top-down approach to child labour is to protect children from employment or at least from exploitive employment, whereas in some situations of extreme poverty children find legal work practical and empowering. Another area revealing the need to consider children's living rights is around participation in conflict. Researchers have offered ethnographic information indicating that children in certain conflict-related roles gain experience and motivation for the future after serving as medics or in other useful roles in armed conflict (Sta Maria, 2006). Rather than justifying the recruitment of child soldiers, such research identifies the competencies and critical capabilities of childhood (James *et al.*, 1998). Analyses of conversations with young people also suggest increased knowledge about society and maturity in dealing with a range of losses, responsibilities and strategies for dealing with injustices including violence (Akinwumi, 2006; Ukeje, 2006). If young people's understandings of rights are affected by the specific circumstances where they live, research questions and methods should usefully broaden beyond abstract experimental, survey or interview techniques to theory-based inquiries in relation to practical activities.

Whether it does not go far enough to ensure children's decision-making (Hart, 2008; Thomas, 2007) or whether the politics of children's rights administration diminish its power (Daiute, 2008), the CRC is perceived as requiring expansion (or revision), in particular in terms of the process of developing rights: 'The concept "translations" is no longer considered as a single, one way act, but as a dynamic, circular and continuous process which takes place between the local and the international levels, relying on interdisciplinary concepts of complexity, circularity and interrelations' (Hanson *et al.*, 2010: 1). Consistent with this view, we should examine living rights in relation to the various contexts where children participate, such as in life on the margins of society with little adult interaction (see Mizen and Ofosu-Kusi, Chapter 3 of this volume), in children's movements (see Liebel, Chapter 11 of this volume) and in educational or community organizations interacting with youth living rights, as in this chapter.

The spontaneous emergence of human rights as an issue in the letter by Fadil, the narrative by Margareta and the reflection by Ljubicica, young people whose lives have been defined by extremely unstable circumstances, is not surprising when we recognize the fact that violence and its aftermath threatened their lives and the lives of their peers. Claiming the right to move beyond victimization in the war, however, Fadil expressed a living history from a 'bottom-up' perspective (Hanson and Nieuwenhuys, Chapter 1 of the present volume) characteristic of those in relatively weak or marginal political positions.

Enlivening developmental theory

A review of relevant understandings of child development is useful for guiding ongoing theoretical and practical integration of living history, living rights and child–society translations.

Several active contemporary theories, including cultural–historical activity theory (Vygotsky, 1978) and childhood studies (James *et al.*, 1998), explain that human development occurs in social practices. Many have explained that children interact with the wider social, institutional and global contexts where young people's voices echo those contexts (Taylor and Percy-Smith, 2008; Tisdall, 2008; Vygotsky, 1978). Consistent in their focus on the child's perspective in material and symbolic circumstances, these theoretical stances also offer different insights to suggest that since living history and living rights are perspectives from below, from less powerful people in society, transitional spaces can be beneficial to their development. We can use these theories to consider how, if children mature gradually at least in some respects (Piaget, 1968), they are able to perceive history and rights in unique and important ways. Drawing on theories that posit children's uses of cultural tools in their environments from very early in life (Nelson, 2003; Tomasello, 2005), we ask, 'How do children develop their claims to living rights, and, more specifically for this inquiry, claims to living history?' Compared with developmental theories positing that children gain the ability to interact socially only eventually (Piaget, 1968), cultural–historical activity theory defines humans as profoundly social from the start:

> Every function in … cultural development appears twice: first, on the social level, and later, on the individual level; first between people (interpsychological), and then inside the child/person (intrapsychological). This applies equally to voluntary attention, to logical memory, and to

> the formation of concepts. All higher functions originate as actual relations between human individuals.
>
> (Vygotsky, 1978: 57)

According to this view, human development is an interactive process of individuals and societies in everyday life. History is thus not an abstract story from the past but a meaning-making process in which individuals and groups contend with perceptions and interpretations of events as they participate in public and private life. On this view, young people's perspectives are important because they are not only *about* problems but also *merged* with them in contemporary life. Among the many symbol systems that create meaning is language – the quintessential human activity. As children develop living histories, they interact with other people and their physical (urban or rural) spaces, built environment (monuments, burial grounds, etc.) and symbolic environments (dinner table conversations, media, church).

Socio-historical activity theory (Vygotsky, 1978) explains development in terms of the 'relation of the child to reality' (Veresov, 2006: 14). Development occurs not only in terms of maturation of the individual as cognitive and other abilities unfold in relation to biology, but in the social situation also referred to as the child's 'lifeworld' (Nieuwenhuys, 1994), especially after early childhood:

> [This] social situation of development is the starting point for all the dynamic changes that occur in development during the given age period. It fully determines those forms and that path that by following the child successively acquires new properties of his personality, drawing them from social reality as the main source of development, that path along which the social situation becomes individual.
>
> (Vygotsky in Veresov, 2006: 15)

This view is consistent with theories explaining that mundane activities in actual situations become meaningful and developmental in discourse (and other symbolic systems).

If 'all higher functions originate as actual relations between human individuals' (Vygotsky, 1978), we must understand contexts, including social institutions, in order to understand people. The idea presented here is that thought is integrated in activity in the world, not only as abstract representations but also as 'social relations in goal-directed activity' (Engestrom, 2009). Thought is thus culturally developed, that is, meaningful, shared and repeated in discursive interaction. Discourse is oral, written or non-verbal symbolic expressions that function as 'links in a chain of communication' in which 'no utterance is the first to break the silence of the universe' (Bakhtin, 1986: 69). Discourse activities, such as writing letters, sharing narratives and offering responses to questions on surveys, are social relational behaviours embodying values, power dynamics and other processes that not only express knowledge but also guide perception, action and interpretation (Bakhtin, 1986; Bamberg, 2004; Bruner, 1986; Harre and Van Langenhove, 1999). Letters like Fadil's, narratives like Margareta's, and commentaries like Ljubicica's all link young people's knowledge and experiences with the multiple histories circulating in their environments. These discursive enactments of youth perspectives are, moreover, tools for collective control over their environments (Middleton, 2004; Saljo, 2004; Tudge, 2004).

This use of language and other symbol systems to perceive, manage and develop self–society relations is referred to as *mediation*. Since children use whatever cultural tools are available in their environments to mediate (understand and act upon their environments and themselves), they can begin from a very early age to perceive history and needs for rights. Mediation involves connecting one's own consciousness to the consciousness of others. Mediation is the 'conductor[s] of human influence on the object of activity' (Vygotsky, 1978: 55). On this view, discourse and other symbol systems do not simply transmit meanings or reveal individual character and intentions. Instead, beginning at an early age, children use cultural tools, at first with gestures and sounds, then single words, and eventually complex genres like narratives in ways that are 'externally oriented … aimed at mastering and triumphing over nature' *and* as 'a means of internal activity aimed at mastering oneself' (Vygotsky, 1978: 55).

We saw the mediation process at work in the letters by youth activists who understood from participating in projects to benefit the community that collective systems can be strategies for achieving social change – not only complaining about it or asking for it. We also saw the mediation process in Margareta's narrative of the homeland war above, as she used the narrative to identify with her new country *and* to critique it. Such multiple positioning illustrates how living history combines perspectives, time periods (past, present and future) and politics. Margareta uses the narrative to connect with her family's hopes for (and perhaps justification of) the war sympathetically and in contrast to her family's adversaries. But then she offers her narrator perspective in stark contrast to the results of the hopes. Such uses of narrating to position one's self across time is neither a counter script nor simple resistance (as sometimes stated) but a working of history with an eye toward future development.

The more abruptly and dramatically the environment changes, the less young people can rely on interpretations from the past. From this perspective, we consider how a young person raises questions about contradictory knowledge, as stated by one girl who has lived in various places across the region: 'How is it that different ethnic groups lived peacefully in Yugoslavia for so many years, then one day began killing neighbours they didn't even think of as different the day before?' Because of the shared consciousness and mutual influence of individuals in society, this girl, like her peers, can reproduce the commonly accepted narrative of war in her homeland ('different ethnic groups lived peacefully in Yugoslavia'), a motto of 'brotherhood and unity' that some say is a myth, while also critiquing that myth ('then one day began killing their neighbours'). In the absence of adult explanations for such unexpected and, for some, inexplicable events, young people create their own interpretations as 'active, responsive, transformative orientation' (Bakhtin, 1986: 68).

Understanding discourse in this way provides a bridge among researchers, educators and community leaders working with young people. When we define language as a cultural tool for doing something in society, rather than as a mere transmitter of information, we inquire into the dynamics of social relations and social change. Qualities of life during armed conflict and the aftermath, like displacement, poverty, political and economic instability make children's lives extremely challenging. Because of such challenges, children use their intelligent resources, like language, to perceive needs and rights to improve their situations.

Conclusion

Data from the study described in this chapter support the concepts of living rights, translations and social justice via youth expressions of living history in conflict-affected settings. I offer this case study to illustrate how children's discourses develop in society and integrate living rights from multiple perspectives, as we saw here in community organizations but also presumably with parents, peers and the media. Analyses assessing young people's uses of cultural tools (letter-writing and community participation) offer examples based on a developmental approach assuming their intense interaction with socio-political institutions.

I offer this discussion to illustrate the kind of knowledge we can elicit if we bring context into our conceptions of young people's living rights, not as background influences or cultural diversity, but as critical engagements in society and potential social change. I have offered this analysis of such critical engagement in a practice-based design wherein young people express their expertise in letters to public officials and an examination of their use of community centre participation to translate bottom-up and top-down perspectives about what is salient in their society. Writing letters is one among many activities for youth activism, and community organizations are one among many contexts for collective action and reflection. With this combination of tools for expanding living rights practices, we have seen how such participations can lead to young people's new ways of conceptualizing human relations. That participants defined societal problems and solutions in terms of socio-political systems offers concrete evidence of the developmental gains of enacting living rights and young people's capacities to translate across various actors. From the perspective of this social–relational theory of development, we observe a case of childhood interactions in society for mutual individual–societal change. Because living history can be examined systematically, we must do so across contexts, rather than make universal assumptions about what children understand, need, can do and can contribute. We can, moreover, draw on these results to argue that research and practice should provide concrete context-embedded opportunities for children to raise their voices about living history as a case of context-sensitive living rights. When we examine living history in terms of young people's translations via their participation in community organizations, we advance the concept of translation as well.

Young people interact with the circumstances in their environments, including the problems, not only by observing but also by organizing their perceptions, interactions and interpretations in important activities. From the cross-site analysis we learn that youth of the same age focus on different locally relevant issues in society, not only identity and peers, as has been posited in much prior research. When youth in Serbia focus intensely to assess their own responsibility, as in the commentary by Ljubicica, they are managing the international history of Serbia as a major aggressor, the local history that Serbia suffered too when Serbs were expelled from what is now Croatian territory and in the 1999 bombing of Belgrade. In contrast, a young Bosnian echoes the powerful narrative both internationally and locally that Bosnians were the major victims in the war, suffering a three-year siege of their capital city and a majority of deaths in the wars during the 1990s. Such differences enter into the living histories of young people in different areas but they do not totally define them. These illustrations offer a glimpse into how young people are sensitive to political–economic issues not only from their personal perspectives but also in relation to the material and symbolic circumstances where they live and in relation to activities that encourage their activist stances.

References

Akinwumi O (2006) Youth participation in violence in Nigeria since the 1980s. In: Daiute C, Beykont Z, Higson-Smith C and Nucci L (eds.) *International Perspectives on Youth Conflict and Development.* New York: Oxford University Press, pp. 73–85.

Bakhtin M M (1986) The problem of speech genres. In: *Speech Genres and Other Late Essays.* Austin: University of Texas Press, pp. 60–102.

Bamberg M (2004) Positioning with Davie Hogan. In: Daiute C and Lightfoot C (eds.) *Narrative Analysis: Studying the Development of Individuals in Society.* Thousand Oaks, CA: Sage Publications.

Barber B (ed.) (2009) *Adolescents and War: How Youth Deal with Political Violence.* New York: Oxford University Press.

Bonanno G L (2004) Loss, trauma, and human resilience. *American Psychologist* 59(1): 20–8.

Boyden J (2003) The moral development of child soldiers: what do adults have to fear? *Peace and Conflict: Journal of Peace Psychology* 9(4): 343–62.

Bruner J (1986) *Actual Minds, Possible Worlds.* Cambridge, MA: Harvard University Press.

Collier P (2003) *Breaking the Conflict Trap: Civil War and Development Policy.* Washington DC: The International Bank for Reconstruction and Development/The World Bank.

Daiute C (2008) The rights of children, the rights of nations: developmental theory and the politics of children's rights. *Journal of Social Issues* 64(4): 701–23.

(2010) *Human Development and Political Violence.* New York: Cambridge University Press.

Daiute C and Lucic L (2010) Situated cultural development among youth separated by war. *International Journal of Intercultural Relations* 34(6): 615–28.

Daiute C and Turniski M (2005) Young people's stories of conflict in post-war Croatia. *Narrative Inquiry* 15(2): 217–39.

de Berry J (2008) The challenges of programming with youth in Afghanistan. In: Hart J (ed.) *Years of Conflict: Adolescence, Political Violence and Displacement.* New York: Berghahn Books, pp. 209–29.

Edelstein W (2006). Extremist youth in Germany: the role of history, development, and cohort experience. In: Daiute C, Beykont Z, Higson-Smith C and Nucci L (eds.) *International Perspectives on Youth Conflict and Development.* New York: Oxford University Press, pp. 43–56.

Engestrom Y (2009) The future of activity theory: a rough draft. In: Sannino A, Daniels H and Guitierrez K (eds.) *Learning and Expanding with Activity Theory*. Cambridge University Press, pp. 303–28.

Freedman S W and Abazovic D (2006) Growing up during the Balkan wars of the 1990s. In: Daiute C, Beykont Z, Higson-Smith C and Nucci L (eds.) *International Perspectives on Youth Conflict and Development*. New York: Oxford University Press, pp. 57–72.

Freedman S W, Weinstein H M, Murphy K and Longman T (2008) Teaching history after identity-based conflicts: the Rwanda experience. *Comparative Education Review* 52(4): 663–90.

Goehring J (ed.) (2007) *Nations in Transit: Democratization from Central Europe to Eurasia*. New York: Freedom House.

Gutiérrez K, Baquedano-López P and Turner M (1997) Putting the language back into language arts: when the radical middle meets the third space. *Language Arts* 74(5): 368–78.

Hanson K, Darbellay F and Poretti M (2010) *Living Rights/Translations: An Interdisciplinary Bottom up Approach to the Study of International Children's Rights*. Sion, Switzerland: University Institute Kurt Bosch.

Harre R and Van Langenhove L (1999) *Positioning Theory: Moral Contexts of Intentional Action*. Malden, MA: Blackwell Publishers.

Hart J (2008) Children's participation and international development: attending to the political. *The International Journal of Children's Rights* 16(3): 407–18.

Hart R A (1997) *Children's Participation: The Theory and Practice of Including Young Citizens in Community Development and Environmental Care*. New York: UNICEF.

James A, Jenks C and Prout A (1998) *Theorizing Childhood*. Cambridge: Polity.

McMahon P (2009) *Much ado About Nothing? Civil Society and the NGO Embrace in Bosnia*. Paper presented at the Association for the Study of Nationalities (ASN) 2009 World Convention. Available at: www.nationalities.org (accessed 1 December 2011).

Middleton D (2004) Talking matters: studying the use of interdependencies of individual and collective action in youthful learning. In: Perret-Clermont A N, Pontecorvo C, Resnick R B, Zittoun T and Burge B (eds.) *Joining Society: Social Interaction and Learning in Adolescence and Youth*. Cambridge University Press, pp. 204–15.

Nelson K (2003) Narrative and self, myth and memory: emergence of the cultural self. In: Fivush R and Haden C (eds.) *The Development of Autobiographical Memory: Memory and Self-understanding*. Mahwah, NJ: Lawrence Erlbaum Associates, pp. 3–28.

Nieuwenhuys O (1994) *Children's Lifeworlds, Gender, Welfare, and Labour in the Developing World*. New York/London: Routledge.

Parish M (2010) State-building in post-war Bosnia: the legacy of failure. Paper presented the Harriman Institute, Columbia University Seminar Series: *Limited Sovereignty and Soft Borders in Southeastern Europe and the Former Soviet States: The Challenges and Political Consequences of Future Changes in Legal Status.* October 28.

Percy-Smith B (2006) From consultation to social learning in community participation with young people: creating 'spaces' for young people's participation in neighbourhood development using dialogue and social learning. *Children Youth and Environments*, 16(2): 153-179.

Perret-Clermont A N (2004) Thinking spaces of the young. In: Perret-Clermont A N, Pontecorvo C, Resnick R B, Zittoun T and Burge B (eds.) *Joining Society: Social Interaction and Learning in Adolescence and Youth.* Cambridge University Press, pp. 3–10.

Piaget J (1968) *Six Psychological Studies.* New York: W W Norton.

Saljo R (2004) From learning lessons to living knowledge: instructional discourse and life experiences of youth in complex society. In: Perret-Clermont A N, Pontecorvo C, Resnick R B, Zittoun T and Burge B (eds.) *Joining Society: Social Interaction and Learning in Adolescence and Youth.* Cambridge University Press, pp. 177–91.

Silber L and Little A (1995) *The Death of Yugoslavia.* London: BBC Press.

Sta Maria M A (2006) Paths to Filipino youth involvement in violent conflict. In: Daiute C, Beykont Z, Higson-Smith C and Nucci L (eds.) *International Perspectives on Youth Conflict and Development.* New York: Oxford University Press, pp. 29–42.

Summerfield D (1999). A critique of seven assumptions behind psychological trauma programmes in war-affected areas. *Social Science and Medicine* 48(10): 1449–62.

Taylor M and Percy-Smith B (2008) Children's participation: learning from and for community development. *The International Journal of Children's Rights* 16(3): 379–94.

Thomas N (2007) Towards a theory of children's participation. *The International Journal of Children's Rights*, 15(2): 199–218.

Tisdall E K M (2008) Is the honeymoon over? Children and young people's participation in public decision-making. *The International Journal of Children's Rights* 16(3): 419–29.

Tomasello M (2005) *Constructing a Language: A Usage-Based Theory of Language Acquisition.* Cambridge, MA: Harvard University Press.

Tudge J (2004) Practice and discourse as the intersection of individual and social in human development. In: Perret-Clermont A N, Pontecorvo C, Resnick R B, Zittoun T and Burge B (eds.) *Joining Society: Social Interaction and Learning in Adolescence and Youth.* Cambridge University Press, pp. 192–203.

Ukeje C (2006). Youth movements and youth violence in Nigeria's Oil Delta Region. In: Daiute C, Beykont Z, Higson-Smith C and Nucci L (eds.) *International Perspectives on Youth Conflict and Development*. New York: Oxford University Press, pp. 289–304.

Veresov N (2006) Leading activity in developmental psychology. *Journal of Russian and East European Psychology* 44(5): 7–25.

Vygotsky L S (1978) *Mind in Society*. Cambridge, MA: Harvard University Press.

Winnicott D W (2005) *Playing and Reality*. Oxford: Routledge Classics.

10

Inclusive universality and the child–caretaker dynamic

EVA BREMS

This chapter addresses conflicts between the rights of children and those of their caretakers with respect to their positioning vis-à-vis cultural or religious rules and practices. A model (legal) approach to deal with such conflicts is developed, in which the theory of inclusive universality is integrated, as well as the specifics of the children's rights approach. In the final section, the model is tested through its application to a number of hypothetical cases.

Human rights and cultural and religious diversity: inclusive universality

Human rights per definition claim universality, in the sense of worldwide and general applicability to all human beings. Yet the circumstances in which human beings live differ enormously from one part of the world to another. Human rights have roots in natural law; they attempt to capture a common human nature and to express universal conditions for human dignity. Human rights supposedly are context-neutral, yet at the same time they are man-made. Without doubting the good intentions of the drafters of human rights declarations, it is obvious that there is no such thing as an objective viewpoint from which to picture an abstract human being, and that the pretence of context-neutrality is an illusion. As the drafters of the 1948 Universal Declaration of Human Rights were predominantly white, well-off, adult Western men, the rights it protects are inevitably tailored more to the needs and aspirations of that group than to those of – relatively unknown – others. If the Universal Declaration, as the founding moment of the international human rights system, was inspired mainly by ethical concerns, human rights in their further development got caught up in the power relations characterizing international relations in general. At the level of standard setting, as well as at the levels of interpretation and application of human rights standards and in the context of determining human rights priorities, Western dominance in international power relations has often translated into a disproportionate Western influence in shaping international human rights.

Non-Western societies could not fail to react to this evolution. A critical discourse developed in several parts of the world, stating that international human rights are 'too Western', and demanding changes that take into account the reality of life in other societies. Both the dominance of human rights discourse and its potential as a tool to realize some of the goals of non-Western states and societies may explain why their diagnosis that human rights are 'too Western' does not generally lead to a rejection of the concept. Instead, the emphasis is on redefining, reinterpreting and reprioritizing. For this reason, it is not appropriate to label contemporary non-Western critiques of international human rights as 'cultural relativism'. This is because the term 'cultural relativism' denominates in the first place the position of anthropologists and philosophers who claim that moral values are necessarily relative, and that as a result it is not possible to use uniform criteria for judging human behaviour across a diversity of contexts, which means that universal norms are not desirable. Originally, 'cultural relativism' is the name of a school of anthropology that had its peak in the first of half of the twentieth century. While the United Nations Commission on Human Rights was drafting the Universal Declaration of Human Rights in 1947, a leading cultural relativist, Melville Herskovits, wrote a statement on behalf of the American Anthropological Association (1947), in which the whole idea of universal human rights was plainly rejected.

Although some of the arguments of cultural relativism can still be heard in contemporary discourse, the main debate today is a different one. Whereas the debate over 'cultural relativism versus universal human rights' took/takes place mainly among Western academics, this other debate is partly also academic, but is fought to an important degree in the political arena. The main difference, however, is that it is not a debate within the West about the theoretical possibility of universal human rights, but rather a debate between representatives of the West on the one hand and of non-Western societies on the other, about the modalities of universal human rights.

The main challengers in this debate are found in Southeast Asia, Sub-Saharan Africa and the Islamic world. While the Islamic critique is a genre of its own – addressing issues on which Islamic teachings conflict with human rights norms – the Asian and African critiques are remarkably similar as to the cultural particularities they invoke. The central theme is the rejection of the perceived overly individualistic character of human rights in favour of a focus on community. This leads to a support for collective rights and for restrictions of individual rights in the interest of the community, as well as for individual duties and responsibilities.

The reaction in the West and in the mainstream human rights community to non-Western particularist critiques of human rights is generally one of rejection. The critiques are seen as an attack on the universality principle and therefore as a threat to the basis of the international system of human rights protection.

I submit that this is a wrong reaction, as at least parts of the critiques are justified. In the view that I propose, the universality of human rights can be promoted better by attempting to accommodate some of the claims of non-Western societies in a flexible and dynamic human rights system than by rigidly defending the status quo.

Obviously, cultural and other particularist arguments are sometimes abused by authoritarian rulers with the sole purpose of avoiding or countering international scrutiny of their human rights record. Yet this does not do away with the fact that on the one hand international human rights have a strong Western flavour, and on the other the differences between life in the West and life in non-Western societies are real and manifold. It is hard to deny that a lot of the arguments that are put forward by academics, governments and other elites, who undoubtedly have their own agendas, nevertheless express real sentiments toward human rights that are widely shared in the societies concerned: many Africans do feel more at ease with communal concepts and consensus-based mechanisms than with individual rights, just as many Muslims are reluctant to accept human rights that contradict their religious duties.

In the literature a consensus is forming around the crucial insight that universal human rights can accommodate cultural and other contextual differences. It is not an either/or issue: we can promote universal human rights and respect diversity at the same time. Universality does not require uniformity. It is interesting to find that across academic disciplines similar conclusions are reached through different methodologies. A distinction can be made roughly between authors who have examined the issue in a top-down manner and others who have used a bottom-up approach. The former, mainly lawyers and political scientists, have taken international human rights standards and the international human rights protection system as a starting point and have argued that it is both desirable and feasible to integrate contextual diversity within them. Donnelly (1984), one of the leading voices in this debate, has long defended 'weak cultural relativism'. Recently he proposed the concept of 'relative universality of human rights' to express the view that 'universal human rights, properly understood, leave considerable space for national, regional, cultural particularity and other forms of diversity and relativity' (Donnely, 2007). Others (Cohen-Jonathan, 2003: 11; Delmas-Marty, 1998) prefer to talk about 'a pluralist conception of human rights', conceived as a combination of common leading principles with a national margin of appreciation in recognition of a right to be different.

At the same time, those examining human rights in action in the field – mainly anthropologists – have described how local communities instrumentalize and adapt human rights discourses, norms and procedures in their quest for justice and fairness, and have argued the value and legitimacy of such 'vernacularisation' (Merry, 1997: 29, 2006) or 'localisation' (De Feyter, 2006) of human rights. It is stated (Merry, 1997: 30) that 'human rights is an open text, capable of appropriation and redefinition by groups who are players in the global legal arena'. Goodale (2007: 22) has situated human rights 'between the global and the local', in an 'intentionally open conceptual space which can account for the way actors encounter the idea of human rights through the projection of the legal and moral imagination'. Hellum (1999: 96) has used the term 'cultural pluralism' to describe the space 'between universalism and relativism as well as individualism and communalism' where human rights and non-Western cultures can be reconciled.

Crucial learnings from anthropology have gradually been integrated into legal and political debates on human rights and cultural diversity. Their main point is that representations of culture as static and homogenous cannot hold. Anthropology (Merry, 2003: 67) uses a far more sophisticated and complex concept of culture:

> Over the last two decades, anthropology has elaborated a conception of culture as unbounded, contested, and connected to relations of power … Its boundaries are fluid, meanings are contested, and meaning is produced by institutional arrangements and political economy. Culture is marked by hybridity and creolization rather than uniformity or consistency. Local systems are analyzed in the context of national and transnational processes and are understood as the result of particular historical trajectories.

In this light, mainstream human rights views of culture as 'a barrier to the reformist project of universal human rights' (Merry, 2003: 72) soon reveal themselves as overly simplistic. Merry (2003: 72) has provided the vital insight that 'recognizing the extent to which the human rights project is itself a cultural one, and that it can build upon culture rather than only resist it, would foster its expansion and use by local activists'. Indeed, many in the mainstream human rights world have now come to the conclusion that the accommodation of cultural diversity is key to strengthening the universality of human rights as a real factor for the good in people's lives – as opposed to a mere theoretical construct. What is more, the continuing tension between the uniformizing tendencies inherent in universalism and the vocal – at times assertive or even aggressive – claims for contextualization and diversity need not be a cause for alarm or even be identified as a problem. Rather it should be seen (Cowan *et al.*, 2001: 6) 'as part of the continuous process of negotiating ever-changing and interrelated global and local norms'. Rather than bemoaning this tension, or trying to ignore it, human rights advocates must recognize it and deal with it.

In this context, the universality concept I propose is based on the central idea of the inclusion of all people in the human rights framework. This 'inclusive universality' goes beyond general and worldwide applicability of human rights standards. Underlying it is the recognition that human rights are not context-neutral, and that for that reason people who do not correspond to the implicit point of reference of human rights (a human being who is male and Western) experience a form of exclusion. The exclusion consists of the fact that when human rights standards are formulated or interpreted, and when human rights policies are determined, the needs, concerns and values of members of non-dominant groups are not taken into account to the same extent as those of the members of dominant groups. Inclusive universality proposes to remedy this situation by accommodating particularist claims from excluded people. The awareness that the 'abstract human being' does not exist and that neutrality and objectivity are impossible, even in human rights standards, leads to the recognition that equality of all human beings cannot be realized by consistently eliminating all context-related factors. Equality requires not only that similar situations be treated in the same way, but also that different situations be treated differently. Context matters. If human rights are to be universal in the sense that they apply in an equal manner to all human beings, they must take into account specific circumstances relevant to the lives of these human beings.

Thus, inclusive universality wants to close – or at least narrow – the gap between international human rights and non-Western societies. It proposes to make human rights more universal by making them more relevant for more people. Human rights have to be more open to cultural and other differences.

Yet this should not be a one-way effort. The efforts of the human rights system to become more receptive to differences among societies should be matched by efforts inside societies to make them more receptive to human rights. Respect for difference should not stand in the way of a critical view. Human rights have a revolutionary calling; they challenge the laws and practices of societies, even if these are long-standing. A commitment to human rights inherently entails a commitment to change certain laws and practices. For example, Article 5(1) of the Convention on the Elimination of All Forms of Discrimination against Women (CEDAW) obliges States Parties to 'take all appropriate measures to modify the social and cultural patterns of conduct of men and women, with a view to achieving the elimination of prejudices and customary and all other practices which are based on the idea of the inferiority or the superiority of either of the sexes or on stereotyped roles for men and women'.

Hence the gap between human rights standards and certain cultural practices or views has to be bridged by a simultaneous effort from both sides.

The fundamental commitment to inclusive universality, as well as the difficult balance between the necessity to change societies in the name of human rights and the need to change human rights in the name of the diversity of societies, must result from a dialogue among civilizations. Yet it is important to emphasize that both types of change are possible.

On the one hand, cultures and societies are dynamic and heterogeneous; they change constantly. Hence there is no inherent reason why changes that improve respect for human rights would threaten cultural integrity or other cherished aspects of a society's identity. How such changes are to be effected is in the first place a matter for internal debate within the relevant societies. It is crucial that societies allow for such a debate to be conducted freely, as well as for everybody to participate in it.

On the other hand, human rights can accommodate diversity without fear that this would undermine their integrity. As a lawyer and an outsider to non-Western cultures, I have focused in my work on this aspect. The fear that 'giving in to' non-Western critiques would undermine human rights can be easily undercut by pointing at two under-recognized qualities of international human rights: their flexibility and their dynamic character. Hence a lot can be realized in terms of the accommodation of diversity by simply using the possibilities that the legal framework of human rights already offers.

In the first place, and maybe contrary to popular intuition, there is an important degree of flexibility inherent in human rights standards. Flexibility may exist at the level of the formulation of standards: when human rights lists found in regional conventions or in national constitutions are compared, there are differences with regard to the inclusion of certain rights, as with regard to the level of detail at which rights are formulated and with regard to certain emphases in formulation. Yet besides these regional or local expressions of universal standards, we expect states also to subscribe to universal human rights instruments. It is therefore perhaps even more important to stress the flexibility that exists in the interpretation and implementation of universal standards. Flexibility is accepted amongst others in the interpretation of general concepts and in the balancing between competing interests. As a result, the application of the same rule leads to different outcomes in different contexts.[1]

In the second place, human rights are dynamic. Since the adoption of the Universal Declaration of Human Rights in 1948, the international human rights system has not stopped expanding in a myriad of directions. New instruments are being created, new control mechanisms are being devised, 'old' standards get new meaning through interpretation, and so on. Some of the more 'structural' claims of non-Western societies can be accommodated through transformations of the international human rights system. Examples of transformations that would respond to non-Western claims are the upgrading of economic, social and cultural rights, the recognition of more collective human rights and the recognition of human duties in addition to rights. With regard to each of these, there are sceptics who fear that these changes would undermine existing human rights.[2] However, it is perfectly feasible to avoid that risk in the manner in which the changes are effected. For example, duties do not threaten rights as long as it is clear that a duty should never replace a right, and that the enjoyment of a right should never be dependent on the performance of a duty.

An inclusive approach to human rights is also relevant at the national level, when dealing with cultural minorities. It requires a willingness of

[1] An example is the use of the so-called 'margin of appreciation doctrine'. See amongst others Schokkenbroek, 1998, as well as the other articles in this special issue of the *Human Rights Law Journal*; Yourow, 1996; Brems, 2003.

[2] E.g. with respect to the recognition of duties: Van Hoof, 1998; Koven, 1998; with respect to collective human rights: Donnelly, 1990; Haarscher, 1990; Graff, 1994.

the cultural majority to open up long-standing interpretations of fundamental rights to accommodate new claims. For example, if the dominant religion does not have any dietary rules, the accommodation of a minority religion that imposes such rules on its members requires new interpretations of religious freedom in its relation to other interests.

Children's rights and the child–caretaker dynamic

Claiming and proclaiming specific human rights texts and mechanisms for specific groups such as children, women or people with disabilities in response to claims of non-dominant groups, can be seen as another expression of inclusive universality. Indeed, children may rightly claim that the implicit image of the human being in 'human rights' corresponds to an adult human being, and therefore ignores some of the specific ways in which children experience a need for human rights protection (Brems, 2002/2007). The CRC corrects the adult bias of mainstream human rights amongst others through its choice of topics. These highlight issues that are not as such addressed in general human rights treaties, for example child abuse, child labour, child soldiers, adoption, right to play and so on. Moreover, the CRC includes rights corresponding to the broad spectrum of children's needs. In particular, these include not only protection rights, corresponding to the specific vulnerability of children, but also development rights – guiding children towards adulthood – and participation rights, recognizing children's capacity for autonomy.

Yet even more interesting is its development of a number of legal interpretation techniques designed to accommodate children's specificities. Developed in the context of the CRC and in the practice of its monitoring body, these techniques can easily be integrated into domestic legislative and judicial practice as well as into the argumentation of other international human rights bodies, thus accommodating children's specificities throughout human rights protection.

A prominent feature in this respect is the triangular relationship child–adult caretakers–state that replaces the binary individual–state relationship characterizing other human rights treaties. As stated in Article 5 CRC, adult caretakers have a responsibility, right and duty 'to provide, in a manner consistent with the evolving capacities of the child, appropriate direction and guidance in the exercise by the child' of its human rights. The first interpreters of a child's need with respect to human rights protection are therefore his or her adult caretakers. They assist the child in his or her claims (both positive and negative) toward the state authorities. These authorities have a secondary duty to provide assistance and structural arrangements facilitating the caretakers' task, as well as a responsibility to intervene when caretakers fail in their efforts or act against the child's interests. The principle of the 'evolving capacities of the child'[3] allows the translation into legal terms of an essential feature of childhood, that is a child's gradual and growing capacity for autonomy. It circumscribes the room for parental paternalism. While abandoning a young child to autonomously exercise his or her rights would be a shortcoming in a caretaker's protective duties, a refusal to make room for such autonomous exercise as the child grows up violates his or her participation rights.

In addition, the Committee on the Rights of the Child has upgraded four provisions of the CRC – Articles 2, 3(1), 6 and 12(1) – to the level of general principles, to be taken into account whenever CRC rights are being interpreted or applied.

Article 3(1) reads: 'In all actions concerning children, whether undertaken by public or private social welfare institutions, courts of law, administrative authorities or legislative bodies, the best interests of the child shall be a primary consideration.' Taken in the abstract, the 'best interests principle' does not offer any substantive guidance; what is in the best interests of a particular child or children in general in a particular situation will depend on the context. As a central yet indeterminate concept, the 'best interests principle' allows for the accommodation of cultural diversity in the context of inclusive universality. Cultural views and common societal practice may indeed – implicitly as well as explicitly – determine decisions as to what is or is not in a child's best interests. In the first place, the 'best interests principle' is a procedural requirement. Whenever children are concerned, explicit attention has to be paid to their interests in the course of the decision-making procedure. In many cases the best interests principle will be invoked together with one or more specific children's human rights provisions. When balanced against other interests, human rights carry a priori more weight, even though they will not always prevail in the end. The best interests principle may be seen as simply confirming this in the area of children's human rights – to the extent that human rights should always by definition be a primary consideration – and as extending this to cases where no specific human rights can be invoked by the child.

[3] On the adaptation of the content of CRC rules to the child's evolving capacities as a general rule of interpretation underpinning the entire Convention, see Van Bueren, 1995.

Article 12(1) is likewise a procedural principle: 'States Parties shall assure to the child who is capable of forming his or her own views the right to express those views freely in all matters affecting the child, the views of the child being given due weight in accordance with the age and maturity of the child.' Whenever children are concerned, they must be consulted. This provision is key to a bottom-up construction of children's rights. Applicable to norm-making procedures as well as to decision-making in individual cases, it opens up space for children to contribute in shaping their fundamental rights. When Article 3(1) is read together with Article 12(1), it transpires that the interpretation of what is or is not in the child's best interests cannot be undertaken by adults alone without consulting the children concerned (unless they are too young to express their views). While Article 12(1) does not give children a right to have their views prevail, the 'due weight' clause does offer them a guarantee that their views cannot be ignored. The consultation of children cannot be an empty formality; children's views have to be taken into account in the actual decision-making. The 'evolving capacities' principle plays a double role in this respect: in the first place, the exercise of the Article 12(1) right requires a capacity to express one's views; hence as long as a child does not possess this, it cannot enjoy this right. In addition, the weight to be accorded to the child's views grows according to the capacities of the child (Van Bueren, 1995).

Article 2 reaffirms the non-discrimination principle, which in fact functions as a general principle throughout human rights protection, and is therefore not as such characteristic of children's rights reasoning.

Finally, Article 6 focuses on the survival and development of the child. The duty to maximize children's survival and development opportunities functions as a guideline in particular in determining the required extent of a state's positive efforts in an environment of competing resource claims.

To the extent that human rights claims are made vis-à-vis state authorities, the protection of children's rights normally coincides with the protection of the rights and/or interests of the children's adult caretakers. For example when a state does not recognize education in a minority language, the parents – though not in need of education themselves – find their own interest in maintaining their cultural identity and transferring it to the next generation affected.

In the large majority of situations in which children's rights are relevant, caretakers support children in the exercise of their rights. Yet emancipation of non-dominant groups inevitably leads to conflicts with the rights of members of dominant groups. Emancipation of children occurs in the first place vis-à-vis their adult caretakers.

The loss of parental power through the recognition of children's rights can be illustrated by the comparison of Article 18(4) International Covenant on Civil and Political Rights (ICCPR) and Article 14(2) CRC. The former enshrines 'the liberty of parents and, when applicable, legal guardians to ensure the religious and moral education of their children in conformity with their own convictions', whereas the latter refers to 'the rights and duties of the parents and, when applicable, legal guardians, to provide direction to the child in the exercise of his or her right [to religious freedom] in a manner consistent with the evolving capacities of the child'. Between 1966 (the ICCPR) and 1989 (the CRC), parents have lost the right to determine the religious education of their children. They are left with an accessory right to support the child in the exercise of his or her own right. The child has been promoted from a passive beneficiary of a parental right to an autonomous rights bearer in this field. This implies the possibility for a child to invoke his or her religious freedom not only against the state authorities but also against his or her caretakers (see Brems, 2006). A child rejecting parental views on religious education or practice seems to find support for his or her dissident position in the CRC. As Article 14(2) only confirms the cross-cutting principle of Article 5 that restricts caretakers' roles as the child grows older, this issue may occur in many other fields as well.

The focus in this chapter is on conflicts between children and caretakers relating to their positioning vis-à-vis cultural or religious traditions. In some cases caretakers may want their children to embrace a dominant tradition or practice, whereas their child may want to opt out of it. In other cases caretakers may wish to opt out of a tradition that their child prefers to go through with. Such conflicts oppose the cultural or religious right of the child to the cultural or religious rights of the adult caretaker(s). Whereas the child's right concerns religious and cultural autonomy (the right to make one's own choices), the caretaker's right is of a different nature, concerning on the one hand the secondary right to support the child in the exercise of his or her religious freedom and on the other hand the caretaker's own right to teach one's religion to one's children, as well as rights concerning the communal aspects of religious and cultural rights: exercising one's religion in/with the family, and assuring the survival of a minority religion or culture.

As I contend in what follows, a model for approaching such conflicts starts from a general approach to competing human rights. As we are dealing with a field in which minority and majority cultures conflict, to this must be added a concern of inclusive universality. Finally, the specific interpretative tools of children's rights protection need to be integrated into the model.

Dealing with conflicting rights

Both the list of interests recognized as human rights and the number of individuals empowered to claim their rights have a tendency to continuously expand. Hence, situations multiply in which human rights claims compete against each other. While some of the most hotly contested contemporary human rights dilemmas concern conflicts between human rights, both legislators and judges resort to ad hoc solutions in approaching them. The main disadvantage of ad hoc solutions is their vulnerability to criticism of bias, which may result in failure to pacify the conflict. If a model approach for dealing with conflicting human rights could be developed, both legal certainty and the conflict reducing capacity of the law would be improved. This is the object of this section.

Three-step model

In my research (Brems, 2005, 2008) in this field, I have attempted to develop some initial guidelines for dealing with conflicting human rights. They are based on a three-step model. First, it has to be ascertained whether we are dealing with a real or 'fake' conflict. The latter have to be eliminated. If it is a real conflict, the preferred solution should be one of compromise between competing rights. One right should get priority over the other only when a compromise is not possible. In that case, criteria have to be developed on which to base prioritization.

Step 1: Eliminate fake conflicts

In some cases the conflict between fundamental rights is not a necessary feature of the issue concerned, but rather results from a particular approach to that issue. When a claim is made for the restriction of one human right in the name of the protection of another human right, it has to be examined whether it is possible to *avoid* the conflict between these two rights. Can a solution be found that leaves both rights intact? If this is the case, that solution will have to be preferred in most cases. An example in the context of criminal procedure is a legal provision attempting to realize the right to a trial within a reasonable time by imposing strict procedural time limits only on the accused and not on the prosecutor. This is a restriction of the accused person's right of equality of arms. Both the reasonable time requirement and the requirement of equality of arms are sub-rights of the right to a fair trial. The European Court of Human Rights in *Wynen* v. *Belgium* (2002)[4] held that the reasonable time objective can – and therefore should – be realized without impinging upon the equality of arms.

Step 2: Preference for compromise

Most of the time, however, it will not be possible to fully protect both rights, which means there is a 'real' conflict between human rights. In those cases it is important to avoid having to sacrifice one right for the sake of the other. By definition, each of the interests involved is considered particularly important, such that under normal circumstances it is given priority over other claims. Hence a solution that completely forsakes the protection of either one of the rights is undesirable. When both rights are put in the balance, the challenge is to find equilibrium, rather than making the balance tilt to one side or the other. Preference has to be given to a solution that does not subordinate one right to the other, but rather finds a compromise with concessions from both sides for the purpose of guaranteeing maximum protection of both rights.

Step 3: Criteria for prioritization

It seems inevitable that a substantial number of conflicts will not be susceptible to either elimination or compromise, and may only be solved by according priority to one right over the other. In this respect it is useful to inventorize relevant criteria that may guide this exercise. Some examples:

- A distinction between the core and the periphery within each right. In a conflict between rights A and B, it is possible that realizing A infringes upon the core of B, whereas realizing B would only infringe upon a peripheral zone of A, which would argue in favour of that solution. A related criterion is the severity of the interference caused by the exercise of one right in the exercise of the other and vice versa. If the exercise of the right is rendered utterly impossible, this will carry more weight than if it is 'only' made more difficult;

[4] European Court of Human Rights, *Wynen* v. *Belgium*, 5 November 2002, *Reports of Judgments and Decisions*, 2002-VIII.

- the indirect involvement of other rights, due to the involvement of third parties or to the 'leverage' effect of a particular right (e.g. the right to a fair trial acts as a lever for the enforcement of all other rights); if an infringement on right A indirectly results in infringements upon rights C and D, there is increased reason to avoid this infringement;
- the distinction between positive and negative obligations. Direct interferences by state authorities are more serious than shortcomings of the authorities in their obligation to fulfil rights.

Taking into account inclusive universality and children's rights

The above basic model can be improved and refined to adequately address the type of conflicts with which we are concerned, which involve cultural diversity on the one hand and children's rights on the other.

The best interests principle

The conflicts we are dealing with oppose a child's right to the right of his or her adult caretaker(s). The rule of Article 3(1) CRC claims that the best interests of the child should be a primary consideration. Hence, when looking for an appropriate compromise between conflicting rights, a solution that arguably fits the best interests of the child should be preferred. As mentioned earlier, this is mostly a procedural or formal requirement. As far as substance is concerned, the child may claim that his or her best interests are strongly related to his or her autonomy claim, whereas the caretakers may claim that it is in the best interests of the child to follow their guidance. At the same time as the child's best interests are required to be 'a primary consideration', rather than 'the primary or ultimate consideration', the criterion leaves room in principle for a solution that does not serve the child's best interests, even if this would require to be justified with very strong arguments. When no compromise is possible and prioritization is therefore required, each side will have to try and convincingly argue that their claim coincides with the child's best interests. I expect that in most cases both the child and the caretaker will be successful in this respect. Hence the only case in which the best interests criterion will have a substantive effect in a prioritization exercise is when the caretaker is arguing only on the basis of his or her own right to have the child conform to his or her wishes. In such a case the best interests argument will strengthen the child's claim without an equivalent strengthening of the caretaker's position.

Participation

As indicated above, the general principle of Article 12(1) CRC is a procedural guideline. That does not make it any less crucial. When general norms are made on issues that may oppose children and their caretakers with respect to their cultural or religious positions – for example a law determining the procedure to opt in or out of religious education in public schools, or a school rule on participation in school prayer – children have to be consulted in the course of the drafting procedure. Caretakers violate a child's right if they take a decision about a child's participation in a religious or cultural practice without first hearing the child's opinion. A mediator or court dealing with a case in which the right of a child conflicts with that of his or her caretaker will have to actively involve the child in its proceedings. This procedural requirement may affect the substantive outcome in the sense that a caretaker position will be weakened – in the negotiations toward a compromise or in the balancing exercise leading to prioritization of rights – when it has been reached without consultation of the child concerned, and will be strengthened to the extent that it has incorporated and given due weight to the child's views. Whenever children's participation is at stake, the adults in charge will have to show that they have taken the degree of maturity of the child into account and have given due weight to the child's views in accordance with that degree of maturity. When children of different ages are involved, differentiation in the degree or means of participation and in the weight accorded to the child's views is to be expected; where there is no differentiation, this will have to be justified.

Insider perspective

A methodological consequence of the choice for inclusive universality is the need to adopt an insider perspective: the perspective of the individuals who risk seeing their human right restricted if their claim does not prevail. Inclusive universality wants to correct distortions in human rights interpretation that have occurred by ignoring the views of non-dominant groups in shaping and applying human rights norms. This can only be done by taking seriously the views of the people concerned. In conflicting rights cases the insiders are obviously plural, but that does not do away with the necessity of interpreting cultural and religious rules, as well as the human suffering that is caused by their application or by their lack of application, through the eyes of the individuals concerned. In cases concerning religious or cultural rules or practices the risk of external paternalistic interpretations is a real one. This is the case in particular when minority groups are concerned, and when those making norms or dealing with a case of conflicting rights do not belong to that minority group. Anti-minority prejudice as well as plain ignorance may create obstacles to a fair approach. In addition to that, in the South a clash between rural and urban styles of living may interfere, with elites set on enlightening 'backward' peasants (see Droz, Chapter 6 in this volume). In this context, the concept of 'the best interests of the child' risks being abused, in the sense that the views of external individuals doing the interpreting may overpower both the child's and the caretaker's views of what is in the child's best interests. Paternalistic interventions set on 'liberating' children ignore the autonomy rights of caretakers as well as children and are therefore anti-emancipative.

The weight of the group

The insider perspective is conceived as an individual perspective, yet in the field under discussion the role of the cultural or religious community cannot be ignored. When children and their caretakers disagree on these issues, this usually implies that the child or the caretaker is dissenting – opting out of a community tradition – or that the child or caretaker is switching from one cultural or religious (sub-)community to another. The group may claim a right to cultural conformism of its members. In a conflict between the rights of two individuals, one side may thus be backed by a community while the other stands isolated. In my opinion, it would be wrong to a priori give more weight to the former. I submit that group rights derive their value from the meaning they present for individuals; in the cases we are concerned with here, the individual's position toward the group is precisely what is at stake: an autonomous position and a conformist position should a priori carry equal weight.

Yet there should be room for some contextual flexibility as 'Western' and 'non-Western' cultural traditions differ mainly on the importance they give to the interests of individuals versus those of communities. Most non-Western cultures value harmony and community and deplore the antagonistic assertion of individual claims that would characterize Western human rights debates. Community pressure can be a strong factor in some societies' everyday life. This cannot be ignored when looking for a compromise among conflicting rights or when balancing rights with a view to prioritization. Whereas in Western societies the mainstream or dissenting character of a child or caretaker's position might in principle be left out of the debate, taking it into account would be justifiable in more community-oriented societies. When a child dissents against strong community pressure, the age and maturity of the child will be a decisive factor. If the child is mature enough to understand the consequences of his or her position yet remains consistent in his or her position, this claim will carry a lot of weight. Yet for a younger child, in addition to his or her expressed preferences, the cultural context will have to be taken into account when identifying the best interests of the child. It may be that the child's best interests lie in cultural conformism in accordance with the wishes of his or her caretakers (Alston and Gilmour-Walsh, 1996; Armstrong, 1994; Rwezaura, 1994).

Cases

The proof of the pudding is in the eating – hence the following test of the model in a number of hypothetical cases. As in real life, most of these cases are not situated before a legal forum such as a court. This implies that it is not possible to impose any solution; the idea is rather to come up with an adequate proposal and persuade the parties to accept it. At first sight it may seem as if, rather than solutions that prioritize one right over the other, this would lead to solutions that reach a compromise between conflicting rights. Yet the human mind is more complex than that and persuading one of the two parties to give in may be easier than reaching a compromise. However, it should not be the weakest party (in terms of power relations, negotiation skills etc.) who gives in, but rather the one with the weakest claim.

The first two cases are situated in the northern hemisphere, and involve individual children whose cultural/religious rights claims conflict with those of their parents. The first of the cases that are situated in the South opposes a child to her caretakers, while the second concerns a collective claim of all the children in a village against their parents and caretakers. In this last case – the case of village Y – the collective dimension is most explicitly present, as a collective action of children directly threatens the cultural status quo in the community. Yet the communal dimension is an essential feature of the other cases as well. The case of Marie-Rose concerns a harmful cultural practice – denial of inheritance rights to females – that by its nature affects large numbers of individuals, yet only a few at the same time. If Marie-Rose wins her case in court, therefore, this will empower other girls in her situation to challenge the same cultural practice, which as a result will become untenable. The effect of an individual action would thus be the empowerment of a relatively disempowered segment within the cultural group. As we shall see, the cases of Malika and Ruben do not in the first place concern the issue of cultural change within a community, but rather allegiance to one community or another in a culturally pluralist setting. In both of these cases the autonomy claim of a child concerning one particular practice has wider implications, as it may imply a shift of allegiance of the child from one cultural group to another. In Ruben's case, complying with his demand would effectively require him to shift from the non-believing segment of Belgian society to the Catholic community. In Malika's case, her parents may fear that her decision to take off the hijab might be a first step away from the Muslim community in Germany to which she belongs.

Malika (Germany)

Malika is a 12-year-old Muslim girl. She attends a public school where around one-third of the pupils are Muslims. Some of the Muslim girls in school wear a hijab, others don't. Malika wears a hijab, just like her mother, because that is what her parents tell her to do. Malika is very much interested in religion and in expressions of cultural and religious diversity as she experiences them in her daily life. She has a lot of discussions about these with her school friends, and when teachers address these issues in class, Malika is an eager participant in debates. All this has led her to reflect on her own position vis-à-vis Islam. She is now certain that she never wants to have a boyfriend who is not Muslim, that she will never drink alcohol or eat pork (except in hotdogs, but that is not really meat, is it?), and that she will no longer wear a hijab. When she communicates the latter decision to her parents, they do not agree. They make her wear the hijab when she leaves home, but she takes it off as soon as she arrives in school. The parents blame the school for indoctrinating their child and for leading her away from her religion. The school's ombudsperson wants to address the issue from a human rights angle. Quid? [And what if it were the other way around: the girl wanting to wear the hijab against her parents' wishes?]

After hearing both parties, the ombudsperson will find that there is a conflict between Malika's right to religious freedom (Article 14(1) CRC) and her parents' right to provide direction to Malika in the exercise of her religious freedom (Article 14(2) CRC) and their liberty to ensure Malika the religious and moral education in conformity with their own convictions (Article 18(4) ICCPR). They disagree on the interpretation of Malika's best interests: according to Malika it is her best interest to make her own choices with respect to the different modalities of the exercise of her religion; according to her parents it is in living according to their interpretation of their religion at least as long as she lives at home. This is related to their disagreement with the interpretation of Malika's maturity: she claims she is old enough to make her own decisions in this matter, whereas they claim she is not and that she will probably later change her mind and regret her decision. This is not a fake conflict, yet it might be possible to solve it by way of a compromise. After a discussion that takes the views of both parties seriously, the parents may agree that Malika take off her hijab in school as long as she wears it on the street; or they may convene that Malika comply with her parents' wishes for the time being and if she still feels the same way in a year's time, her parents will lift their objections. Proposing a compromise should be the ombudsperson's first option. If it comes to prioritizing claims, it seems that Malika's claim is the stronger one. Despite her relatively young age, she is quite mature and has thoroughly reflected on her position. Hence her autonomy claim is quite strong. On the other hand, the parental claim is weakened by the fact that taking off the hijab is not an irreversible decision – she can decide to start wearing it again at any time. Moreover, while autonomous choice in matters such as religious dress is an important element in the exercise of religious freedom (as in other human rights), and this level of decision coincides rather well with what a 12-year-old can handle, it is arguably less essential in the exercise of the parental right to impose their choice in this field. The key issue for the girl is to define her own path as a believer and to live accordingly. The key issue for the parents is to teach their child the tenets of the religion; while they are disappointed that the child's choice in this matter does not coincide with their own, the core issue for them is that she remains a believer. Hence the issue touches upon a more crucial element of Malika's right than on that of her parents.

If the issue were the other way around, Malika wishing to wear a hijab against the wishes of her parents, that would not change the arguments to a decisive extent.

Ruben (Belgium)

Ruben is a 6-year-old boy. He attends a Catholic school. Catholic schools are very popular in Belgium and also attract many pupils who are not Catholic. According to Catholic rites, at age 6 or 7 children are allowed to receive the Holy Communion for the first time during Mass. This First Communion is a festive occasion. Children get new clothes, a big party and a lot of presents. During a whole term the schoolteacher

> prepares the children for the First Communion: they learn songs, they make drawings of Jesus and they listen to stories from the Children's Bible. In Ruben's class, out of twenty children, fifteen will have their First Communion in May. In February Ruben realises that he is not to be among them. His parents explain that they do not believe in God or Jesus, and that for that reason their children are not baptized. Ruben is very angry and insists that he wants to be a Catholic and have the Communion just like the other children in his class. Two months later, in April, he is still crying for this reason every day after school. Several parents of other children have spoken to Ruben's mother about this issue, claiming that she is violating her child's human rights. Ruben's mother, a UNICEF employee, is very sensitive to this argument. Quid? [And what if it were the other way around?]

In this case, a compromise is not possible. For Ruben to have his Holy Communion, he will have to be baptized first, which means that he will be initiated into the Catholic religion; in principle a baptism can be undone, but in practice that is very rare. His parents will, in that case, not only experience a strong restriction of their right to guide their child in the exercise of his religious freedom, they will in addition face a duty to guide him in the exercise of this freedom, which will involve supporting him in his exercise of the Catholic religion. Ruben is very young, arguably too young to autonomously make up his mind on an issue that concerns the essence of religious freedom: whether or not to join a particular cult. A serious discussion with Ruben on this issue may show that his real wish is to participate in school preparations for Holy Communion and to have a party. In that sense, we may be dealing with a fake conflict, that can be avoided by letting Ruben have a party (for this specific purpose, the organized non-religious community in Belgium has created 'Spring Parties') and letting him join the Catholic children in the preparation activities. If it is not a fake conflict because Ruben insists he wants to be a Catholic, in this case parents' rights should be prioritized. Ruben's claim is weakened because he is not sufficiently mature to make the choice he wants to make, and because he will have many other opportunities to make the same choice later on in life. The parents' claim is strong because of the irreversible nature of what Ruben wants, and because their duty to support their young child in the exercise of a religion they do not themselves adhere to, also affects also their own religious freedom.

In the opposite situation, the parental rights would also prevail. In that case Ruben would normally already be baptized yet refuse to take part in the Holy Communion. A discussion with the boy would have to point out the reasons. If these do not indicate a fake conflict, prioritization would favour the parents, since the Holy Communion in itself does not restrict the child's future choices with respect to religion, whereas not participating in the First Communion would strongly affect the parental rights with respect to their child's religion, and arguably even their own religious freedom, as they might argue that First Communion for children is part of the collective dimension of the exercise of their own religious freedom.

Marie-Rose (Democratic Republic of Congo)

> Marie-Rose is 14. After the death of her parents in a robbery, her relatives come in and divide the family property among her brothers and uncles according to customary rules. She is told that she will receive nothing because she is a girl. Her uncles say that from now on they will take care of her. She is afraid that will mean that she will become a maid in their household until they find her a husband. The sister of Marie-Rose's friend is a lawyer. She asks her advice.

As this case is about property, cultural rights enter only in second place from the child's perspective. In the first place the case opposes Marie-Rose's right to inherit (property right and right to protection of family life) and her right to protection against gender discrimination against the family's (including her guardians') rights to inherit and their right to live according to their cultural traditions. In the second place, Marie-Rose rejects the cultural traditions and wishes to change them or opt out of them because of their discriminatory character. She will claim that her best interests are not in becoming dependent on her uncles and future husband, but rather in having her share and making her own decisions. The adoption of an insider perspective requires that we do not reject African customs too easily. In this type of case, the South African Constitutional Court in 2004[5] pointed toward a solution that avoids the conflict: through a reinterpretation on the basis of the inherent dynamic character of customary law, it is possible to apply customary law that does

[5] Constitutional Court of South Africa, 15 October, 2004, *Bhè and Others* v. *Magistrate, Khayelitsha and Others* CCT49/03; *Shibi* v. *Sithole and Others* CCT69/03; *South African Human Rights Commission and Another* v. *President of the Republic of South Africa and Another* CCT50/03; CCT49/03; CCT69/03; CCT50/03.

not discriminate.[6] Hence Marie-Rose's rights would be compatible with the cultural rights of the family and the community. As this involves a reduction of the inheritance rights of the other family members, this solution is better qualified as a compromise than as one of identifying a fake conflict.

The boys from village Y (South Africa)

> *Ulwaluko* is a Xhosa male initiation rite, consisting of ritual circumcision, performed in 'initiation schools' where boys spend a few weeks in a hut in 'the bush'. Some of these initiation schools are illegal and unsafe, leading to the death of numerous young boys. Yet after the intervention of government regulation, in village Y all boys are sent to an initiation school that respects medical standards. Nevertheless, all thirty-six boys (aged 12–17) of village Y refuse to undergo the practice. They are afraid because of media stories of penile amputation as a result of badly performed circumcision, and they think the cultural rites surrounding the ritual are 'bullshit, old-fashioned stuff from the elderly, who think the New South Africa should look just like Africa before colonisation'. The adults in the village put a lot of pressure on the boys, and the boys consult a lawyer with the question: can our parents force us to undergo *ulwaluko*?

Gauging from the way this case is described, the practice is not harmful as such. Hence it concerns a conflict between the boys' right to opt out of a cultural practice and the right of the parents to initiate their children in their culture. The collective dimension cannot be ignored in this case. If all the boys of a generation refuse to be initiated into Xhosa traditions, these traditions will extinguish in that particular community. Hence the parental rights express also a group right of that community to keep Xhosa traditions alive. The establishment of legal and medical control over *ulwaluko* can be seen as a compromise that probably would suffice

[6] In the Bhè case, the Constitutional Court of South Africa stated that: 'Customary law has ... been distorted in a manner that emphasises its patriarchal features and minimises its communitarian ones' (§ 89). The Court finds that the rule of male primogeniture in heritance is incompatible with the prohibition of gender discrimination in the South African Constitution. However, this does not lead it to reject customary law. Instead, the Court emphasizes its positive features, amongst which its flexibility. However, in the South African context, while the circumstances of family life have changed strongly, customary law has not been able to keep pace; the amendment of customary rules by the Constitutional Court is thus not presented as a rejection of customary law, but rather as a contribution to its dynamic role of adaptation to new circumstances.

to overcome the objections of many boys who would otherwise opt out. It would be necessary to talk to each boy; the younger ones in particular may change their minds after adequate information. Yet if their objection persists based on the rejection of the cultural practice as such, prioritization would favour the claim of the boys. In addition to their cultural rights, their right to physical integrity is involved, and arguably also their protection against gender discrimination. On the parental/community side, the parental claim to guide the children in the exercise of their cultural rights is weakened because of the maturity of the children, whereas the community claim is weakened by the collective nature of the protest. As all or the majority of the boys of a generation join in the protest, it is clear that the community preference is shifting. In such a situation, the argument that the best interests of the child require cultural compliance loses ground.

Conclusion

Human rights are universal, yet in their interpretation and implementation there is significant room for cultural diversity. Moreover, cultural and religious rights are included within the international human rights protection system. When children mobilize their human rights to engage in action for the realization of their conceptions of social justice, this may involve choices in the field of culture and religion. The recognition of children as autonomous rights-bearers empowers children to opt in or out of cultural or religious rules and practices, to shift allegiance from one cultural community to another, and through their individual or collective action to challenge the cultural status quo in the family or the community.

This chapter has focused on situations in which children's choices in the realm of cultural and religious practices conflict with those that their parents make on their behalf. As both children and parents can rely on human rights, such situations involve conflicting or competing human rights. Adopting the legal approach, this chapter has worked on the basis of a general three-step model that allows us to deal with conflicting rights, enriched with the concept of inclusive universality on the one hand, and of the specificities of children's rights on the other, with a number of essential procedural requirements. The resulting model, tailored to address conflicts between the human rights of children and those of their caretakers concerning their respective positioning vis-à-vis cultural and religious rules and practices, has been tested through its application to a number of hypothetical cases. The test shows that the model makes room for a broad range of considerations both at the individual as well as the group level and can serve as a framework for addressing cases of conflict between the rights of children and those of their caretakers with respect to their positioning vis-à-vis cultural or religious rules and practices.

References

Alston P and Gilmour-Walsh B (1996) *The Best Interests of the Child. Towards a Synthesis of Children's Rights and Cultural Values*. Report, UNICEF ICDC, Florence.

American Anthropological Association (1947) Statement on Human Rights. *American Anthropologist* 49(4): 539–43. Reprinted in: Winston M E (ed.) (1989) *The Philosophy of Human Rights*. Belmont: Wadsworth, pp. 116–20.

Armstrong A (1994) School and sadza: custody and the best interest of the child in Zimbabwe. In: Alston P (ed.) *The Best Interests of the Child. Reconciling Culture and Human Rights*. Oxford: Clarendon Press/UNICEF.

Brems E (2002/2007) Children's rights and universality. In: Willems J C M (ed.) *Developmental and Autonomy Rights of Children. Empowering Children, Caregivers and Communities*. Antwerp/Oxford/New York: Intersentia, (2002) pp. 21–45 and (2007) pp. 11–37.

(2003) The margin of appreciation doctrine of the European Court of Human Rights: accommodating diversity within Europe. In: Forsythe D P and McMahon P C (eds.) *Human Rights and Diversity: Area Studies Revisited*. Lincoln/London: University of Nebraska Press, pp. 81–110.

(2005) Conflicting human rights: an exploration in the context of the right to a fair trial in the European Convention for the Protection of Human Rights and Fundamental Freedoms. *Human Rights Quarterly* 27(1): 294–326.

(2006) Article 14. The right to freedom of thought, conscience and religion. In: Alen A *et al.* (eds.) *Series: A Commentary on the United Nations Convention on the Rights of the Child*. The Hague/Boston/London: Martinus Nijhoff Publishers.

(2008) Introduction. In: Brems E (ed.) *Conflicts Between Fundamental Rights*. Antwerp/Oxford/New York: Intersentia, pp. 1–16.

Cohen-Jonathan G (2003) Universalité et singularité des droits de l'homme. *Revue Trimestrielle des Droits de l'Homme* 53: 3–13.

Cowan J K, Dembour M B and Wilson R A (2001) Introduction. In: Cowan J K, Dembour M B and Wilson R A (eds.) *Culture and Rights: Anthropological Perspectives*. Cambridge University Press.

De Feyter K (2006) *Localizing Human Rights*. Institute of Development Policy and Management, Antwerp University. Available at: www.ua.ac.be/objs/00152976.pdf (accessed 15 January 2012).

Delmas-Marty M (1998) De la juste dénomination des droits de l'homme. *Droit et Cultures* 35: 105–16.

Donnelly J (1984) Cultural relativism and universal human rights. *Human Rights Quarterly* 6(4): 400–19.

(1990) Human rights, individual rights and collective rights. In: Berting J *et al.* (eds.) *Human Rights in a Pluralist World. Individuals and Collectivities*. London: Meckler.

(2007) The relative universality of human rights. *Human Rights Quarterly* 29(2): 281–306.

Goodale M (2007) Locating rights, envisioning law between the global and the local. In: Goodale M and Merry S E (eds.) *The Practice of Human Rights: Tracking Law Between the Global and the Local*. Cambridge University Press.

Graff J A (1994) Human rights, peoples, and the right to self-determination. In: Baker J (ed.) *Group Rights*. University of Toronto Press.

Haarscher G (1990) Les droits collectifs contre les droits de l'homme. *Revue Trimestrielle des Droits de l'Homme* 3: 233–4.

Hellum A (1999) Women's human rights and African customary laws: between universalism and relativism – individualism and communitarianism. In: Lund C (ed.) *Development and Rights: Negotiating Justice in Changing Societies*. London: Routledge.

Koven R (1998) Diluting a declaration of universal rights. *International Herald Tribune*, 28 January.

Merry S E (1997) Legal pluralism and transnational culture: the Ka Ho'okolokolonui Kanaka Maoli Tribunal, Hawai'i, 1993. In: Wilson R (ed.) *Human Rights, Culture & Context. Anthropological Perspectives*. London: Pluto Press.

(2003) Human rights law and the demonization of culture (and anthropology along the way). *Political and Legal Anthropology Review* 26(1): 55–85.

(2006) Transnational human rights and local activism: mapping the middle. *American Anthropology* 108(1): 38–51.

Rwezaura B (1994) The concept of the child's best interests in the changing economic and social context of Sub-Saharan Africa. In: Alston P (ed.) *The Best Interests of the Child. Reconciling Culture and Human Rights*. Oxford: Clarendon Press/UNICEF.

Schokkenbroek J (1998) The basis, nature and application of the margin-of-appreciation doctrine in the case-law of the European Court of Human Rights. *Human Rights Law Journal* 19(1): 30–36.

Van Bueren G (1995) *The International Law on the Rights of the Child*. The Hague/Boston/London: Martinus Nijhoff Publishers.

Van Hoof F (1998) A universal declaration of human responsibilities: far-sighted or flawed? In: Bulterman M, Hendriks A and Smith J (eds.) *To Baehr in Our Minds. Essays on Human Rights from the Heart of the Netherlands.* Utrecht: Studie- en informatiecentrum mensenrechten, SIM Special No. 21, pp. 57–62.

Yourow H C (1996) *The Margin of Appreciation Doctrine in the Dynamics of European Human Rights Jurisprudence.* The Hague/Boston/London: Martinus Nijhoff Publishers.

11

Do children have a right to work? Working children's movements in the struggle for social justice

MANFRED LIEBEL

Introduction

The UN Convention on the Rights of the Child (CRC) confers upon children the right to protection from economic exploitation. This guarantee for protection is often understood as the obligation to prevent situations in which children have to work. In this sense the prohibition of child labour – for example in the International Labour Organization's (ILO) conventions or national legislation – is being understood as the manifestation of a specific human right of the child, whose implementation is a prerequisite to the realization of other children's rights, such as the right to education. Such interpretations tacitly assume that children's work called child labour is synonymous to exploitation. What is more, they suggest that the prohibition of child labour and subsequent enforcement measures serve the interests of working children by putting an end to their exploitation. In this way the right to be protected from economic exploitation is reinterpreted to mean the (alleged) right to be 'free of child labour'.

In opposition to this interpretation, working children's organizations claim the 'right to work'. This does not mean that any person has the right to demand that a child works, nor that children have to be guaranteed employment. As opposed to the right to employment, the right to work is understood as an individual child's right to freely decide whether, where, how and for how long they would like to work. It goes beyond employment under the regime and dependency of an employer in a capitalist economy as well as beyond all kinds of economic activities outside the 'official' labour market (e.g. in the informal economy or private households) that children are obliged to carry out by persons who have power over them. The *raison d'être* of the claim is to broaden children's scope for decision-making and to strengthen their social roles as acting subjects. It challenges the dominant legal conception that children's rights are first and foremost the rights of adults to set a framework that fosters children's best interests (see Liebel, 2012). Likewise, it opposes a conception of child protection that relies on exclusion measures and prohibitions to prevent children's exposure to exploitation.

The chapter is based on my work as a consultant and researcher of the working children's movements and organizations that came into being first at the end of the 1970s in Latin America and later from the beginning of the 1990s in Africa and Asia as well. These movements developed from small informal mutual aid groups of children, but also from initiatives of young people and adults[1] who encourage children to claim their rights themselves. Activists in these children's organizations are usually between 12 and 18 years old and work in the informal urban economy. The working children's movements are both acting and learning environments in which children take decisions and have the final say. This is where children find and develop their own social spaces and age-specific forms of communication by which they can better understand their situation, search for solutions to their problems and develop their identity. As a general rule the children ask adults for support and they are usually dependent on this help. Usually the adults do not play a leading role but act as consultants to the children.[2]

This chapter examines how the children in these movements understand and claim the right to work. The study is based on statements by the working children's organizations mentioned above in the period from 1988 to 2008. I take these statements as expressions of the collective will of working children, derived from active reflection on their life situation and work experience. The analysed documents contain both explicit and implicit messages, which I will discuss while highlighting the issues that arise concerning children's right to work. After describing in which specific ways the demand for this right arose in the working children's movements of each continent, I explain how this claim became part of the worldwide movement. In the subsequent sections I take a more analytic view and discuss why the right to work can be understood as a living

[1] In most cases, NGOs working on children's rights or which centre their social and educational work in children's participation and self-organisation encourage these projects.

[2] On the development and structure of these movements and the role of adult co-workers see the articles in Liebel *et al.*, 2001.

right and can contribute to the realization of social justice. Finally, I ask where and in which way, until recently, the claim for the right to work has become reality.

Talking about the right to work in Latin America, Africa and Asia

The attitudes and mindsets that crystallize in the claim to a right to work are common among working children, but have not ceased to surprise researchers working on child labour.[3] When children are given the opportunity to comment on their work and their attitude to work, most of them show a positive attitude towards the fact that they are working. Others comment that they would like to work if presented with a reason or an opportunity to do so. It is remarkable that children always attach certain images and expectations to work.

When children talk about their notions of work, they do not necessarily refer to work openly. Many times they talk about how they would like to earn money, be helpful, support their families or gather experience in the 'adult world'. Before children can start to view their own activities as work and to distinguish between work and working conditions, they have to rid themselves of the predominant notion that what children do is not work, that it is 'unseemly' for children to work, or that children 'help' at most. In order to claim a right to work, children have to reflect upon their work, develop their own concept of it and, most importantly, they have to learn how to express themselves in the 'language of the law'. This is why it is no coincidence that this claim is mainly voiced by children who are already organized. They are living in a context where joined reflection processes take place and they can develop new competences to analyse their own situation, to understand their own interests and rights and to formulate their own views and wishes. In this section I explain the way in which the claim for the right to work developed in the movements of the different continents and how it is understood by the children.

In Latin America the claim to a right to work developed during the 1980s. The Peruvian children's movement MANTHOC[4] was the first to campaign for more acceptance and appreciation for the work children are doing and to fight for an improvement in their working conditions. A

[3] Evidence can be found in Boyden *et al.*, 1997; Liebel, 2004; Hungerland *et al.*, 2007; Bourdillon *et al.*, 2010.

[4] Movimiento de Adolescentes y Niños Trabajadores Hijos de Obreros Cristianos.

major step was the founding meeting of the Latin American children's movement in the Peruvian capital Lima in 1988. In an 'outcry' the delegates lamented:[5]

> Some of us have to steal or beg, because we cannot work. If we work we receive bad pay, we are chased from the squares and markets, because they do not want us to steal. How can we make our living? We don't want to be chased from our work places only to be called dodgers later on. We girls are not given employment. We are being exploited as objects of sexual desire. We have to run away when the police come. Many times, we work till late at night, and then it is dangerous for us to be out on the streets. We know that many girls from the countryside are working in rich people's households. They are told that these people are their godparents and things like this. They promise these girls that they can go to school. But the rich people do not keep their promise and they mistreat the girls. It is difficult to reach out to these girls so that they can organize themselves.

During the meeting the right to work was not made explicit, rather the wish to have a free choice to work and to have better working conditions, for example better pay, a more favourable treatment and the possibility to go to school, being emphasized. The claim was only made explicit during the 6th Latin American meeting, which took place in Asunción, Paraguay in 2001. The delegates stated that work dignifies people and is 'a form of cognitive apprenticeship and a source of education and family income'. Children should work in dignity and under good conditions, their right to work should be recognized, but at the same time there should be no obligation to work, their work should be protected and regulated by national law and it should not be discriminatory or exploitative. The delegates demanded the creation of workshops for children, free-of-charge apprenticeships for further qualification imparted by qualified teachers, and an education that leaves room for 'protagonism'.[6] In addition they demanded a good health care system. School education is not seen as good and positive in itself, but should meet minimal conditions, just as work should. Seven years later, in March 2008, the 7th Latin American meeting in Cachipay (Colombia) emphasized the need for policy measures which:

> alleviate poverty and improve our working conditions as well as fighting social exclusion and violence against children, especially working children. We lobby for the right of children to work in dignity and we defend

[5] This and the following documents originally in Spanish or French were translated or existing translations were revised by the author.

[6] On protagonism see Liebel, 2007; Liebel *et al.*, 2001.

> this work. For us, work is one of many mediums to foster children's active participation ... We are the most important actors in the improvement of our living and working conditions. This is why we fight for alternatives in worthy work and better possibilities to further qualifications and active participation by children.

This is the first occasion on which a 'solidarity economy' is being highlighted as the basis of improved living conditions, 'which we ourselves, as working children, have to develop and practice'. When the Latin American working children's movements talk of *economía de solidaridad* or *economía solidaria*, they refer to small enterprises that are based on principles of mutual help and solidarity, and are managed by the children themselves (see Liebel, 2006: 227–53; Schibotto, 2009). In most cases these companies are organized as cooperatives (though usually not in terms of their legal form), where consumer goods for the neighbourhood (such as furniture, soap, bread and other foods) or for tourists (such as jewellery and candles) – sometimes even for export (such as greeting cards, handicraft products) – are produced. Sometimes the children work together with family members or other adults from their neighbourhood (e.g. transport service from marketplaces to households and public houses) or they pursue a type of tourism by showing visitors and tourists hidden locations of their region and by allowing them to participate in their everyday life (e.g. by providing alternative hostels administered by children and youth). Sporadically, banks and microcredit funds have been founded, which are managed by or with the assistance of children. Most small-scale enterprises of that kind emerge from associations of working children or on the initiative and with the support of child aid foundations (NGOs) or neighbourhood associations. These enterprises are understood as collective attempts to replace types of labour that are based on exploitation by other forms of work that ensure the ethical maxims of solidarity, respect and dignity. In that way, elements of economic practice emerge that allow children to work under largely self-determined circumstances to make a living. They manage their working conditions and time in a way that allows them to visit schools, to relax or to participate in the activities of child aid organizations. Some enterprises founded by children or adolescents are purposefully associated with educational facilities and training programmes where learning and working are reciprocally connected. Such forms of economy are not only created by working children's movements in Latin America, but in Africa and Asia as well.

The African Movement of Working Children and Youth, in its funding document ('12 Rights') adopted in Bouaké (Ivory Coast) in 1994 (see

ENDA, 2001), postulated the 'right to light and limited work'. The document reads:

> When we take up the work, we negotiate the type of work that is appropriate to our age, but this agreement is never respected. There are no fixed hours, we start early and finish late. We ask that we not be given hours of work and tasks that you would not ask your own children to do.

The right postulated is closely related to other rights such as the 'right to security when working', which is explained in the following manner: 'To work without being harassed by the authorities and people in general (not to be man-mistreated, but be trusted).' Other rights relevant to the right to work which are stated in the document are 'to respect', 'to rest when sick', 'to health care', 'to be taught a trade', 'to play' and 'to learn to read and write'. The African children's movement holds that these rights are interrelated and mutually supportive. In the words of the final declaration of the 6th Meeting of the African children's movement, which took place in Thiès (Senegal) in 2003:

> For nine years now, we have been organized in order to build and implement our rights to education, vocational training, health care, respect, dignity, safety, organization, equitable justice, return to our villages, leisure, light and limited work.

In addition the declaration stresses that the 'implementation of our rights' includes fighting against poverty and for 'income-generating activities'. The aim is 'for our work to gain dignity and for exploitation to be eradicated'. Alluding to the ILO's Convention 182 (1999), the document points out:

> We are fighting against the worst forms of child labour, which lead to exploitation and to very hard and dangerous work. We totally condemn child labour trade through trafficking. We are fighting against this trade. This fight will be taken further.

Three years later, during the 7th Meeting in Ouagadougou (Burkina Faso), the interrelatedness of the proclaimed rights is underlined with the following words:

> Wherever we are organized, our rights have progressed, such as the right to learn to read and write, to cure ourselves in case of illness, to work less hard … The development of our Income Generating Activities (IGA) is enabling us to struggle against poverty and to fund our rights. We have begun struggling against exploitation, violence, early migration with good results, but we are training ourselves in order to develop this indispensable activity so that African children will never continue to be victims.

From Asia as a whole there are few statements of working children's organizations. The children's movements are based in individual countries or regions inside these countries. International networking is still in its beginnings. Where the organizations exist, for example in India, they insist on the necessity to fight against discriminating and exploitative labour conditions. This is in parallel to early developments in Latin America. A regional meeting of children's movements from South and Central Asia, which took place in Kathmandu (Nepal) in 2005, formulated for instance:

> We believe that we need to come out of the hazardous working situations by means of appropriate alternatives such as respectful, paid work with minimum wage, standard and equal opportunity of quality education without discrimination.

Besides poverty, 'low quality education, violence and humiliation at schools' is held responsible when children 'drop out of school and get involved in hazardous work'. About their work experiences the delegates mentioned both positive and negative aspects:

> Amongst the good things that work brings for us is that we work to meet our livelihood and survival needs, meet health support for self and family. Sometimes the work we do gives us the skills and training. By working we learn to cope with the challenges and hostility. Work also gives us self-dignity, feelings of solidarity, we take pride in resolving some of our family problems, for example, repayment of loans taken by our parents. At the same time we found many painful experiences which are part of our working life and which are common to all working children in South and Central Asia. Our friends here shared some of those experiences. Many of us are involved in hazardous work, many of us are at risk of meeting serious accidents and amputations. We are compelled to be engaged in hazardous work because sometimes it brings more money to meet out extreme poverty and other times because no other options are available. Working children all over South and Central Asia are more exposed to being misled by drugs, gambling, exposed to sexual abuse and abuse by adult employers. Street children face typical street hazards such as being at the risk of false accusation of theft. Employers never look at the cause of why children have to work. On top of this, economic exploitation; discrimination including gender discrimination, physical, sexual and mental torture and exploitation; and feelings of insecurity are common in South and Central Asia.

The delegates did not claim a right to work, but they criticized existing laws and contended that the prohibition of child labour ignores the real conditions in which children work and was adopted without children's participation:

> Although there are laws and acts on children and child labour existing in many countries in South and Central Asia, these are not always congenial towards children. We are never consulted while formulating laws and policies although we know best about the problems we face. In particular, children from the so-called 'untouchable' caste, who comprise the majority of the working children, face extreme discrimination. The laws are also not accessible to the uneducated community and some members of the law-enforcing agencies are not aware of the law.

Children's movements from these three continents concur in asserting that child labour should not be generally banned under all circumstances. On the contrary, they stipulate that exploitation and ignoble conditions should be counteracted by improving work conditions. But there are differences in the priorities they set as well. The African and Asian children's movements stress the importance of action against 'hazardous work' and, especially in Africa, of fighting child trafficking. Only the African and Latin American movements claim an explicit right to work. While in Africa this claim refers to 'light and limited' work, in Latin America the right to 'work in dignity' is given priority, which raises the question whether these specifications should be implemented by imposing age restrictions or through a restructuring of labour conditions. I come back to this question in 'Some achievements and challenges' below. In what follows, I first describe the process in which the right to work became one of the fundamental and common claims of the worldwide emerging network of the working children's movements.

Towards a worldwide working children's movement

Since the mid 1990s the different children's movements from the three continents have been working on establishing international networks. Their aim is to form a 'world movement' of working children. During these past years a number of meetings have taken place at which delegates of the different movements tried to formulate common positions. From the statements published at the end of these meetings, one can gather whether the claim to a right to work, put forward first in Latin America and then in Africa, has been adopted by all children's movements, in which way they interpret it and how they judge this right.

A first manifestation of international networking was a meeting held in the Southern Indian town of Kundapur in 1996, where elected delegates from thirty-three countries took part. The final declaration of the meeting (see for a detailed interpretation Bonnet, 2006) is not formulated in legal language but states in simple words what children *want* and *do not want*. Since it is the first intercontinental position paper and is seen as a declaration of basic principles by all movements, I reproduce it here:

- We want recognition for our initiatives, suggestions and organization processes.
- We are against the boycott of products made by children.
- We want respect and safety for our work.
- We want an education with methods adequate to our situation.
- We want professional training suited for our context.
- We want to have access to good health systems.
- We want to be consulted for any decision that affects us, whether local, national or international.
- We want a fight to be initiated against the reasons that are at the origin of our situation and first of all poverty.
- We want more initiatives in rural areas so that children do not have to go to the city.
- We are against the exploitation of our labour, but we are in favour of a dignifying job with a schedule suited for our education and spare time.[7]

Two smaller, rather informal meetings ('Mini-Summits') followed. The first one was held in Huampaní (Peru) in 1997, the second one took place in Dakar (Senegal) in 1998. Unlike Kundapur, these summits stipulated the *right to work*. Ascertaining that 'work dignifies the human being', the declaration of Huampaní stipulates a right to work under humane conditions and the recognition of working children as persons 'who contribute economically, socially and culturally to society'. The delegates demand to eradicate 'the deep roots of poverty and the poverty itself, the debt, the sanctions rich countries impose upon poor countries, unemployment and corruption'. The children say that they are willing to fight for better working and living conditions and for their rights, namely the rights to 'good and free education, health care, freedom to get together and share our actions'. The 'Mini-Summit' of Dakar concludes: 'We want all the world's children to be able one day to decide whether to work or not.' This claim is specified in two ways: the work children do should be adequate to the individual child's abilities and development and – in obvious contrast

[7] A final demand stipulated in the declaration is: 'For the next meetings to be held from now on, we want to be present at the same level as other participants (if 20 ministers, then 20 working children).'

to ILO Convention 138 – there should be no fixed age limit to children's right to work.[8] With a view to the imminent adoption of ILO Convention 182 and its definition of 'worst forms of child labour', the delegates insist that a difference be made between the work of children and crimes against children.[9]

On the occasion of the 2nd World Meeting,[10] which took place in Berlin in 2004 – for the first time ever in a European city – the thoughts formulated in the Huampaní and Dakar declarations were elaborated upon and specified. The delegates declared:

> We value our work and view it as an important human right for our personal development. We oppose every kind of exploitation and reject everything that hurts our physical and moral integrity. In our lives our work allows us to resist with dignity the economic, political and suppressing model that criminalizes and excludes us and continues to worsen the living conditions of ourselves, our families and our communities … Furthermore, we create forms of dignified work deriving from our organizations that make it possible for us to show society just and political, economic and social relationships based on solidarity.

Again the delegates stress the importance of fighting against the causes of poverty and 'for the full recognition of our rights and our cultural and ethic values'. The 'current neo-liberal system' was being accused of bringing poverty to the countries of the South and of privatizing basic services such as health care, education and recreation. In addition, multinational corporations were accused of 'viewing children only as consumers, not as living spirits and transformers of society'. With reference to the International Labour Organization (ILO) the congress rejected any policy 'that promotes the abolition of children's work' and 'undermines our dignity as working children and jeopardizes our rights'. The 3rd World Meeting, which took place in Sienna (Italy) in October 2006, reinforced this position using the following words:

> Through our World Movement, we are committed to promoting our rights, developing actions aimed at reducing poverty, and improving

[8] The minimum age legislation on child labour was recently questioned by Bourdillon *et al.*, 2009: 106–17; see also Chapter 12 by Hanson and Vandaele in this volume.

[9] The ILO Convention 182 – adopted in 1999 – did not take up this claim. Child trafficking, forced recruitment in armed conflicts, forced prostitution and child pornography and the use of children for drug production and drug trafficking were stated as forms of child labour against the express will of the children's movements.

[10] The 1st World Meeting was that of Kundapur, which, originally, was called 'International Meeting'.

> our working conditions; we are committed to fighting against child trafficking and exclusion, and also against violence perpetrated against children – and working children in particular. We promote and defend the dignified work of children. We are the main actors in changing our working and living conditions.

The following announcement was new: 'We have decided to create a label of protection for the products that we produce.'

The declarations made during the three world meetings and the two mini-summits intimate that since the middle of the 1990s common goals and demands have developed across continents and cultures. I know from my own experience with these meetings that it was not always easy to agree upon the wording. During the world meeting in Berlin a heated discussion ensued between the Latin American and African delegates as to whether collaboration with the ILO makes sense and in what manner criticism against the ILO's child labour policies should be expressed. A number of Asian delegates advocated a stronger focus on brutal forms of exploitation and abuse against working children. They were doubtful as to the possibility of creating dignified employment opportunities for working children. Translation of official documents proved to be problematic because of culture-specific interpretations of certain key words and phrases.[11] These controversies and communication difficulties reflect differences in living and working conditions but also different forms of communication and modes of interaction. In addition, the children's movements were founded under distinct conditions and have diverse historical backgrounds. Their positions reflect their diverse experiences. Despite differences in opinion and misunderstandings, the delegates always found ways of compromising and reaching final consensus. In Berlin they agreed to respect differences and concentrate on shared convictions instead.

Comparing the different declarations the notion of *rights* is arguably increasingly used to legitimize and emphasize wishes and demands. The claim to a right to work in the meantime unites all working children's movements. The terms 'dignified work' and 'work under human conditions' have been established as common points of reference. Neither of these terms should be understood as a restriction, limiting the right to work to certain 'child-friendly' activities or labour conditions but as a stance in favour of improving working conditions and guaranteeing

[11] The final declarations of all world meetings were drawn up in English, Spanish, French and, in some cases, also in Portuguese.

future employment relationships. As a means to realize these positive labour relations, mention is increasingly made to the need for fundamental and comprehensive changes that challenge dependency and inequality in the global economic context.

From the Berlin world meeting onwards, the demand on society and the state to provide for dignified working conditions has been supplemented by references to initiatives and 'projects' for dignified work that the children's movements have been undertaking. What the African children's movement used to call 'income-generating activities' is increasingly now realized through the starting of production workshops and cooperatives inspired by the ideas of an economy based on principles of solidarity (see the previous section). At the Sienna meeting, these initiatives inspire for the first time the idea of a label of approval for products of workshops where children produce goods for export. The label is conceived as a project organized and supervised by the children's movements themselves. It should certify dignified work, self-determined by the children. The label is a practical positive alternative to the boycotting measures against products containing child labour, already rejected in the Kundapur declaration, because they hurt children. But is the right to work to be understood as a *living right*? Would its realization contribute to social justice? What achievements can be observed so far? It is to these questions that I now turn in the following sections.

A living right

In contrast to the right to be protected from economic exploitation – codified in Article 32 of the UN Convention on the Rights of the Child – the right to work is a claim put forward by *children* themselves. The demand is a result of working children's experiences that legislation and policy measures devised to protect them from exploitation contributed rarely if ever to ameliorate their situation. Quite to the contrary, whenever the prohibition of child labour contained in national law and ILO Convention 138 ('minimum age' for access to labour) was translated into concrete measures, their situation became more complicated and difficult. Even ILO Convention 182, which aims specifically at combating the 'worst forms of child labour', turned out to be an instrument that created more problems for working children than it helped to solve. Without consulting the children and their families, arbitrary definitions were made as to what should be considered the 'worst forms of child labour'. In many cases this

Convention was used as a means to justify dispelling working children from their places of work.

These negative effects are on account of laws and measures intended to protect children from exploitation that regard child labour as harmful and fail to take the reasons motivating children to take up work into account. The belief is that, children being unfit to work, there is no need to try to understand children's views and feelings. The children are seen as victims and objects in need of help, not as subjects with thoughts about their situation and ideas about how to solve their problems that they wish to articulate.

There is likewise also a neglect of the cultural contexts in which children grow up and the existing diverse concepts of 'childhood' and 'work' in which children's work is not seen as a defect but as a contribution to 'shared responsibilities', something to be appreciated. Of course, this entails the danger that in a situation of poverty children are only seen in terms of their labour force and little attention is paid to their rights and needs. But this danger can only be counteracted if children's work is not defined as intrinsically negative. Instead, critique against working conditions must be paired with recognition of the value of children's economic activity. One can simply not ignore that children like to help their families and that they are proud of contributing to the family's needs and income.

The claim to a right to work results from the desire of working children for social recognition of their work. It is put forth, first and foremost, by children who have experience with work and exploitation as well as with the inadequacy of measures taken for their protection. The children want solutions that take into account their living conditions and their experiences. They want to be respected as subjects who take an independent interest in solving their problems. In this sense, the right to work is an instrument of empowerment in which children take command of their situation.

Especially because children do not have political rights yet, that is are not yet 'citizens' who 'give rights' and can 'rule the law or judge',[12] there is special meaning in their statement of will backed up by their social movements. It demands that adults, who are in a privileged situation compared to children, are made accountable:

[12] The 'participation rights' foreseen in the CRC, as well as the right to get together peacefully or to found an association, are in accordance with classical civil rights, yet fall short of granting children political rights such as the right to vote.

> Some danger lies in our use of rights to abstract and universalize at the expense of efforts to imagine the stake we have in mutual comprehensibility and to be responsive to other forms of life, especially those under construction by the young.
>
> (Reynolds *et al.*, 2006: 300–1).

From this understanding, when children formulate rights of their own, they find legitimacy in seeking an answer to urgent needs and demand that the social reality in which they find themselves be improved. The rights they demand have a relation to their concrete life experiences and are claimed because they are seen as relevant. Because it results from the experiences of children, particularly of working children, and is claimed by them, the right to work that I discuss here can be understood in this sense as a living right.

Contribution to social justice

To understand the right to work as a possible contribution to social justice, it is important to note that up to now it has been claimed by children who already work. In doing so, these children wanted to contest their work being often illegal and the disadvantages connected to their subordinated social status in order to achieve a stronger position to negotiate better working conditions and limit exploitative practices. In the children's organization's documents, the right to work is portrayed as a prerequisite to be able to exercise other rights, be it protection or participation rights at work, or those granted by the CRC such as the right to organize and to be heard.

As long as the children remain factually dependent on the benevolence of adults, the fundamental shift that the CRC promises by granting children the right to a humane and dignified life and a self-determined social identity remains in essence a dead letter. Only when they are lawfully recognized as economically active and can dispose of their own income, can children achieve the independence and social weight necessary to realize their rights in society themselves.

For working children, the lack of social justice is not that they are working, but that they are regularly working under conditions of subordination and exploitation. The special meaning of the right to work is to give them a better standing in the dual sense of guaranteeing protection and participation, and recognizing their human dignity. Like the economic exploitation of adults, the exploitation of children is a 'structural feature of modern capitalist economies' (Lavalette, 2000: 214). But a general reference to the structures and modes of functioning of capitalist economies is not sufficient to explain the particular risks of the exploitation and disadvantaging of children. Nor can it explain the varying degrees of risk and the specific and quite different forms and degrees of exploitation to which children are exposed.[13]

The low social status of children within the age hierarchy constitutes a special risk factor that exposes children to exploitation that does not directly follow from the laws of capitalism. Terming this a 'weakness', as is commonly done, is unsatisfactory, inasmuch as it suggests that what is involved is primarily a biological phenomenon. In fact, the 'weakness' of children is the result of a 'social construction', that is it results from social power relations and is thus also susceptible to change. The 'weakness' of children manifests itself in two ways: as a failure to respect their subjectivity, and as exclusion from social responsibility and participation.

In her now classical theoretical study on 'The differentiation of children's labour in the capitalist labour market', Diane Elson (1982) attributes the 'dominant' forms of work that disadvantage children to three 'authority sources' that, according to her, mark the 'seniority system' of contemporary capitalist societies: 1. the authority of adults in the family; 2. the requirements of the educational system, which is also governed by adults; 3. the 'needs' of capitalism for the easy and profitable utilization of labour power:

> The seniority system obviously encompasses a range of gradations, not simply the division between children and adults, but children are at the bottom of it. And this means it is extremely difficult for them to secure full recognition in monetary terms for the skills they possess and for the contribution they make to family income.
>
> (Elson, 1982: 493)

Children being primarily given tasks that are considered economically less valuable, their low status results in a low valuation of their abilities. Despite the large quantity of work that they do, children are not recognized as workers in their own right.

Elson describes the seniority system as a socially constructed age hierarchy 'in which those in junior positions are unable to achieve full social status in their own right. They are not full members of society' (Elson,

[13] On the question of children's economic exploitation see also Liebel, 2004: 194–215.

1982: 491). Their subordination does not mean that they lack the personal capacity for autonomous behaviour; indeed, many children have more ability than many adults. Subordination means the 'lack of public means for recognition of the right to autonomy; and the lack of public means to sustain and extend autonomy' (Elson, 1982: 492). Adults are typically not inclined to question their own power over children:

> The desire of adults to preserve adult power over children, through constructing certain forms of family, for instance, and certain forms of education, has given children an unenviable choice between exploitation at work and subservience in home and school.
>
> (Elson, 1982: 494)

By contrast, Elson states, children should be granted an appropriate income of their own as their right, as well as the connection between education and income-generating activities. The exclusion of children from the sphere of work, even if it is the capitalist labour market, 'simply changes the way in which children are subordinated, rather than ending that subordination' (Elson, 1982: 495).[14]

As it is meant to protect working children from the special forms of exploitation that they experience, the right to work is an economic right promoting equal participation of children in society. The concept of protection that I use here differs from its common usage of avoidance and prevention of endangering situations ('protection from …') but is rather a concept that seeks to build on active involvement of those most concerned by it ('protection by …'). This has its dangers. We may question children's ability to judge the dangers underlying certain economic activities, to identify their 'best interests' or to weigh short-term and long-term interests when having an opportunity to earn money. At issue is also the question whether they really can gather sufficient power to resist unacceptable working conditions and realize the necessary changes.

As it strengthens children's dependency to the detriment of their freedom and participation rights, understanding protection as avoidance and sheltering children from danger entails risks as well. It may make it more difficult for children to develop necessary competences to react to new situations or make them blind and inflexible toward the living conditions

[14] The social philosopher Nancy Fraser (2000, 2003) undertook the noteworthy attempt, with regard to 'subordinated status groups', to conceptualize social justice as the combination of recognition and redistribution, where the ideas of 'participatory parity' play a central role. It would certainly be of interest to apply her considerations to children and their right to work.

and specific, culturally defined positioning. Understanding protection as avoidance and sheltering means throwing out the baby with the bathwater; it makes it impossible to analyse the context in which children's work is inserted, which role work plays for children and what they can contribute to their own protection. As a kind of self-fulfilling prophecy, the avoidance concept may well contribute to the state of 'helplessness' that serves as evidence of children's putative 'need of protection'.

Once children are granted the right to work, however, they can become familiar with challenges they may encounter in life and can possibly rely on the help and support they need to protect themselves from dangers or to improve their situation. In addition, labour law could be extended to regulate maximum working hours, parallel schooling or protection and participation rights at the workplace for jobs accessible to children. In addition, for children who are willing to work, work opportunities could be arranged that abide by these regulations and take the wishes of children into account. This would be possible also in the frame of public institutions or in view of developing new forms of solidarity and non-profit economies.

In the declarations of the working children's movements the right to work is not related to any kind of work, but is, as emphasized over and over again, about 'work in dignity', a 'light' or 'not too hard' work, in sum work that is 'adequate according to capabilities'. At first glance this could be understood as if children were asking for a limited right to work in 'child-specific jobs'. From the context in which the demands are put forward, however, it is clear that guaranteeing human dignity and not age is taken as the criterion for adequacy. In the understanding of the children's movements the right to work means that children should be able to carry out 'as good as possible' work and that any kind of exploitation and debasement at work should actively be confronted. This entails a 'utopian surplus', an understanding of work that goes beyond wage work, which is the dominating form of work in capitalist societies. In addition, children claim the right to decide themselves whether the work they are offered abides by the self-set criteria.

In a societal situation in which the working relations worldwide are being 'deregulated' and made more 'flexible' and more and more people are expected to be satisfied with precarious jobs, these criteria carry a special weight. They underline that children, in contrast to common assumption, are not willing to be utilized as cheap competitors in the labour market, and that they are well aware that they are in one boat with people of other ages, who depend on their own labour as the children do. But children insist that they should not be excluded merely on the ground of their age from social practices from which adults draw a sense of fulfilment and self-respect. According to the understanding of working children's movements, the right they claim is not at all limited to wage work, but refers to all activities that are important for human life. It expresses the desire not to be set apart in a limited 'childhood' dependent on the goodwill of adults, but to be involved in the struggle for a more equitable and fair world on equal par with them.

Some achievements and challenges

In order to become effective, the right to work must, as must all human rights of children, be socially appreciated and recognized. One way to achieve this is its codification in legal norms. Yet even before that adults may acknowledge and respect it in everyday life. In this sense, the African children's movement engages in regular inventories of the extent to which its '12 Rights' are fulfilled, and accordingly gives grades or marks to the responsible adults and governments in the countries in which it is present.

It would certainly be useful if international labour law would follow these developments (see Hanson and Vandaele, Chapter 12 in this volume). The right to work claimed by the organizations of working children represents a strong counter-current to international labour law as codified in ILO Conventions 138 and 182, and to the corresponding international and national action programmes that aim at a complete eradication of all forms of child labour (see ILO, 2010). Even so, organizations of working children have succeeded, at least in some Latin American countries, in making a certain impact on national legislations.

The first country in which children were accorded the right to work explicitly in legislation is Peru. The Children and Adolescents Law (Código de los Niños y Adolescentes, Decreto Ley No. 26102), which the Peruvian government promulgated on 28 December 1992, states:

> The state recognizes the right of adolescents to work under the provision that their work activity does not present any danger to their development, both physical and mental and their emotional health, and that it does not impair their school attendance.

In accordance with ILO Convention 138 ratified by the Peruvian state, and contrary to the request of the national organizations of working children not to tie the right to a minimum age, the law limited the right to work to children above 12 and took care to speak of 'adolescents' rather than 'children'. The law stipulated that children between 12 and 14 years old may work up to four hours a day and twenty-four hours a week, and that adolescents between the ages of 15 and 17 may work for up to six hours a day and thirty-six hours a week. Despite numerous protests by the organizations of working children, in the amended version of the law of 21 July 2000 (Código de los Niños y Adolescentes, Ley No. 27337), the minimum age for the right to work was raised to 15 years for agricultural employment, to 16 years in industry, commerce and mining, and to 17 years in the fishing industry. The state's obligation to provide school timetables that make it possible for working children to attend school recognizes indirectly, as did the earlier law, the work of younger children (without naming an age limit). This is no longer the case in the recently discussed new draft of the Children and Adolescents Law, where the minimum age for all kinds of work will be fixed at 15 years in general, without any consideration for special rights of working children below this age.

Another important achievement can be reported from Bolivia. The new Constitution of this country, which was approved by a referendum on 25 January 2009, distances itself for the first time from a general ban on child labour and aims at distinct regulation. Article 61, which in paragraph 1 forbids 'all forms of violence against children, in the family as well as in society' and threatens punishment for disregarding it, states in paragraph 2:

> Forced labour and the exploitation of children are forbidden. Activities, which children perform in the family and their social environment, are in the interest of their integral development [*formación*] as citizens and have an educational function.

This phrasing recognizes that the work of children can also be beneficial for society and the children themselves. What is decisive are the conditions under which it is undertaken. By referring to 'family and social environment', a positive stance is taken on the active role of children in the family- and community-based economy, as practised for centuries in indigenous communities. However, even if supporting the ambition to develop, for and with children, new forms of self-determined and cooperative work, the article creates the questionable impression that a ban can rid the world of exploitation. An earlier draft of the Constitution foresaw a general ban on child labour but the intervention of the Bolivian Movement of Working Children and Adolescents (UNATSBO), supported by some indigenous representatives of the Constitution task force, led to a revision. The influence of the movement can also be gauged from Article 46, where every person, irrespective of his or her age, is accorded the 'right to dignified work'. Whereas labour law in general and the regulation of child labour particularly is only applicable to waged work in employment for a third party, the Bolivian Constitution seeks in addition to pay attention to and regulate working relationships that are organized in cooperative or communal ways. This is particularly important for the work of children, as it is often not carried out in formally regulated employment. This recognition intimates the emergence of a vision that transcends labour relationships and economic exploitation under capitalism.

With reference to the new Constitution, UNATSBO recently presented a draft law on the rights of working children and adolescents (UNATSBO, 2010). In contrast to the ILO conventions and the current Bolivian legislation on child labour, this draft sets no minimum age for children's paid economic participation. The rights and regulations are supposed to apply to all children from birth until 18 years of age. Only some regulations differentiate between working children (below 12 years) and working youth (from 12 to 17 years). Working children and youth are understood as 'social subjects in their own right', who have the right and the capacity to 'actively take part in the productive dynamic and the servicing of society' in equal measure. The state is ascribed the duty to recognize and value the economic, social and cultural contributions that children and youth make through their work. Included in this recognition and valuation is the acknowledgement that the work of children and youth is a constituting element of their identities and a form of participation, as well as providing a context for socialization and acquisition of values and norms. Every child and adolescent is entitled to be protected at work, as well as to obtain an integral education and vocational education that corresponds to his or her wishes, qualities and capabilities and that are required for working. The state is obliged to protect children against any form of exploitation and against types of work that are dangerous, or that harm their education or threaten their health and mental and social development.

In the UNATSBO draft the children and adolescents are assured equality before the law and are entitled to the same protection and guarantees as adults. No child shall be excluded, discriminated against or favoured for reasons of age, gender, colour, sexual orientation or identity, origin, culture, nationality, language, religious beliefs, political opinions, affiliations to political parties, civil status, economic and social situation, profession, degree of education, attributes perceived as disabilities, pregnancy or any other reasons. Beyond equal rights and the general prohibition of any discrimination, working children and adolescents are entitled to special rights at their work. Seven groups of rights are explicitly named: the right to health, education, sports and leisure time; the right to freedom and dignity at work, in school and in society in general; the rights linked to the expression of one's culture, as manifested in language, clothing, world-view (cosmology) and values; the right to organize in the workplace, to join trade unions and to conclude collective agreements; the right to social, psychological and legal assistance, especially in cases of work-related conflicts; the right to special assistance and protection at work for children with 'other abilities';[15] the right to generally accessible vocational education provided by the state. In relation to the more specific regulation of the rights of working children and adolescents, the draft legislation differentiates different types of work: (a) dependent, monetarily remunerated work; (b) apprenticeship; (c) self-employment; (d) work within one's own family and household; (e) work in the context of indigenous communities.

This legislative drafting initiative by the Bolivian Movement of Working Children and Adolescents is a novelty both in terms of the history of children's rights and in relation to labour and social law-making. While it is true that in the last two decades children have sometimes been consulted in the drafting of law concerning children and adolescents, a drafting process has never before been predominantly in their hands. Another innovative aspect is that the draft legislation embodies the perspective of working children's organizations on the topic of children's work and is based on the notion that children have a right to work. As currently drafted, the legislation is supposed to enable children themselves to take action against exploitation and abuse, to preserve their dignity and to exercise their rights. The mere existence of such a drafting process involving working children is owed to a uniquely conducive historical situation. For several years now Bolivia has experienced sizeable social and political transformations, in the course of which a heterogeneous alliance of formerly marginalized groups is trying to overcome a past characterized by racism and extreme socio-economic inequality. The new Constitution is a product of these transformations. But in view of the local and international resistance against its vision of children's right to work, it is uncertain whether the UNATSBO draft will eventually be enacted into law.

[15] To be understood in the sense of abilities that are usually considered abnormal or as disabilities.

Conclusion

The working children's movements' claim for the right to work in general, and the legislative processes and initiatives from Peru and Bolivia in particular, are both remarkable achievements and challenges to both national labour law and law concerning children and adolescents. Importantly, to become effective, the right to work need not necessarily be first codified in law. As with all human rights, the right to work can become a legitimate claim before being formally codified in state law or interstate conventions. It obtains its legitimacy by being increasingly articulated by children themselves in an ever more organized way. This is not to say it lacks any legal foundation. For instance, the '12 Rights' formulated in the founding document of the African Movement of Working Children and Youth, or the law proposal on the rights of working children drafted by the Bolivian Movement of Working Children and Adolescents, even if not incorporated into any 'official' legal document, do find a legal foundation in some articles of the CRC. But what is more important is that the claim to the right to work is directly and concretely related to the living situations and needs of working children, who formulated them or are represented by the children's movements. The initiatives of the children organized in these movements to develop cooperative and self-determined forms of work of their own testify to their bringing their right to work into practice in ways that secure them a living and provide at the same time spaces for their development and education. As they realize the right of children to be active in socially useful ways and to develop novel forms of work that are not exploitative but rather beneficial to them, these practices pose a challenge for legal regulation which go beyond codification in labour law.

The demand for the right to work, as well as the attempt by the movements of working children to bring it into practice, both call into question widespread ideas about childhood as a stage of 'becoming' and preparation for the future as well as the state of being cared for. By understanding children's rights as agency rights and steps on the way to equality, the demand also implies rethinking the subordinated status of children as a social group and addressing its implicit injustice (see Liebel, 2012). For this purpose, working children's movements challenge widespread concepts of protection, which primarily involve regulations that impose bans and exclusion. In practice this means recognizing working children and their organizations as equal partners in the struggle for fairer living conditions. This is a challenge both to trade unions that have to unlearn considering working children as victims and unwelcome competitors, and also to social movements and NGOs that have to accept that working children are not merely objects of supportive measures. Children whose right to work has been recognized and who are supported in realizing this right could play a much greater active role in the process of social transformation towards a more just world than they have done so far.

Quoted documents (declarations) of working children's movements

Latin America:

1st Latin American Meeting ('outcry'), Lima, Peru, 1988. Source: Author's archive (Spanish), or ask at: molacnatsecretariado@hotmail.com.

6th Latin American Meeting, Asunción, Paraguay, 2001. Source: Author's archive (Spanish), or ask at: molacnatsecretariado@hotmail.com.

7th Latin American Meeting, Cachipay, Colombia, 2008. Source: http://molacnats.org/index.php?option=com_content&task=view&id=74&Itemid=81 (accessed 14 June 2012).

Africa:

1st African Meeting ('12 rights'), Bouaké, Ivory Cost, 1994. Sources: www.maejt.org/page%20anglais/English%20about%20us%20objectives.htm (accessed 14 June 2012), or: ENDA (2001), p. 96.

6th African Meeting, Thiès, Senegal 2003. Source : Author's archive; or ask at: ejt@enda.sn.

7th African Meeting, Ouagadougou, Burkina Faso, 2006. Author's archive; or ask at: ejt@enda.sn.

Asia:

Regional Meeting, Kathmandu, Nepal, 2005. Source: www.pronats.de/materialien/deklarationen/kathmandu-2005/ (accessed 14 June 2012).

World Movement:

1st (international) Meeting, Kundapur, India, 1996. Sources: www.workingchild.org/ (accessed 14 June 2012); or: ENDA (2001), pp. 127–8; or: Liebel *et al.* (2001), p. 351.

1st Mini Summit, Huampaní, Peru, 1997. Source: Liebel *et al.* (2001), pp. 352–3.

2nd Mini Summit, Dakar, Senegal, 1998. Source: Liebel *et al.* (2001), p. 354.

2nd World Meeting, Berlin, Germany, 2004. Source: www.enfants-actifs.org/?p=868 (accessed 14 June 2012).

3rd World Meeting, Sienna, Italy, 2006. Source: www.italianats.org/index.php?option=com_content&view=article&id=51:siena&catid=40:dichiarazioniufficiali&Itemid=62&lang=en (accessed 14 June 2012).

References

Bonnet, M (2006) La 'Déclaration de Kundapur': et si on écoutait les enfants travailleurs? In: Bonnet M, Hanson K, Lange M-F *et al. Enfants travailleurs: Repenser l'enfance*. Lausanne: Page deux, pp. 59–100.

Bourdillon M, White B and Myers W (2009) Re-assessing minimum-age standards for children's work. *International Journal of Sociology and Social Policy* 29 (3/4): 106–17.

Bourdillon M, Levison D, Myers W *et al.* (2010) *Rights and Wrongs of Children's Work*. Brunswick, NJ and London: Rutgers University Press.

Boyden J, Ling B and Myers, W (1997) *What Works for Working Children*. Stockholm: Save the Children.

Elson D (1982) The differentiation of children's labour in the capitalist labour market. *Development and Change* 13(4): 479–97.

ENDA (ed.) (2001) *Voice of African Children: Work, Strength and Organisation of Working Children and Youth*. Occasional Papers no. 217. Dakar: ENDA Third World.

Fraser N (2000) Rethinking recognition. *New Left Review* 3(May/June): 107–20.

(2003) Social justice in the age of identity politics: redistribution, recognition and participation. In: Fraser N and Honneth A *Recognition or Redistribution? A Political-Philosophical Exchange*. London and New York: Verso Books, pp. 7–109.

Hungerland B, Liebel M, Milne B *et al.* (eds.) (2007) *Working to Be Someone. Child Focused Research and Practice with Working Children*. London and Philadelphia: Jessica Kingsley Publishers.

ILO (2010) *Accelerating Action Against Child Labour. Global Report under the Follow-up to the ILO Declaration on Fundamental Principles and Rights at Work*. Geneva: International Labour Office.

Lavalette M (2000) Child employment in a capitalist labour market: the British case. In: Schlemmer B (ed.) *The Exploited Child*. London and New York: Zed Books, pp. 214–30.

Liebel M (2004) *A Will of Their Own: Cross-cultural Perspectives on Working Children*. London and New York: Zed Books.

(2006) *Malabaristas del siglo XXI: Los niños y niñas trabajadores frente a la globalización*. Lima: Ifejant.

(2007) Paternalism, participation and children's protagonism. *Children, Youth and Environments* 17(3): 56–73.

(2012) in collaboration with Hanson K, Saadi I and Vandenhole W *Children's Rights from Below: Cross-Cultural Perspectives*. Basingstoke: Palgrave Macmillan.

Liebel M, Overwien B and Recknagel A (eds.) (2001) *Working Children's Protagonism. Social Movements and Empowerment in Latin America, Africa and India*. Frankfurt and London: IKO.

Reynolds P, Nieuwenhuys O and Hanson K (2006) Refractions of children's rights in development practice: a view from anthropology. *Childhood* 13(3): 291–302.

Schibotto G (2009) El niño trabajador y la 'Economía de Solidaridad': del umbral de la sobrevivencia al horizonte del projecto. *NATs – Revista Internacional desde los Niños/as y Adolescentes Trabajadores* 13(17): 109–28.

UNATSBO (2010) *'Mi Fortaleza es mi Trabajo'. De las Demandas a la Propuesta. Niños, Niñas y Adolescentes Trabajadores y la Regulación del Trabajo Infantil y Adolescente en Bolivia*. Cochabamba: Union de Niños, Niñas y Adolescentes Trabajadores de Bolivia.

12

Translating working children's rights into international labour law

KARL HANSON AND ARNE VANDAELE

Introduction

As discussed by Manfred Liebel in Chapter 11, the statements and declarations issued by the movements of working children cover at least two different but related claims. First, working children demand participation in the discussions on how child labour is regulated nationally and internationally. Second, working children want recognition of their living right to work in dignity. Phrasing the right to work in dignity as a living right, next to stimulating the social imagination about alternatives for the actual conception of childhood and present social and economic relations (Liebel, 2003), also inspires rethinking how international labour law could accommodate working children's rights. This is the subject of the present chapter.

According to Bernard Schlemmer (2000: 11), a 'genuine conceptual revolution needs to occur before people accept that the child really is a subject and not just the object of specific measures, a responsible social actor perfectly capable of exercising rights which are, or should be, the rights of every human being and, in particular, every worker.' In this chapter we make a modest contribution to such a conceptual revolution and explore ways of looking at the existing international labour law framework taking working children's perspectives on child labour into account. In contrast with the dominant abolitionist approach to child labour, international labour law can offer an emancipatory perspective on the protection of children's work-related rights. In what follows, we first clarify resemblances and differences between working children and working

An earlier version of this chapter has been published previously as part of an article analysing international labour rights applicable to working children (Hanson and Vandaele, 2003). Related ideas to those expressed in the chapter have been published in separate contributions in French (Hanson, 2006) and in German (Hanson, 2008).

adults, relying on the *difference dilemma* to discuss issues of equality and difference between adults and children and in particular between adult labourers and child labourers. Next, we conceptualize working children's participation rights and their right to work in dignity within the existing international human rights and labour law framework. In the third section we suggest ways of rethinking international labour law with regard to age limitations, rights in work and instrumental work-related rights. We finally discuss a pragmatic and a comprehensive strategy for the regulation of child labour.

Children's rights and the *difference dilemma*

This section proposes a contextualized view on differences and resemblances between children and adults. We first address the indeterminacy of the principle of non-discrimination and then discuss children's equal rights and special rights. After that, we contend that when discussing resemblances and differences between working children and working adults, the dilemma of difference is a helpful tool to use to take context into account.

The complexities of child labour in Western history raise different questions relevant for today's working children. Historical research suggests that working children in nineteenth-century industrializing Europe were part of different categories at the same time. The 'master story' of child labour mainly gives evidence of the miserable conditions in which children were working and living, and contends that children were abusively put on a par with adults. The period in Western societies during which children laboured in the same factories and worked the same land as their adult contemporaries is generally analysed as a faux pas in the process of industrialization. However, more recent historical research that studies working children as active participants indicates that work for children could sometimes and somewhere be 'normal'. For instance, in the family wage economy that was the prevalent social and economic structure in nineteenth-century Norway, paid or unpaid activities within or outside the household formed an integral part of both children's and adults lives (Schrumpf, 2001). In addition, in Belgium in the first half of the nineteenth century, working children's aspirations and claims, such as the reduction of working hours, a better wage and the improvement of working conditions, were about the same as those of other workers. The abolition of their paid work did not form part of working children's demands. It is more likely that working children saw themselves as constituting an integral part of the working class, even if considering themselves at the same time as a separate, though equal, group. Adult workers saw working children as competitors who were feared and whose support was sometimes bought, for instance by resorting to bribery in order to assure their solidarity with particular protest actions (De Wilde, 2000). In sum, working children formed part of the mass of the labouring classes, and as such shared the same working and living conditions of all labourers. They belonged to several distinct professional groups, with whom they had in common the particularities or privileges attached to their profession. Children worked and lived in specific regions and were subject to local conditions, which, together with gender, influenced their wages, working conditions, status and so on. Finally, working children also belonged, in some circumstances and for certain aspects, to the group of workers epitomized by their particular age. This contingent status of working children has today largely disappeared in the West, the child having acquired a separate status and for whom work is either a marginal activity to be carried out after school, or an anomaly when the child works and is not in school. But in the developing world the situation is, as working children's movements testify, not as clear-cut.

Given the specific historical and geographical Western origins of much thinking on child labour, working children problematize with their demands the way the child's status is being conceptualized in both research and policy. Do we have to see them as children who happen also to work? Or are they male or female workers exercising a particular profession in a specified region who are, incidentally, also children? In legal terms, questions about whether working children belong to the category of workers or to the category of children have to come to terms with the principle of non-discrimination and equality of treatment. Herbert Hart (1961/1994) formulates the guiding principle of non-discrimination as 'treat like cases alike, and treat different cases differently'. The author states that although the non-discrimination principle is a central element to the idea of justice, it is in itself incomplete. Until supplemented with criteria used to give guidance to the 'treat like cases alike' principle, it cannot provide any clear guide for conduct:

> This is so because any set of human beings will resemble each other in some respects and differ from each other in others and, until it is established what resemblance and differences are relevant, 'Treat like cases alike' must remain an empty form. To fill it we must know when, for the purposes in hand, cases are to be regarded as alike and what differences are relevant.
>
> (Hart, 1961/1994: 159)

Hence, one of the central issues of the child labour debate is the criteria used to compare the situation of working children with that of working adults. Is it, for example, the types of activities or, on the contrary, the age or capacity of the person who performs the activities that make a difference? In the former case, child work should be treated on a par with adult work; in the latter, it should be treated differently. In this respect the abolitionist position towards child labour rests on the presupposition that children are inherently different from adults, and hence looks upon children's work as essentially different from the work performed by adults. Working children's organizations, by contrast, stress the similarities between their situation and the situation of some categories of adult workers, and challenge the dominant viewpoint that children's work is essentially different from adult work.

The discussion on children's labour rights is related to the distinction between the 'equal rights' and 'special rights' of children. Hillary Rodham (1973), for example, distinguishes two general approaches to children's rights: the extension of adult rights to children and the search for legally enforceable recognition of children's special needs and interests. She illustrates the demand for the extension of adult rights to children by referring to the proposals to extend all the rights of adult criminal defendants to accused juvenile delinquents. However, it is not her intention to simply put children on par with adults. In some cases the rights of adults can be applied to children, whereas in other cases they must be adjusted to the needs and situations of children. The second approach of children's rights, which seeks to legally enforce children's special needs and interests, 'begins with the belief that even if all adult rights were granted to children and were strictly enforced, this would not guarantee that certain critical needs unique to children would be met' (Rodham, 1973: 495–6). Consequently, children have additional, special rights based on their young age. In this respect it is significant that the notion of children's rights comprises a double claim, that is the claim for the recognition of general (adult) rights for children, as well as the claim for the recognition of the special rights of children. According to this approach, working children have a right to 'equal rights' as well as to 'special rights'. The two claims, however, do not always coexist smoothly. An interesting example thereof in the area of international labour law is provided by the discussion on the protection of women against night work, something many national laws indeed do. According to Christian Tomuschat (1990), concern for the health of women should not be used as a pretext to create and defend labour monopolies for men. The author notes that, in the case of female labour, protection may degenerate quite easily into discrimination. By relying on the principle of non-discrimination and the equality of treatment, women successfully challenged the prohibition of night work for women as a general principle. In order to mitigate prohibitions that were established earlier, the International Labour Organization (ILO) adopted in 1990 a Protocol on Night Work (Women) to ILO Convention No. 89 (Revised) of 1948. Following the adoption of Directive 76/207 concerning the principle of equal treatment of men and women in conditions of work, the European Union Member States went even further and denounced Convention No. 89 (Drzewicki, 1995). Claims of working children's organizations similarly pose the question whether, as was the case for night labour by women, protection regarding child labour via prohibitive legislation does not also degenerate into discrimination on the basis of age, that is whether working children's 'equal rights' have been sufficiently taken into account when giving them the 'special right' not to work at all.

Discussions on working children's rights may gain from broader discussions among feminist lawyers about the *difference dilemma* (Brems, 1997; Minow, 1986; Raes, 1992). Should working children (or those who defend them) choose a treatment similar to the treatment of working adults, with the risk that this equal treatment is not adjusted to children, but follows the same pattern as the treatment of adults? Or should they defend special treatment and run the risk that this may lead to discrimination? As for all dilemmas, there is no definite solution. In some cases working children may benefit from being granted special rights, whereas in other cases it may be important to defend their equal rights. In other words, rather than making general abstractions to resolve the *difference dilemma*, an assessment of concrete situations is required. The *difference dilemma* does not refute the idea that there are differences between working adults and working children. However, what it contests is the idea that these differences must lead in all circumstances to the same response, regardless of the situation. There are probably cases where working children's particular position, for instance as an apprentice or domestic worker, may best be dealt with by a completely different legal framework than the existing adult labour legislation. Conversely, there may be instances where working children's rights are best supported by relying on general labour law principles and legislation. Rather than relying on a standard response that seems to disregard that work is the daily reality of masses of children, the *difference dilemma* framework may be a better way to take the many different situations of working children into account. At stake, then, are the mutual contribution and the interrelation of working children's general and special rights. When and how far should working children's special rather than general rights be recognized? Which rights should be given priority, and to what extent, if there is a conflict between them? In what cases, to what extent and based on which criteria should working children's preferential rights extend or otherwise restrict their general labour rights? These questions will be addressed in what follows from the vantage point of children's equal rights, in particular by asking how general international labour law could apply to the situation of working children. Before doing so, we will first contend that international human rights law grants children the right to participate in matters that affect them and that this justifies taking their perspectives on work into account.

Children's participation rights as a 'cluster of rights'

This section argues that international norms justify the participation of working children in debates on child labour. In particular, it provides a legal analysis of the relevant provisions in the 1989 UN Convention on the Rights of the Child (hereafter: CRC) and lists the rights and obligations in the field of children's participation rights. Also in the field of child labour, children's participation rights imply that working children's perspectives on their work should be taken into account.

Women's organizations successfully challenged the supposedly protective and preventive nature of the prohibition of women's night work (Drzewicki, 1995). Women's voices were crucial for reinterpreting how to balance women's right to freedom to work without discrimination with their special right to protection at work. In the same vein, working children's organizations now claim the right to participate in developing international child labour standards. Relying on their participation rights, they are particularly critical of restrictions placed on children's freedom to work and challenge existing restrictions on the freedom to work that impose strict minimum ages for admission to employment (Hanson and Vandaele, 2003). The claim of working children's organizations to participate in meetings of international bodies such as the ILO and the United Nations is not an end in itself but an attempt to influence how questions related to the *difference dilemma* will be settled.

Working children's organizations rely on various provisions of the CRC to support their claim to participate in the child labour debate. They can indeed refer to the right to express an opinion and to have that opinion taken into account, in any matter or procedure affecting the child (Article 12), the right to freedom of expression (Article 13), the right to freedom of association and of peaceful assembly (Article 15) and the right to freedom of information (Article 17). For many actors in the children's rights field, children's participation rights are the most innovative of the principles contained in the CRC and function as a key concept for its understanding and implementation. Several commentators find support in these CRC provisions for the need to approach the issue of child labour from a perspective that includes working children's views (see, inter alia, Bonnet, 1998; Bourdillon *et al.*, 2010; McKechnie and Hobbs, 1998; Miljeteig, 2000). Conceptually, however, there is a considerable degree of confusion about the meaning and the implications of children's participation. According to Schlemmer (2000), the CRC has the merit of declaring principles that aim at imposing themselves on the international community. Nevertheless, the author also notes that the CRC sometimes remains stuck in general wordings, betraying a lack of sufficient reflection on the subject. Michael Freeman (1998) observes that even after the adoption of Article 12 of the CRC, the implications of recognizing children as social actors and subjects in their own right have not been properly elaborated. Problems related to the principle of participation are not only extremely complex to implement in practice (David, 2002), but also encounter significant objections as they do not give real power to children and fail to include certain groups of children (Thomas, 2007). As children stay excluded from the real centres of power-making, the globalization of social and economic policy and decision-making processes contribute to reduce children's participation practice to a marginal activity (Tisdall *et al.*, 2006). For Thomas, 'there is very little sign of children and young people really participating in the processes that actually produce important political decisions, or in contributing to defining the terms of policy debate' (Thomas, 2007: 207). This conceptual fuzziness has consequences for the implementation of working children's participation rights. In this respect Boyden *et al.* (1998: 183) comment: 'While the right of children to participate in decisions concerning them is today widely touted and officially recognized by almost all countries ... action to put that right into practice in the formulation of laws and standards is still incipient at best.'

A legal analysis of the relevant CRC provisions on children's participation rights poses particular problems. In contrast, for instance, to the 'right to freedom of expression' contained in Article 15 CRC or the 'right to protection of privacy' in Article 16 CRC, a 'right to participation' is not a separate article or provision of the Convention. Hence, children's participation rights can best be viewed not as a single legal precept but as a 'cluster of rights' that contains several closely related notions. Amartya Sen's (1999) framework on freedom provides a useful theoretical point of departure to conceptualize the meaning and functioning of children's participation rights. The author's distinction between the 'constitutive role' and the 'instrumental role' of freedom helps to distinguish, for the purpose of this analysis, between two different features of participation rights, namely a constitutive and an instrumental one.[1] Central elements that make up participation rights are the rights as contained in Articles 13, 15 and 17 CRC to freedom of expression, to freedom of information, to freedom of association and to peaceful assembly. These rights are of intrinsic importance in guaranteeing the substantive freedom that enriches children's lives and can therefore be considered as forming the *constitutive dimension* of participation rights. To state that children have the right to freely express their views or to form an association, as Articles 13 and 15 of the CRC normatively affirm, also means that children can use their participation rights to make their opinions on other rights known. Working children can, for instance, make use of their right to freedom of expression to convey their meaning about their right to access to good health care (something they indeed did in the Kundapur Declaration, 1996 mentioned in Chapter 11 of this volume). In the sense that children – in the same way as other persons or groups – can make use of their participation rights to try to influence the outcome of certain decisions or policies related to the exercise or realization of their rights, children's participation rights consequently also contain an *instrumental dimension.*

Articles 13, 15 and 17 CRC accept that the exercise of participation rights may be subject to certain restrictions. However, such restrictions have to be provided for by law and have to be necessary for the respect of the rights or reputation of others, for the protection of national security, of public order (*ordre public*) or of public health or morals. Furthermore, Article 12 CRC imposes a duty on States Parties to provide for adequate structures or mechanisms to enable children, who are capable of forming their own views, to express these views freely (Committee on the Rights of the Child, 2009; Lücker-Babel, 1995). Hence, states have to provide

[1] Sen attempts to see development as a process of expanding the real freedoms that people enjoy, viewing the expansion of freedom as both the *primary end* and the *principal means* of development. The constitutive role of freedom relates to the importance of substantive freedom in enriching human life, whereas its instrumental role relates to the argument that these freedoms and rights may *also* be very effective in contributing to economic progress.

adequate structures via which working children can also exercise their participation rights.

The recognition of the constitutive and instrumental features of children's participation rights does not imply, by itself, conferring decision-making power to children. Article 12 of the CRC, however, not only recognizes the right of the child to express his/her views freely, but adds that, providing that the child is 'capable of forming his or her views' and that these views concern 'a matter affecting the child', due weight has to be given to the child's views in accordance with the age and maturity of the child. In other words, children's views should be a consideration in certain decisions, but at the same time they are not the only element (Lücker-Babel, 1995). According to the CRC, the opinions of working children are not to be given pre-eminence over other justified interests per se, but have to be taken into consideration when deciding on matters that affect them. Furthermore, the 'due weight clause' arguably implies that decision-makers should disclose the different elements and interests that were taken into consideration when a particular decision was made. Without such an obligation, the requirement that, under certain circumstances, due weight should be given to the child's view would be meaningless, because it would be unclear to what extent children's views have played a role in the decision-making process. Of importance for working children is that debates on child labour standards should be public and that decisions should be motivated. Indeed, although working children's views cannot take precedence over other opinions or interests, a decision has to indicate how their views have been taken into account.

An examination of the content of the relevant CRC provisions reveals, as a result, that at least the following rights and obligations can be considered part of the existing normative cluster of children's participation rights:

- **Subjective rights of the child, both in their constitutive and instrumental dimension:**
  - freedom of expression
  - freedom of information
  - freedom of association
  - freedom of peaceful assembly

- **Restrictions and obligations for states**
  - the above-mentioned subjective rights of children can be restricted only under precise conditions

- the obligation to encourage the dissemination of appropriate information via diverse means
- the obligation to provide, under certain circumstances, for adequate structures or mechanisms to enable children to express their views

- **Obligations in the decision-making process**

- the obligation to give due weight, under certain circumstances, to the views of the child
- the obligation for debates to be held in the open, and for decisions to be motivated

The participation of working children in the debates on child labour can then provide new perspectives on the place of children in international labour legislation. In doing so, working children's organizations can rely on the prevailing international normative framework on children's participation rights. They can, in particular, refer to the instrumental dimension of the right to freedom of expression and the right to freedom of association to convey an opinion about the way their work-related rights should be interpreted and applied. Subsequently, working children's participation rights can lead to a reconsideration of whether and the extent to which their rights have to be taken into account when deciding on how they may work. States have to refrain from unlawful intervention in children's exercise of their participation rights, and must provide adequate structures to enable working children to express their views. Moreover, due weight has to be given to children's views. Finally, even if it is uncertain whether working children's views on their rights will have a real impact in the decision-making process, their participation rights at least require a disclosure of the criteria and interests that prevailed for settling matters that affect them. More generally, recognizing working children's participation rights leads to taking working children seriously as social actors (Hanson and Vandaele, 2003).

Relying on the participation rights in the CRC, working children do have the right to participate in discussions on child labour. This general requirement includes, according to the Committee on the Rights of the Child (2009: 26), that 'representatives of working children's associations should also be heard when labour laws are drafted or when the enforcement of laws is considered and evaluated'. We now turn to international labour law in order to analyse how this particular legal framework could accommodate working children's views on their labour and on their living right to work in dignity.

Rethinking international labour law

Working children's most fundamental claims, that is for participation rights and for the recognition of their right to work in dignity, question the current international labour law framework with respect to child labour. In this section we explore how these claims can stir up our legal imagination, and provide some alternatives for looking at working children's rights.[2] After a critique of the current abolitionist interpretation, we look in particular at how international labour law can provide a reference framework for taking the freedom to work (age limitations), rights in work and instrumental work-related rights into account.

The current international legal framework with regard to child labour, including Article 32 CRC and ILO Convention No. 182 on the abolition of the worst forms of child labour, is clearly abolitionist and takes an unambiguous position in the *difference dilemma*. The position entails that the particularities of children makes it imperative for international labour law to deal with working children in a completely different way than with adults. However, such a different treatment is not without problems and can lead to new forms of discrimination, as the formal ban on child labour restricts the possibilities for working children to invoke fundamental workers' rights to counter exploitation. From a legal point of view, children under the established age limits do not exist as workers. If they work, they do so clandestinely and are outside the law and its protective frameworks (Bonnet, 1998). Some even argue that legislation prohibiting child labour, even if intended to protect children, 'often turns out in practice to be regressive and counter-productive, driving child work underground and making children even more vulnerable to exploitation' (International Working Group on Child Labour 1997). In addition, international child labour law leaves only very limited space for working children to have a say in matters that concern them. The discussion on how to combine respect for both working children's equal rights and their special rights to protection has taken place almost without any consultation with working children's organizations.

Age limitations

The recognition of the freedom to work does not stand in opposition to restricting this freedom, for instance by the enactment of legislation with

[2] For a more extensive account of the existing international legal framework on child labour, see Hanson and Vandaele, 2003, in particular Section III.2 on pages 97–121.

a view to protecting vulnerable persons from working in certain conditions. In principle, then, limitations on child work such as the setting of a minimum age for admission to employment do not per se curtail the right to work. From a labour law perspective, the prohibition of child labour is to be considered part of protective and preventive restrictions of the freedom to work (Drzewicki, 1995). Prohibition of child labour usually takes the form of requiring a certain age in order to legally work. Age limitations are part of the comprehensive framework of work-related rights and freedoms. They serve a similar goal as other rights in work. They are to be considered as special measures for the protection of the young and vulnerable workforce, preventing them from working in poor working conditions. The initial contradiction between the prohibition of child labour and the recognition of children's rights in work thus has to be put into perspective; or, as suggested by Aimé Bada *et al.* (2000: 20): 'The common objective of protecting working children from abuse and exploitation appears to us to be stronger than the apparent contradiction between minimum age and light work.'

When analysing child labour from the perspective of specific international law with regard to child labour, however, the right to freedom to work has been ignored. ILO Convention No. 138 does not contain any reference whatsoever to this principle. The aim of the Convention, read together with the accompanying Recommendation No. 146, is the total abolition of child labour. This is presented as a goal in itself. The 1998 ILO Declaration on Fundamental Principles and Rights at Work also proclaims the effective abolition of child labour, thus granting it the status of a fundamental human right. The overall approach of these instruments is that work performed by children is an exception to the prohibition of child labour. This is most clearly illustrated in Convention No. 138. Hence, the current view is that the imposition of age limitations itself does not constitute an exception to the right to freedom to work. This is, however, open to discussion. Are age limitations the best way to protect children from exploitation?

The African movement of working children disagrees with the way their right to freedom to work has been restricted. They 'wish that the work required from them be adapted to their development, and especially that it be determined according to their capacities and not their age' (Bada *et al.*, 2000: 10). The example of the prohibition of night work for women shows that it is not impossible to review existing protective measures regarding the right to freedom to work. In any event, reframing the debate in this line of reasoning would be conceptually more in line with existing legal principles of international labour law.

Rights in work

Within the international labour law framework, rights *in* work form an integral part of the body of work-related rights. The recognition of an individual's right to work, both as a right to employment and as a freedom to work, implies the recognition of his or her right to just conditions at work (rights *in* work). But as international labour law legislation with respect to child labour takes the prohibition of child labour as a starting point, the question arises whether something that is legally prohibited, but occurs in practice, can be regulated. Entangled as the issue may seem, in the conflict between the prohibition of child labour and the recognition of children's rights in work, it is important to take into account that the prohibition of child labour is itself an exception to the freedom to work. Such exceptions, interpreted restrictively, cannot deny the freedom to work. Protective measures thus have to be interpreted in light of the purpose they serve. Restrictions on the freedom to work must be proportional to the aim of protecting the child. Hence, within this framework, the prohibition of child labour is not contradictory to the freedom to work. On the contrary, the prohibition of child labour is in fact a particular way of organizing the freedom to work. In addition, the recognition of children's rights in work is not contradictory to the prohibition of child labour. As is the case for the prohibition of child labour, the recognition of rights in work aims to protect the child. Indeed, the underlying assumption is that the regulation of child labour can change exploitative working circumstances into acceptable and decent working conditions. It is *only* when rights and principles related to just conditions in work are granted that the judicial concept of exploitation can be changed to a concept of acceptable and decent working conditions. Hence, both the prohibition of child labour and the regulation of labour conditions originate from the same fundamental principle and can even be considered as mutually reinforcing. Again, the condition is that one accepts that the freedom to work of children is not denied as a matter of principle.

International labour law instruments with respect to child labour leave very limited room to discuss children's rights in work. The improvement of their working conditions may be acceptable only as a temporary measure awaiting the total abolition of child labour. Conceptually, they are to be seen as exceptions to an overall general principle. Exceptions that generally require a restrictive interpretation offer a very weak basis for the foundation of rights in work. It can therefore be argued that the international labour law with respect to child labour needs rethinking.

It is in any event difficult to use age restrictions as an argument against the possibility for working children to rely on rights in work. This kind of interpretation would hamper the possibilities of reducing the exploitative character of child labour, a goal that is pursued by legislation prohibiting child labour. Pushing the argument only a little further, when child labour prohibition is used as an excuse for denying the possibility of elaborating legislation that imposes certain minimal working conditions for children, one may ask whether protecting working children is still the main concern of the law. Ben White (1994) asks what would be achieved by insisting on the general prohibition of children's employment if respect for children's work-related rights is to be realised. The author contends that nothing more would be attained than the abolition of children's right to earn money. This suggests that rather than for the prevention of the exploitation of child labour, legal arguments may be used for pursuing other concerns, such as the elimination of competitors in the labour force, mainly low-paid workers in the developing world.

Instrumental work-related rights

Within the general labour law framework the rights to freedom of expression and freedom of association are considered as fundamental principles. By referring to these rights, workers can influence the content of other rights in work, for instance conditions of employment and remuneration. Instrumental work-related rights apply in principle without discrimination. As emphasized in the CRC, the recognition of these rights for children corresponds to the instrumental dimension of participation rights.

In the same way as rights of children in work can protect children, so can instrumental rights of children protect the young workforce. A regulatory and empowerment perspective implies the recognition not only of rights in work, but also of instrumental rights to strive for rights in work. However, the actual recognition of instrumental rights in work is not always easy. Trade union membership can certainly be beneficial for the recognition and enhancement of children's instrumental work-related rights and, consequently, for all work-related rights. However, it is not always possible for children to become members of a trade union[3] or for working children's movements to be formally

[3] See for example the situation in India (Venkata Ratnam, 1999).

recognized as a union.[4] Serious doubts also arise as to the willingness of trade unions to take working children's claims on board. Bessell (1999: 97), for instance, observes that 'allowing children to join unions would be in direct conflict with the objective of eliminating child labour, to which many unions are fully committed'. The view that opposes the prohibition of child labour against the recognition of children's work-related rights is only one possible interpretation of current international labour law. The same line of reasoning as adopted before also applies to instrumental work-related rights. Both age limitations and instrumental work-related rights serve a similar goal, namely to address working children's exploitation. Consequently, the recognition of children's right to join unions is not necessarily in contradiction with minimum ages to admission to employment.

The history of working children's organizations suggests that not all trade unionists are deaf to children's work-related rights claims. Bhima Sangha, an Indian union of working children, came into being as the result of actions of trade unionists who sought to organize adult workers in the informal unorganized labour sector. Confronted with a high percentage of child workers present at the meetings, the union decided to undertake specific action towards the category of child workers (Swift, 1999). In this respect McKechnie and Hobbs (1998: 75) recommend trade unions to 'seek to recruit all workers irrespective of age. Where organizations of child workers exist, trade unions should enter into cooperative agreements with these organisations.' According to Bessell (1999: 97), this recommendation 'could do a great deal to improve the conditions in which children work and contribute to preventing exploitation and abuse by providing children with avenues of complaint and support mechanisms'.

Worldwide, most children work in the agriculture and informal sectors. Economic globalization has made particularly this work a major concern of trade unions, leading them to reconsider such issues as workers' interests and solidarity (Leisink, 1999). According to an ILO publication:

> for several years the discussions and work of trade union organisations have displayed highlighted interest in the informal sector, nationally and internationally. There has been more and more agreement within the trade union movement on the need to provide appropriate responses

[4] This is the case in India for the working children's organization 'Bal Mazdoor', which the Indian High Court and Supreme Court refused to formally recognize as a union (McKechnie and Hobbs, 1998).

> to the problems facing workers in the informal sector and this need is a pressing concern for many trade unions in developing countries.
>
> (Velasco, 1999: V–VI)

The case of workers in the informal sector, and especially the necessity of taking their views into account, have also been addressed by the Commission of Experts on the Application of ILO Convention No. 122 on employment policies. The Commission expressed its concern that, next to organized labour, other sectors of the active population should be involved in the debate on employment policy. These may include workers from the rural areas, the informal sector and unemployed people (Aries, 1995). For this debate to take place, working children can hardly be excluded for the simple reason that they form an important part of the unorganized, active population. Recent ILO statistics show that of all child labourers aged 5 to 17, 60 per cent are involved in the largely unorganized agricultural sector (Diallo *et al.*, 2010: 13). In developing countries, where there are more children than adults, all those under the age of 18 cannot be excluded from economic activities and be cared for by society (Bourdillon, 2007: 1206). It will therefore be difficult for labour unions and the ILO to sustain in the long term their 'official' position that, child labour being prohibited, they cannot discuss labour issues with working children.

Strategies for the regulation of child labour

If we admit that children can claim the right to work in its wider meaning, the question arises how international labour law rules on child labour may be adapted in practice to these claims. We consider in what follows two possible strategies. Firstly, child labour could be pragmatically regulated apart from the actual recognition of children's right to work. Secondly, child labour could also be regulated in the context of a comprehensive approach based on the recognition of children's right to employment and freedom to work.

Pragmatic strategy: granting rights in work and granting instrumental rights

In a first and most pragmatic strategy, children's rights in work and instrumental rights could be regulated independently from the recognition of their right to employment and to freedom to work. This would include recognizing working children's rights to decent working conditions and remuneration, the freedom of expression and to organize and to join or form unions. The aim of recognizing these rights would be to give a legal foundation for working children's actions that now take place in a legal vacuum. The rationale behind this proposition is consistent with Supiot's standpoint on unremunerated work, that '[w]ork-related human rights must extend to each and every form of activity that a person may carry on in the service of another' (1996: 611). He continues: 'any socially useful work should … be underpinned by a coherent set of labour rights and a legal status that would recognize it as being part of a normal working life without detriment to its distinctiveness. Such rules would have to provide for rights already enshrined in labour law' (Supiot, 1996: 612). The elaboration of such a set of rights would have to start from the observation that children perform activities that are socially useful and that they are therefore de facto workers. It should be possible to elaborate rights for every specific context. The advantage of this pragmatic strategy is that it seems compatible with the overall ILO legal framework. Even if we should not forget that surprisingly 'a right to work is not mentioned anywhere in the Constitution of the ILO or in any of the conventions drafted and concluded under its auspices' (Tomuschat, 1990: 175), the ILO has, since its inception, created several legal instruments regarding rights in work. Moreover, the ILO's International Programme on the Elimination of Child Labour (IPEC), which was created in 1992 with the overall goal of the progressive elimination of child labour, has advocated especially during its early years the adoption of measures aimed at protecting working children and improving existing working conditions of children, albeit as a transitional measure and without mentioning children's freedom to work (International Labour Office, 1992; White, 1994). Such an approach, it can be argued, leaves space for the recognition of rights in work of working children of even a younger age than the age limits imposed via the 1973 ILO Minimum Age Convention.

Choosing a separate set of rights for de facto working children has the advantage that it may be instrumental in challenging exploitative situations, something that would meet most claims of working children's organizations. It also complies with the basic philosophy of labour law to protect workers, *in casu* young workers, who are often more vulnerable than adults. As the activities are no longer clandestine, outside the law and outside all protection networks, the prohibition of child labour would then no longer be an obstacle for recognizing children's claim to the right to work 'in dignity' (Bonnet, 1998). A coherent set of separate rights gives children who perform 'socially useful activities' a legal existence. According to Freeman (1997), true protection of children also protects their rights. This strategy takes into account that children are entitled 'to have both their present autonomy recognised and their capacity for future autonomy safeguarded' (Freeman, 1997: 40).

There are, however, serious objections to the elaboration of a separate set of 'activity-related' rights for children, the main one being that it leaves unanswered questions about the status of childhood itself. A separate set of rules governing children's activities may fail to take the status of minors in society into account and could therefore boil down to an 'improved paternalistic stance' that mitigates children's *exploitation* but fails to address their *oppression* (Schlemmer, 2000). Moreover, the pragmatic strategy further alienates children's activities from the adult world of work. As Olga Nieuwenhuys (1996) argues, a system that fails to address the exclusion of children from the production of value would even reinforce children's vulnerability to exploitation. It is the exclusion of children from the world of labour itself that needs to be addressed. Friboulet (1998: 245) phrases the risks attached to the exclusion (of adults) from the labour market as follows: 'L'éviction d'un individu du marché du travail signifie en réalité une double exclusion. Une exclusion de l'espace public que constituent les échanges marchands, mais également exclusion de l'oeuvre commune qui résulte du procès de production.'[5] Why would this be less true when children are concerned?

Comprehensive strategy: granting the right to freedom to work

The second, more comprehensive strategy would start from recognizing the right to freedom to work as a fundamental human right of *everyone*. Provisions designed to prevent vulnerable persons, such as women, children and young persons, from working under certain conditions, are in this perspective understood as limitations to the freedom to work (Drzewicki, 1995). Regulating child labour would be warranted only as a particular way of reducing the exploitative character of labour. Such regulation must not run counter to the recognition of children as legal subjects and the recognition of their right to work.

As it would enable children to invoke the right to employment and to freedom to work, as well as rights in work and instrumental work-related rights, this strategy seems conceptually more in line with the principles

[5] 'The removal of an individual from the labour market entails in fact a double exclusion: the exclusion from the public space of monetary exchange but also from the common endeavour that is the result of the process of production.'

of the international labour law framework. It is also more in line with the principles of the 1998 ILO Declaration on Fundamental Principles and Rights at Work. This Declaration is drafted to reaffirm the dignity of the worker, which is also important for young people. Full compliance with three of the principles laid down in the Declaration – the right to freedom of association and the right to collective bargaining, the elimination of all forms of forced or compulsory labour, and the elimination of discrimination in respect of employment and occupation – would eliminate the exploitative character of child work and make the prohibition of child labour superfluous. Because the actual abolition of child labour prevents the exclusion of the exploiting character of work that many children undertake on a day-to-day basis, the ILO Declaration is contradictory. This contradiction can only be resolved by setting the current concepts of minimum age aside.

By granting the whole cluster of the right to work to children, including the freedom to work, rights in work and instrumental work-related rights, children are recognized as legal subjects and real persons. From an anthropological perspective, Nieuwenhuys (1996) argues that children have been set conceptually apart by presuming that they do not make contributions to the economy and that what they do is, by definition, 'non-work'. Labour law scholars argue that, essentially, it is the recognition of a person as worker that makes him or her a human being and a subject with rights, or in Friboulet's (1998: 250) words, the right to work is 'une nécessité impérieuse pour la définition de l'homme comme sujet'.[6]

A comprehensive strategy for the regulation of child labour would lead to recognizing the whole cluster of children's labour rights. In the *difference dilemma* the scale would tip in the opposite direction compared to abolitionism and give priority to working children's equal rights. However, to protect children by providing the whole cluster of work-related rights, some conditions have to be met. There is, firstly, the question of children's right to education, which under no condition should be imperilled by any of the components of the right to work. Secondly, appropriate implementation and control mechanisms have to guarantee that the child's right to work will not justify exploitative practices. In other words, the principles and rights of the 1998 ILO Declaration should be enforced strictly in the case of child work. Thirdly, it can be argued that one of the most urgent actions is the inclusion of working children in the programmes and actions directed towards the agricultural and so-called informal

[6] 'is absolutely necessary for the human being to be defined as subject'.

sector. It is in these sectors that most child workers are to be found, and where work-related rights are severely underdeveloped. According to the ILO, there is a need to grant informal sector workers 'a "voice", to represent their interests and thereby lift the yoke of exploitation. This can be achieved only through the establishment of a legal framework, based principally on labour codes and industrial relations systems as we know them today' (Velasco, 1999: VI). Does it make any sense to exclude child agricultural and informal sector workers from these aspirations? Or to put aside the claims of working children's organizations about their right to participate and their right to work in dignity?

Conclusion

The interpretation by international organizations, especially the ILO, of international human rights law in the field of child labour, in particular the international labour law regime that centres on the abolition of child labour, does not address local perspectives of working children's organizations who ask for their right to work in dignity to be recognized. By ignoring children's agency that lies at the very core of the human rights framework, the abolitionist normative framework overlooks the lived realities of young people's everyday engagement with the world of labour as well as their perspectives on and aspirations for social justice.

In line with findings in the field of international children's rights and armed conflict developed elsewhere (Hanson, 2011), the analysis shows that the dominant interpretation that seeks to abolish child labour is only one possible way of translating international standards into national legislation and policy. An alternative translation of international labour law, compatible with how working children's organizations conceptualize a 'living right to work' and with their view on social justice, is possible, however. Starting from the claim to recognize working children's living right to work in dignity, coupled with their demand to participate in debates on child labour, in this chapter we have explored how these statements can be translated into international labour law. We have argued that regulations regarding age limitations, rights in work and instrumental work-related rights do not make this translation a priori impossible. As alternative strategies for how international labour law could address the challenges posed by working children's organizations, we have made a distinction between a pragmatic and a comprehensive strategy. Only the latter approach leads to fully considering children as legal subjects and as rights holders. The central underlying assumption for such an approach is that if children are recognized as legal subjects, then their work-related living rights also have to be acknowledged.

References

Aries J-P (1995) Droit au travail et droit à l'emploi dans le droit international du travail. In: *Mélanges Pierre Vellas: Recherches et réalisations.* Paris: Pedone, pp. 101–8.

Bada A *et al.* (2000) *The 12 Rights of the African Movement of Working Children and Youth (AMWCY). Juridical Foundation, Platform of Demands or Instrument for Development?* Dakar: Enda Jeunesse Action.

Bessell S (1999) Book review: Jim McKechnie and Sandy Hobbs (eds.) *Working Children: Reconsidering the Debates, Report of the International Working Group on Child Labour.* Defence for Children International and the International Society for the Prevention of Child Abuse and Neglect, 1998, 86 pages. *The International Journal of Children's Rights* 7(1): 91–8.

Bonnet M (1998) *Regards sur les enfants travailleurs. La mise au travail dans le monde contemporain: analyse et études de cas.* Lausanne: Page deux.

Bourdillon M (2007) Children and work: a review of current literature and debates. *Development and Change* 37(6): 1201–26.

Bourdillon M, Levison D, Myers W and White B (2010). *Rights and Wrongs of Children's Work.* New Brunswick: Rutgers University Press.

Boyden J, Ling B and Myers W (1998) *What works for working children.* Stockholm/Florence: Rädda Barnen/UNICEF International Child Development Centre.

Brems E (1997) Enemies or allies? Feminism and cultural relativism as dissident voices in human rights discourse. *Human Rights Quarterly* 19(1): 136–64.

Committee on the Rights of the Child (2009) *General Comment No. 12: The Right of the Child to be Heard* (CRC/C/GC12/2009).

De Wilde B (2000) The voice of working children in Belgium (1800–1914). *Information Bulletin International Conference Rethinking Childhood* 4: 12–19.

David P (2002) Implementing the rights of the child. Six reasons why the human rights of children remain a constant challenge. *International Review of Education* 48(3–4): 259–63.

Diallo Y, Hagemann F, Etienne A, Gurbuzer Y and Mehran F (2010) *Global Child Labour Developments: Measuring Trends from 2004 to 2008.* Geneva: ILO-IPEC (SIMPOC).

Drzewicki K (1995) The right to work and rights in work. In: Eide A, Krause C and Rosas A (eds.) *Economic, Social and Cultural Rights. A Textbook.* The Hague: Martinus Nijhoff Publishers, pp. 169–88.

Freeman M (1997) *The Moral Status of Children: Essays on the Rights of the Child.* Dordrecht: Martinus Nijhoff.

(1998) The sociology of childhood and children's rights. *The International Journal of Children's Rights* 6(4): 433–44.

Friboulet J-J (1998) Le droit au travail, droit fondamental de la personne ou utopie sociale. In: Borghi M and Meyer-Bisch P (eds.) *Ethique économique et droits de l'homme. La responsabilité commune.* Fribourg: Editions Universitaires, pp. 233–52.

Hanson K (2006) Repenser les droits des enfants travailleurs. In: Bonnet M, Hanson K, Lange M-F, Nieuwenhuys O, Paillet G and Schlemmer B (eds.) *Enfants travailleurs – Repenser l'enfance.* Lausanne: Editions Page deux, pp. 101–28.

(2008) Arbeitende Kinder und ihr Rechte. Ein Denkanstoss. In: Liebel M, Nnaji I and Wihstutz A (eds.) *Kinder. Arbeit. Menschenwürde. Internationale Beiträge zu den Rechten arbeitender Kinder.* Frankfurt am Main: Verlag für Interkulturelle Kommunikation (IKO), pp. 249–71.

(2011) International children's rights and armed conflict. *Human Rights and International Legal Discourse* 5(1): 40–62.

Hanson K and Vandaele A (2003) Working children and international labour law: a critical analysis. *The International Journal of Children's Rights* 11(1): 73–146.

Hart H L A (1961/1994) *The Concept of Law*, 2nd edn. Oxford: Clarendon Press.

International Labour Office (1992) *IPEC Programme Document. International Programme on the Elimination of Child Labour. An Action Programme to Protect Working Children and to Combat and Eliminate Child Labour.* Geneva: ILO.

International Working Group on Child Labour (1997) *Have we asked the children? Discussion paper.* Bangalore/Amsterdam: Concerned for Working Children/ Defence for Children International-The Netherlands.

Liebel M (2003) Working children as social subjects. The contribution of working children's organizations to social transformations. *Childhood* 10(3): 265–85.

Leisink P (1999) Introduction. In: Leisink P (ed.) *Globalization and Labour Relations.* Cheltenham: Edward Elgar, pp. 14–20.

Lücker-Babel M-F (1995) The right of the child to express views and to be heard: an attempt to interpret Article 12 of the UN Convention on the Rights of the Child. *The International Journal of Children's Rights* 4(3): 391–404.

McKechnie J and Hobbs S (eds.) (1998) *Working Children: Reconsidering the Debates. Report of the International Working Group on Child Labour.* Amsterdam: DCI/ISPCAN.

Miljeteig P (2000) Children's democratic rights: are we ready? What we can learn from young workers. In: Smith A B, Gallop M, Marshall K and Nairn K (eds.)

Advocating for Children. International Perspectives on Children's Rights. Dunedin: University of Otago Press, pp. 159–75.
Minow M (1986). Rights for the next generation: a feminist approach to children's rights. *Harvard Women's Law Journal* 9(1): 1–24.
Nieuwenhuys O (1996) The paradox of child labor and anthropology. *Annual Review of Anthropology* 25: 237–51.
Raes K (1992) *Ongemakkelijk Recht. Rechtskritische Perspectieven op Maatschappij, Ethiek en Emancipatie.* Antwerpen: Kluwer rechtswetenschappen.
Rodham H (1973) Children under the law. *Harvard Educational Review* 43(4): 487–514.
(ed.) (2000) *The Exploited Child.* London: Zed Books.
Schrumpf E (2001) The working child – enslaved or privileged? Changing perspectives on child labour. *Brood & Rozen. Tijdschrift voor de Geschiedenis van Sociale Bewegingen* 6(4): 35–51.
Sen A (1999) *Development as Freedom.* London: Oxford University Press.
Supiot A (1996) Perspectives on work: introduction. *International Labour Review* 135(6): 603–14.
Swift A (1999) *Working Children Get Organised. An Introduction to Working Children's Organisations.* London: International Save the Children Alliance.
Thomas N (2007) Towards a theory of children's participation. *The International Journal of Children's Rights* 15(2): 199–218.
Tisdall K M, Davis J M, Hill M and Prout A (2006) *Children, Young People and Social Inclusion. Participation for What?* Bristol: The Policy Press.
Tomuschat C (1990) The right to work. In: Rosas A and Helgesen J (eds.) *Human Rights in a Changing East–West Perspective.* London: Pinter, pp. 174–201.
Velasco M S (1999) Editorial. *Labour Education* 116: V–VII.
Venkata Ratnam C S (1999) India. *Labour Education* 116: 25–47.
White B (1994) *Children, Work and 'Child Labour': Changing Responses to the Employment of Children.* The Hague: Institute of Social Studies.

Conclusion

13

Children's rights and social movements: reflections from a cognate field

NEIL STAMMERS

Introduction

If forced to choose one central and underlying conceptual issue that connects my own work to many of the issues that Hanson and Nieuwenhuys raise in the introductory chapter to this volume, it would have to be our shared view on the necessity of breaking with sterile binaries – those strong ontological and epistemological assumptions found in so much academic and popular thought that describe and analyse the world in terms of polarities or dichotomies. Crucial in terms of trying to theorise children's rights in international development is how to conceptualise the relationships between actors, agency and structure. Many attempts to explain the social world still work from a crude binary polarity between agency and structure, either privileging the agency of social actors at the expense of a proper consideration of structural constraint or else privileging structures at the expense of proper consideration of the agency of social actors. While I cannot elaborate the argument here, it seems to me that starting from a triadic conceptualisation of actors, agency and structure within which agency is understood as a potential attribute of both actors and structures and conceptualised as synonymous with power (that is, the dynamic but complex relation between 'power to' and 'power over') might offer a more fruitful way forward for grasping the complexities of the social world (see Stammers, 2009: 25–7).

Applying this approach along with others drawn from some of my recent work (Stammers, 2009; Stammers and Eschle, 2005), this chapter offers some concluding reflections on the three analytic themes of this volume: 'living rights', 'translations' and 'social justice'.

Living rights

In their introductory chapter Hanson and Nieuwenhuys use the concept of living rights to focus on children as active subjects and rights holders and to challenge the assumption that children would be incapable of independent action. But, clearly, this idea of living rights has much wider potential applicability. For example, if we replace 'children' with 'women', the concept of living rights would then help us to focus on women as active subjects and rights holders and challenge the assumption that women are incapable of independent action. So, to develop the point, the concept of living rights directs us to two very important but much more general issues: firstly, that rights exist through, with and in people, and that, secondly, people use and construct ideas of rights for some social purpose. My previous work has stressed the importance of looking at 'pre-legal' and 'non-legal' dimensions of human rights in terms of what I have called the 'instrumental/expressive dynamic of movement activism'. This allows us to transcend another much used binary between 'interests' and 'identities' and to indicate that social relations and individuals are always in a state of both 'being' and 'becoming' (see Stammers, 2009: Chapter 6).

The concept of living rights can be properly and importantly juxtaposed to 'abstract rights' and 'legal rights', offering us an important corrective to dominant ways of thinking about rights derived from the disciplines of philosophy and law. Sometimes, work from these two disciplines interlock in such a way as to almost conceptually exclude any other perspective.[1] In contrast, the concept of living rights is probably best located alongside other alternative sociological and anthropological approaches to the study of rights (Cowan, 2006; Cowan *et al.*, 2001; Turner, 2006; Wilson, 1997). Unfortunately, such approaches remain largely marginalised in the specialist academic literature on human rights. A note of caution is also required here, though, because it is tempting to think of living rights in terms of 'practices', whilst seeing philosophical and legal approaches as embedded in an abstracted realm of 'ideas'. For example, in anthropological accounts, international human rights law is often described as 'abstract' and then counterposed to 'local', 'everyday' or 'grass roots' practices (see for example Chapter 2 by Henderson and Chapter 6 by Droz

[1] In other words, the only legitimate 'ideas' about human rights are seen to be those that emerge from the philosophical disciplinary 'canon' and the only legitimate 'practices' of human rights are those practices embedded in national and international law. An interesting volume that tries to examine this problem from a multidisciplinary perspective is *The Legalisation of Human Rights* by Meckled-Garcia and Cali (2006).

in this volume). But we have to be careful not to fall into a binary polarity of 'ideas' and 'practices'. I think the term 'praxis' (understood as the dynamic interaction between ideas and practices) helps us to avoid that trap. We can then understand what philosophers do when they write about human rights as a form of praxis, that what lawyers do in the juridical arena as a form of praxis, and the construction of international human rights law as a form of praxis. But, in important ways, such forms of praxis are but the tip of the iceberg. The myriad of local, everyday and grass-roots praxis worldwide makes it clear that there is (and has been) a vast and complex web of praxis around human rights that is historical and contemporary, local and global. The extent of this praxis is a key insight highlighted by the concept of living rights. My recent work has focused on one form of this praxis, what I have called the creative praxis of social movement activism.

This has examined the analytical significance of the historical link between human rights and social movements and has tried to identify the contours of a framework through which the potentials and limits of human rights might be better and more effectively assessed. Such reassessment has important implications – not just for thinking about human rights – but also for interrogating other key issue areas, for example, power, globalisation, democracy, participation and contemporary forms of institutions and institutionalisation.

Prior to the mid 1990s any reference at all to a connection between human rights and social movements was a rarity. But the following two decades have witnessed some sort of shift, with well-known scholars at least beginning to acknowledge a historical connection between social movements and human rights. From a critical perspective, Costas Douzinas (2000) and Boaventura de Sousa Santos (1995, 1999) have called for understandings of human rights to be reconstructed through grasping their connections to social movement struggles. Developing that point, Upendra Baxi (2002) has argued that over the last sixty years it has been the oppressed of the world – mobilised in and through social movements – who have been the hidden authors of contemporary developments in human rights. Finally, Balakrishnan Rajagopal (2003) puts social movements at the centre of what he calls 'third world resistance' in his focus on the possibilities for the development of 'international law from below'. Despite these recognitions and suggestions, there remains very little detailed research in these areas.

One theme of my work has been that the historical development of human rights needs to be understood and analysed in the context of social movement struggles against extant relations and structures of power. I have argued that human rights initially emerge as 'struggle concepts' and this has major implications for how we should understand them. I should also emphasise that I use a very long historical perspective and have described the process of the adoption of the United Nations Declaration of Human Rights in 1948 as something of a historical anomaly (Stammers, 2009: Chapter 4). We could make a similar argument about the UN Convention on the Rights of the Child (CRC) because it, too, emerged from a thoroughly institutionalised process (see Holzscheiter, 2010).

Let me come back to the idea of 'living' in 'living rights'. My contention is that social movements – through innovative creativity in both ideas and practices (i.e. praxis) – contribute significantly to the shaping of historical development. Mario Diani has helpfully developed what he calls a synthetic definition of social movements and, interestingly and importantly, he insists that 'social movements are not organisations, not even of a peculiar kind' (Diani, 2000: 166). From this it follows that we need to maintain a clear analytic distinction between organisations and social movements (see Stammers and Eschle, 2005).

Diani's conceptualisation enables us to think about how social movements may straddle the institutional and everyday worlds. For Darnovsky, Epstein and Flacks (1995: vii): 'collective action becomes a "movement" when participants refuse to accept the boundaries of established institutional rules and routinized roles.'

Yet, that said, social movements also often generate organisations that both engage with the institutional world and themselves become institutions. I will come back to this point when I discuss 'translations', but it is these features of social movements that necessitate engagement with the instrumental/expressive dynamic of movement activism. As mentioned above, this allows us to:

- transcend important debates around interests and identities;
- recognise that human life and social relations are always in processes of 'becoming';
- open up crucial ways for exploring how non-institutional and pre-institutional aspects of human rights relate to institutionalised social action around human rights, including human rights as law.

Thinking about creative social praxis in these sorts of ways enables us to re-examine the nature of 'the social' and grasp how the collective agency of social movements may contribute to historical transformations. Put in these terms, the importance of social movements in constructing and reconstructing understandings of human rights becomes clear.

But, if this is right, how is it possible that the mainstream literature on human rights has managed to avoid the subject for so long and what does it mean to have the dominant discourses of human rights so disconnected from the social processes through which human rights emerge and are continually being contested and renegotiated? I have used the metaphor of a 'hall of mirrors' – the ones you find in carnivals and funfairs – to try to depict both this literature and the grotesque caricatures of human rights it produces (Stammers, 2009: Chapter 1). I have already mentioned the dominant role of philosophy and law in human rights scholarship. These disciplines are particularly inhospitable and ill-equipped to provide an analytic focus on social movements. In a similar way, dominant ideological perspectives – including liberalism, social democracy, most forms of Marxism, various forms of communitarianism and many strands of post-structuralist and postmodernist thought – have also been unable, or unwilling, to grasp the link between social movements and human rights. Yet all of these have importantly shaped the mainstream literature.

Furthermore, my metaphorical mirrors have generated a strong and pervasive polarity between those I call 'uncritical proponents' and those I call 'uncritical critics'. There is often no grasp of the complexity of the social world, nor of the ambiguities of power. But, crucially, these 'uncritical proponents' and 'uncritical critics' actually share a range of fundamental assumptions when they study human rights (Stammers, 2009: Chapter 1). Perhaps most importantly, this typically involves a shared, essentialist answer to the question 'what are human rights?' Many liberal, Marxist and some post-structuralist accounts assume that human rights are, and can be nothing other than, the rights of possessive individuals in a capitalist society. This means that other dimensions of human rights, in particular their deep social and collective dimensions, are obscured.

In my view, the mainstream literature on human rights amounts to a set of orthodoxies that should not be taken as a reference point for thinking about 'living rights'. So, instead of thinking about how the concept of living rights might be integrated into or accommodated by those orthodoxies, I would argue that the notion of living rights should be used to critique such orthodoxies and developed according to its own trajectories. In respect of children, one potential way of doing this would be to develop a thorough socio-historical analysis of the children's rights movement, which can be traced back to the latter half of the nineteenth century and led, amongst other things, to a declaration on the rights of the child by the League of Nations in 1924 (Veerman, 1992). So there is a long history to be explored here. What are the implications of this history for understanding contemporary praxis around children's rights and children's participation?

If the orthodoxies of the human rights literature cause problems for thinking about 'living rights', they become a dangerous obstruction when we try to interrogate the complexities and ambiguities involved with another key theme of this volume, that of translations.

Translations

In the introductory chapter to this volume, Hanson and Nieuwenhuys emphasise that the 'translation of children's rights into practice is never solely either a top-down or a bottom-up activity ... but a circular process ... giving rise to unforeseen complexities that produce a state of constant indeterminacy'. The concept of translations, they say, therefore attempts to capture the tensions at work between global and local formulations of children's rights in terms of a multifaceted process that transforms the power relations of all actors involved. Such a dynamic view of translations they suggest, citing Robert J C Young, 'comes close to a foundational idea of postcolonialism: that the one-way process by which translation is customarily conceived can be rethought in terms of cultural interaction and as a space of re-empowerment' (Young cited by Hanson and Nieuwenhuys, Chapter 1 of this volume, p. 21).

Hanson and Nieuwenhuys point to the many instances whereby this general argument is illustrated in specific and rich detail by the case studies included within this volume. But, that said, their line of argument also raises some broad analytic issues that cannot be so easily addressed through the detail of specific case studies.

Firstly, and perhaps most fundamentally, their argument points to the necessity of a broad analysis of relations and structures of power and how these impact on all forms of practices that relate to children's rights. Secondly, the key dynamic relationship between 'top-down' and 'bottom-up' forms of translation needs unpacking, so that the tensions in that relationship can be explored and analysed in terms of existing asymmetries of power in the world. Thirdly, we can ask whether a focus on rights can be an effective tool for opening up a space for re-empowerment and achieving positive transformative change. Finally, we can ask what role children themselves can play in all of this, which poses key questions about children's agency and participation.

While these are important issues as they specifically relate to children and children's rights, they cannot be answered or resolved *solely within* a children's rights framework because they address some of the most fundamental issues in social relations generally: issues about power, democracy, change and agency. None of these can be explored effectively without reference to, for example, history, international geopolitics and the contemporary contexts of political, economic and cultural forms of globalisation. So under this apparently innocent-looking term 'translations', we have a rather large agenda!

Perhaps that agenda may be clarified somewhat by considering, firstly, what I have called 'the paradox of institutionalisation' (Stammers, 2009: Chapter 4) and, secondly, what Upendra Baxi (2002: 53) has called 'the problematic of representational power'. Both of these concepts have broad applicability and point towards complex, but *causal*, relations through which power, democracy, change and agency may be more fully understood. Let me look firstly at the paradox of institutionalisation.

The paradox of institutionalisation

At the heart of the paradox is a combination of the necessity of institutions to human existence with the apparently intractable problem of institutional 'power to' so easily morphing into forms of 'power over'. No political ideology or political programme has ever proposed that humans can or should attempt to live without institutions at all. Indeed, institutions are created because people believe they will generate more 'power to' than if they tried to act outside of institutions. Yet at the same time, once established, such institutions seem to carry an inherent capacity for wielding 'power over', often reaching huge proportions in the case of states, corporations, the global financial institutions and large NGOs.

The use of the term paradox here also points to an important specific dimension of the relation between human rights and social movements. Social movement struggles are typically rooted in the everyday world but, historically, have constructed human rights claims in ways that demand their institutional instantiation. Think, for example, how feminist activism in the West since the 1970s has consistently demanded changes in the law and in institutional practices as ways of improving the position of women. In other words, non-institutional activism has demanded the institutionalisation of human rights. Furthermore, a clear trajectory can be identified in the historical development of social movements themselves, which I have characterised as a tendency towards 'the institutionalisation of activism' (Stammers, 2009: 125–9). It follows that the key strategic question identified by the paradox is the extent to which the emancipatory thrust of human rights and human rights struggles can be sustained through processes of institutionalisation.

Like so many terms in the social sciences, the concept of an institution is wide-ranging and contested. I use it to mean formally organised structures of social relations: political, economic and cultural. Understood in this way, the importance of institutions can hardly be underestimated. Campbell – for example – argues that '[i]nstitutions are the foundation of social life' and that '[w]ithout stable institutions, life becomes chaotic and arduous'(Campbell, 2004: i). Yet, in a range of other important work influential across the whole of the humanities and social sciences, much of what Campbell sees as positive has been dramatically questioned. Institutions are at the heart of that aspect of Weberian sociology that emphasises tendencies towards the rationalisation and bureaucratisation of modern life. The key roles of regulation, discipline and normalisation have been identified in, and through studies inspired by, the work of Michel Foucault. Then, particularly important for the analysis of activism, is the work on the development of oligarchy. Initially identified by Roberto Michels (1962 [1915]), strong tendencies towards oligarchy have been persistently identified and confirmed in studies of social movements and organisations ever since (for example, Davis *et al.*, 2005: xiii). Finally, we might recall Schattschneider's (1960: 71) poignant remark that 'organization is the mobilization of bias'.

From even this brief discussion it is clear that institutions and processes of institutionalisation are of enormous import, which is why I think this concept of the paradox of institutionalisation is a potentially important analytic tool. Further, its emphasis on complexity, on the continuities and discontinuities between the institutional and the everyday worlds, the rejection of naive advocacy and naive critique, the fact that these sorts of issues have been largely ignored by the dominant political ideologies of the last 150 years – all these suggest the potential richness and texture of an analysis of human rights and rights struggles that takes the question of the paradox of institutionalisation seriously.

The problematic of representational power

If the key strategic question identified by the paradox is the extent to which emancipatory struggles can be sustained through processes of institutionalisation, then a fundamental question arises of how various aspects of social relations might be reconstructed and democratised. This brings me to what Baxi calls the 'problematic of representational power', which directly links to some of the most important concerns addressed in this volume.

Leaving aside – as I must – the huge issues of democracy *within* movements and organisations, and *between* movements and organisations, there are many circumstances in which relatively powerful, often at least partially institutionalised NGOs claim to speak on behalf of others. Indeed, significant aspects of work in the 'global human rights industry' rely heavily on the work of large international NGOs, such as Human Rights Watch and Amnesty International – key players in the 'transnational advocacy network' on human rights (Keck and Sikkink, 1998).

Now while there is not necessarily a problem with NGOs speaking on behalf of the oppressed and those whose rights are being violated or threatened, those NGOs must ensure that they properly represent the interests, views and demands of those they claim to be representing. So a key question that then arises is the extent to which there are any democratically constructed channels of communication, participation or representation between NGOs and the people they claim to speak for. Lack of such channels potentially poses extremely serious problems, which is what Baxi's notion of the problematic of representational power tries to capture. Because of the focus in this volume on children's participation and children's rights, we need to consider additionally whether Baxi's problematic is raised in a particularly acute form due to the fact that the vast majority of activism around children's participation and children's rights has been led by adults not children themselves.

Let me try to illustrate the utility of these two concepts by looking at a particularly interesting paper. In 'The politics of child participation in international development: the dilemma of agency', Sarah White and Shymol Choudhury (2007) look at a children's organisation in Bangladesh, Amra, to explore how the dynamics of participation have changed over time and what this has meant for children and their families. Their case study provides fascinating specific detail of the paradox of institutionalisation in action at the interface of the institutional and everyday worlds. The basis of Amra was, they say, a small group of boys aged 7–12 who roamed the streets looking for rubbish that they could sell on. Supported by an adult facilitator, Amra was established in 1995 as 'an organisation *of* street and working children *for* street and working children' (White and Choudhury, 2007: 539, emphasis in original). Apparently, at the heart of this organisation in its early days was a group process:

> in which the boys would reason and argue together, devise their work programme, share and discuss their problems, and thrash out any conflicts that arose. Through this group process they determined their own rules and principles: that only working children could be core members; that the organisation belonged to the children who ran it, referring to adults only when they could not manage something themselves; that the group needed to look after each individual within it; that strength and fun lay in being together, so work should be done and decisions made collectively; everyone should be treated fairly and equally, with no one dominating the others.
>
> (White and Choudhury, 2007: 539)

But as the emphasis on child participation grew in the development community, NGOs involved with children's rights felt increasingly pressurised to 'produce' children's participation. Demands on Amra from such agencies built up. White and Choudhury argue that '[t]he implications for Amra were quite contradictory' and that a shift from action in the everyday world to advocacy in institutionalised settings had a 'treacherous aspect':

> the dynamic towards this model of children's participation itself disassociated the participants from the children they supposedly represent. The essential qualities of *Amra*, its rootedness in the collective identity of the group process and its daily active relationships with other poor children in the wider community were put in jeopardy through their incorporation as child participants.
>
> (White and Choudhury, 2007: 541)

Turning to the problem of representational power, White and Choudhury are very concerned about the way in which children's participation often appears tokenistic and framed by NGOs as theatre or spectacle, arguing that the introduction of 'children's participation' within development programmes does not simply challenge existing forms of power but also becomes a means through which power is expressed. They note that 'development agency staff commonly claim the right to determine both what counts as "participation" (and what kinds of participation count) and how it is represented' (White and Choudhury, 2007: 536).

They also raise the issue of the role of adult facilitators working with children's organisations. Noting that part of the culture of 'child participation' is to emphasize the agency of children rather than adults, they suggest the history of Amra calls this into question because the orientation of the organisation notably shifted in line with the interests of its adult facilitators. White and Choudhury use the term 'facipulation' to indicate *the interplay between* the potential polarity of facilitation and manipulation that could be involved here (White and Choudhury, 2007: 545).

Similar sorts of issues to those raised by White and Choudhury are implied extensively throughout this volume and explicitly discussed in the chapters by Cheney (Chapter 8) and Brems (Chapter 10). Kristen Cheney argues that 'children are being systematically disenfranchised by the translation of rights into a discourse of vulnerability that prevents them from initiating rights claims to ameliorate their own circumstances' largely as a consequence of adults using children's rights to pursue their own self-interest. This, she argues, has driven the children of her study to adopt an identity of victimhood so as to help enable them to secure the resources they need. While Cheney's critical comments are largely directed towards state actors and large NGOs, at the heart of Eva Brems' chapter is a recognition that conflicts of interest and interpretation can occur between children and their direct caretakers within the triangular relationship between child, caretaker and state. While aspects of Cheney's argument again points to the relevance of the paradox of institutionalisation, when taken together with Brems' argument, it is the potential scope and depth of Baxi's problematic of representational power that is then highlighted.

In summarising this section, I would reiterate that both the concepts of the paradox of institutionalisation and the problematic of representational power help to clarify some of the many complicated issues involved in the theme of translations. In practical terms they are also highly relevant to the third key theme of this volume, 'social justice'.

Social justice

Social justice is a slippery term, not because there is necessarily wide dispute about what it *means* but because there is a wide divergence of opinion on *how* to try to achieve it. 'How' questions are often seen as largely strategic, but closer investigation quickly reveals that we are back to those basic ontological and epistemological issues around understanding and studying power, and the disputes about the relationships between actors, agency and structure.

Among specialists in children's rights and childhood studies there is broad agreement on the need to transcend 'old' views of childhood. In the special issue of the *International Journal of Children's Rights* on participation, Anne Smith sums up the 'old' view thus:

> Children have been regarded as the passive recipients of adults' teaching, protection and care, as objects to be shaped and socialised, as the property of their families, and as incomplete beings who are not yet humans.
>
> (Smith, 2007: 1)

She argues that rethinking these traditional views of childhood is an essential project for researchers, policymakers and professionals who work with children. The three key themes of this volume offer innovative approaches to the processes of such rethinking.

Unfortunately, these 'old' and 'new' approaches are still often couched in binary terms where, from the 'old' perspective, children are structurally positioned as victims (or potential victims) with no agency, while, from the 'new' perspective, children are seen as subjects/agents potentially in control of their own destiny with apparently little facing them by way of structural constraint. Michael Freeman comes close to this latter position. He claims, for example, that agents 'can make their own lives rather than have their lives made for them' (Freeman, 2007: 8). Much of Freeman's approach fits very well with the one adopted here, but aspects of his argument are rather too optimistic, perhaps even utopian, because they do not adequately locate children's agency within the broader contexts of political, economic and cultural structures of power.

Gallagher (2008) has identified similar binary narratives around the question of children's participation. One, he says:

> holds that participation is the key to true democracy, the way to transform unjust decision-making structures so that every child's voice can be heard and their wishes acted upon. This is a view of child participation as an ideal to drive democratic renewal and the recognition of children's political rights as human beings.
>
> (Gallagher, 2008: 404)

The other narrative is, he says, much more dismal:

> suggesting that, in reality, participation is often ineffective with adults consulting children but not acting upon their suggestions for change. This is tokenism … not real participation at all.
>
> (Gallagher, 2008: 404)

To break with these sorts of binaries means recognising that children can be both victims and social actors with agency, and that participation entails complex and ambivalent encounters with power. But even having made these necessary ontological and epistemological breaks, we are still left with those 'how' questions in their strategic form. Is it possible to identify ways forward that minimise or mitigate the worst problems of the paradox of institutionalisation and the problem of representational power?

Here I want to draw from a paper that does not focus on children but which, in my view, offers a range of important insights and suggestions. In 'Relocating participation within a radical politics of development', Sam Hickey and Giles Mohan (2005) identify many of the problems discussed above in the context of the wider history of participation in international development. They point out that participation has been mobilised on behalf of a variety of different ideological and institutional perspectives and identify the problem of sterile binaries, which they describe in terms of the uncritical promotion of participation and a similarly (un)critical backlash against it. In a neat summary, they note that the key arguments of critics are that proponents of participatory development:

- Focus on the 'local' as opposed to wider structures of injustice and oppression;
- have an insufficiently sophisticated understanding of how power operates;
- have an inadequate understanding of the role of structure and agency in social change;
- tend to treat participation as a technical method of project work rather than seeing it as the politics of empowerment.

(Hickey and Mohan, 2005: 241–2)

However, rather than assuming – as many critics do – that all forms of participatory development are therefore doomed to failure, Hickey and Mohan try to identify what forms of social praxis might successfully address these sorts of problems. They identify three areas where they feel that policy and practices have created positive transformative potential. The first area relates to attempts to foster participatory governance and decentralisation led by political organisations 'with strong social movement characteristics' (Hickey and Mohan, 2005: 242). The second is where NGOs attempt to align participatory approaches with a rights-based agenda and also, crucially, ensure that democratic principles are foremost in the process. The third area concerns the contemporary role of social movements when, in using identity-based forms of participatory politics, movement actors are able to extend the boundaries of citizenship to previously marginalised groups. Recognising what I have called the instrumental and expressive dynamic of movement activism, they suggest a participatory politics of cultural identity, material redistribution and social justice are not alternatives (as many commentators have claimed) but can be unified in and through movement struggle.

Hickey and Mohan identify four threads of continuity that run through these initiatives. Firstly, any successes have depended on participation being part of a broader project that directly challenges existing relations of power rather than work around such relations for technically efficient service delivery. In other words, it is 'an explicit articulation of a radical project that focuses primarily on issues of power and politics' (Hickey and Mohan, 2005: 250). Secondly, they identify a close engagement with underlying processes of development rather than activists being constrained within a framework of specific policy processes or interventions. By this I understand them to mean a focus on the everyday world within which poor people live and the forms of power that keep them poor, in contrast to the tendency for many NGOs to act as technocratic experts seeking specific outcomes matching the demands of funding bodies. Thirdly, they identify a focus on participation as citizenship, which they specify in terms of Bryan Turner's definition of citizenship as:

> that set of practices (juridical, political, economic or cultural) which define a person as a competent member of society, and which as a consequence shape the flow of resources to persons and social groups.
>
> (Turner cited in Hickey and Mohan, 2005: 253)

The fourth and final commonality appears to be that some structural differentiation between political and economic power needs to pre-exist, so that activists have room to manoeuvre between different forms and sites of power.[2]

Although I have concerns about Hickey and Mohan's reliance on a particularist (that is, a largely national) notion of citizenship, their work does point to some fruitful and practical ways of thinking how to ensure that work around children's rights and participation might be developed in a transformative direction. That social movements are key to their way of thinking is well illustrated when they say that the potentially radical political trajectory of citizenship 'can be read most clearly off the claims and programmes of both old and new social movements over the past two centuries' (Hickey and Mohan, 2005: 258).

[2] This point has resonances with Sydney Tarrow's work on 'political opportunity structures' as a context for understanding success and failure in social movement mobilisation (e.g. Tarrow, 1998: Chapter 5).

But we must now ask how far Hicky and Mohan's proposals have applicability to the field of children's rights and participation. Many of the chapters in this volume point directly or indirectly towards the potential utility of a social movements approach to achieving change insofar as they either explicitly focus on children's movements and organisations or else point towards the creative praxis of children themselves in terms of – for example – developing innovative survival strategies or constructing critical and creative historical knowledge. But it seems to me that there are problems in trying to rely entirely on a social movement struggle model in this specific context.

As already discussed, there is the need to transcend the binary through which children are seen either as victims or else as unconstrained social actors. Given that the history of social movement struggles is largely a history of people seeking ways to prevent themselves or others from being victimised by the predations of social power, I do not see a problem with recognising that children *can* be victims. But when we turn to look at children as social actors with agency, it seems to me that distinct, age-related, limits can be identified. While a social movement approach to achieving change may be entirely applicable to the self-organisation of working children, perhaps even quite young children as in the case of Amra considered above, the utility of a social movement struggle model cannot be applicable to very young children, even though such children still have a degree of agency as any carer of a baby or toddler will tell you.

A second point comes back to the problem of representational power. Again, specific issues arise because we are looking at children's activism. The literature which focuses on children's self-activism in movements and organisations often makes reference to the role of adult facilitators and, when it did not, I felt the need to ponder whether a significant omission was being made. For example, in a paper entitled 'The African movement of working children and youth', Terenzio (2007) says that this movement was created by children and youth of four countries in 1994 'after nine years of efforts'. I was left wondering whose persistent and consistent efforts were involved over such a period of time. The paper was silent on this point.

Without wishing to make a general critique of the role of adult facilitators working with children, I think we have to take the potential relationship between facilitation and manipulation – what White and Choudhury called 'facipulation' – very seriously. Moreover, the younger children are when adults are working with them, then the more problematic this relationship is likely to become. In summary, I think this problem of representational power raises additional and very particular issues in respect of adults working with children.

This brings me to my final point, which concerns the 'evolving capacities' of children. Whilst perhaps offering a way of working through the age-related questions identified above, this notion of 'evolving capacities' might look like something that is very specific to children. Yet perhaps Turner's above definition of citizenship, with its emphasis on developing competences, points us in a different direction. If we start by acknowledging that even very young children are social actors, albeit within particular (and often very differently) structured settings, we could make a conceptual link between the development of citizenship competences and the evolving capacities of children through the notion of 'becoming'. As stressed earlier, it is not just children that 'become'. Adults are also always 'becoming', as – it seems to me – are social relations in general. For sure, there will be no panacea here, but such a linkage does offer some potential way of seeing how a social movements approach might be retailored in ways that address the realities of children's physical, emotional and intellectual development.

So, in summary, there does seem important potential that may be realised through a focus on children's movements and organisations and the application of a social movement approach to achieving social change. But it is not without difficulties and complexities and, at the heart of these, is the relationship between 'power to' and 'power over' and how this is mediated in social praxis.

Conclusion

White and Choudhury (2007: 531) note that '[a]ge is a fundamental axis of social power' and, while I would not dispute that, it is important to bear in mind that relations between adults and children are only one part of that intergenerational axis of power. So, in respect of the relationship between adults and children, it might be more productive to focus on the ways in which 'power to' can morph into 'power over' in both the everyday and institutional worlds. Furthermore, recognising age as a fundamental axis of social power should not blind us to other fundamental axes of power – power organised politically, economically, around sex and gender, around ethnicity and around the control of information and knowledge.

Indeed, it has been emphasised throughout this chapter that the key organising concepts of this volume need to be located and understood within a framework that extends beyond the particularities of the relationships between adults and children. With regard to 'living rights', I discussed the implications of substituting 'women' for 'children' and considered how 'living rights' might be linked to what I have called the creative praxis of social movements. With regard to the concept of 'translations', its potential broader applicability can be illustrated by simply substituting 'human rights' for 'children's rights' in the first part of my discussion. Finally, in respect of social justice, my use of Hickey and Mohan's work was intended to make explicit the link between discussions of participation and social justice in the children's rights field with the broader discussion of the same issues in fields of development studies and international relations.

So, my concluding suggestion here is that, in looking at 'living rights', 'translations' and 'social justice' in respect of children's rights and children's participation, we need to keep in mind the wider applicability of each of these terms and what they imply in terms of seeking – more generally – to challenge and transform existing relations and structures of power in the world.

References

Baxi U (2002) *The Future of Human Rights*. Oxford University Press.

Campbell J (2004) *Institutional Change and Globalization*. Princeton University Press.

Cowan J (2006) Culture and rights after 'Culture and Rights'. *American Anthropologist* 108(1): 9–24.

Cowan J, Dembour M-B and Wilson R A (2001) *Culture and Rights: Anthropological Perspectives*. Cambridge University Press.

Darnovsky M, Epstein B and Flacks R (1995) (eds.) *Cultural Politics and Social Movements*. Philadelphia: Temple University Press.

Davis G F, McAdam D, Scott W R and Zald M N (2005) *Social Movements and Organization Theory*. Cambridge University Press.

De Sousa Santos B (1995) *Towards a New Common Sense: Law, Science and Politics in the Paradigmatic Transition*. New York: Routledge.

(1999) Towards a multicultural conception of human rights. In: Featherstone M and Lash S *Spaces of Culture: City, Nation, World*. London: Sage, pp. 214–29.

Diani M (2000) The concept of social movement. In: Nash K (ed.) *Readings in Contemporary Political Sociology*. Oxford: Blackwell, pp. 155–76.

Douzinas C (2000) *The End of Human Rights*. Oxford: Hart Publishing.

Freeman M (2007) Why it remains important to take children's rights seriously. *The International Journal of Children's Rights*, 15(1): 5–23.

Gallagher M (2008) Foucault, power and participation. *The International Journal of Children's Rights* 16(3): 395–406.

Hickey S and Mohan G (2005) Relocating participation within a radical politics of development. *Development and Change* 36(2): 237–62.

Holzscheiter A (2010) *Children's Rights in International Politics: The Transformative Power of Discourse*. Basingstoke: Palgrave.

Keck M and Sikkink K (1998) *Activists Beyond Borders: Advocacy Networks in International Politics*. Ithaca: Cornell University Press.

Meckled-Garcia S and Cali B (2006) (eds.) *The Legalization of Human Rights*. London: Routledge.

Michels R (1962 [1915]) *Political Parties: A Sociological Study of the Oligarchical Tendencies of Modern Democracy*. Glencoe: The Free Press.

Rajagopal B (2003) *International Law From Below: Development, Social Movements and Third World Resistance*. Cambridge University Press.

Schattschneider E E (1960) *The Semi-Sovereign People: A Realist's View of Democracy in America*. New York: Holt, Rinehart and Winston.

Smith A (2007) Children as social actors. *The International Journal of Children's Rights* 15(1): 1–4.

Stammers N (2009) *Human Rights and Social Movements*. London: Pluto Press.

Stammers N and Eschle C (2005) Social movements and global activism. In: De Jong W, Shaw M and Stammers N (eds.) *Global Activism, Global Media*. London: Pluto Press, pp. 50–67.

Tarrow S (1998) *Power in Movement*. Cambridge University Press.

Terenzio F (2007) The African movement of working children and youth. *Development* 50: 68–71.

Turner B S (2006) *Vulnerability and Human Rights*. Pennsylvania State University Press.

Veerman P (1992) *The Rights of the Child and the Changing Image of Childhood*. Dordrecht: Martinus Nijhoff.

White S and Choudhury S A (2007) The politics of child participation in international development: the dilemma of agency. *European Journal of Development Research* 19(4): 529–50.

Wilson R A (ed.) (1997) *Human Rights, Culture and Context: Anthropological Perspectives*. London: Pluto Press.

INDEX

Page numbers with 'n' are notes.

Lightning Source UK Ltd.
Milton Keynes UK
UKOW03n0134071013

218561UK00001B/26/P

9 781107 031517